The Washington Dissensus

A PRIVILEGED OBSERVER'S PERSPECTIVE ON US-BRAZIL RELATIONS

D1521778

RUBENS BARBOSA

Vanderbilt University Press ■ Nashville

Originally published in Brazil as *O Dissenso de Washington* by Agir, Rio de Janeiro, in 2011. Copyright 2011 by Editora Nova Fronteira Participaçõas S.A.

Translated by Anthony Doyle

This book is printed on acid-free paper.
Manufactured in the United States of America

Library of Congress Cataloging-in-Publication Data on file
LC control number 2014008055
LC classification number E183.8.B7B378513 2014
Dewey class number 327.73081—dc23

ISBN 978-0-8265-2011-1 (hardcover)
ISBN 978-0-8265-2012-8 (paperback)
ISBN 978-0-8265-2013-5 (ebook)

For Maria Ignez

Contents

Preface: Brazil in the World

Twenty years ago Brazil was struggling to survive severe international crises and internal economic instability. The Mexican, Asian, Russian, and Argentinean crises; the mismanagement of the entrepreneurial state; and the disastrous effects of inflation on workers are still fresh in memory.

Thanks to the continuity of the economic policy that started with the Plano Real during the FHC government, the picture in Brazil today is hugely different. Economic stability and social programs have allowed for domestic market expansion, a significant reduction in poverty, and the emergence of a middle class of forty million people that today represents 54 percent of the Brazilian population. At the same time as democracy and institutions were strengthened, Brazil experienced high rates of growth as a result of policies that kept inflation low and stable, the fiscal situation under control, and the floating exchange rate in place.

Brazil's growing international presence beyond the South American continent can be gauged by the internationalization of Brazilian industry, and from the manner in which it asserts its interests in international forums.

Despite their different styles and backgrounds, Fernando Henrique Cardoso and Luis Inácio Lula da Silva, both of whom I had the honor of representing in Washington, made valuable contributions to enhancing Brazil's global visibility through their interactions with other heads of state and the contacts they made and maintained abroad. From the international point of view, the voice of Brazil could no longer be ignored on global issues of interest to the developed countries, such as international trade, climate change, energy (biofuel and oil), agriculture and food security, water, and human rights. The new concept of BRICs, an acronym for Brazil, Russia, India, and China, is an indication of the global significance of Brazil and countries like it.

The traditional involvement of Brazilian diplomacy in multinational institutions strengthened the image of the country as a consensus builder and an honest broker. Brazil's ethnic and religious harmony and the role of moderator it exercises in the troubled context of South America also drew the world's attention.

The greater activism of the Lula government and its focus on foreign policy in South America, Africa, and the Middle East, a reflection of the priority it placed on relations with the geopolitical South (South to South relationship), resulted in Brazil's increasing capacity to perform both regionally and globally.

Unlike the other BRIC countries, Brazil is not a nuclear power. This fact, associated with its independent positions in defense of its interests, opened space for the Brazilian government to make incursions into disputes previously the preserve of the developed countries, such as the Iran-US dispute over the Iranian nuclear program.

Brazil has also been engaged in the global governance discussion on the reform of multilateral institutions. In the context of the G20, the consulting mechanism that has been gradually replacing the G8, Brazil has been a strong voice in favor of a more active participation by emerging countries in the World Bank and the IMF. Brazil has also long defended a comprehensive reform of the political and economic mechanisms of the UN and supports UN Security Council expansion to include a greater number of permanent and nonpermanent members in order to increase the weight and representativeness of this overseer of world peace and international security.

Brazil's growing foreign presence as a "soft power" can only be sustained if economic stability and growth and domestic market expansion are consolidated and if its foreign policy remains proactive and consistent.

There is domestic consensus for the growing role of Brazil as a global player and global trader. The time is ripe to focus on those issues that might secure a place for Brazil among the most relevant players on the political and economic world scene.

São Paulo, July 1, 2014

DURING MY NEARLY FIVE YEARS as ambassador in Washington, between 1999 and 2004, I kept a systematic record of all the main events with which I was involved, directly or indirectly, or on which I exercised some influence.

The account presented herein follows the chronology of these records. It is not intended to be either exhaustive or especially meticulous, but merely an objective description of a particularly eventful period of diplomatic life in Washington. The idea is not to make an academic treatment of Brazil-United States relations, but when it is pertinent to do so, synthetic analyses or assessments will be made. Nor is it the purpose here to analyze broader aspects of Brazilian foreign policy not directly related to Brazil-US relations.

From the privileged vantage point of an embassy in DC, this book draws a panorama of the diplomatic relations between Brazil and the United States and the main regional and global issues that came to bear during my service to Brazil and Itamaraty, as the Brazilian Foreign Ministry is also known. In addition, I have seen fit to include a brief look at relations between the period April 2004, when I left the embassy, and May 2011, when this book was completed, as well as a closing chapter that puts the events discussed into wider historical perspective.

An ambassadorship, even in posts of the utmost political and diplomatic importance, does not always coincide with milestone events in the histories of the host or home country. In my case, however, I witnessed facts of particular relevance, such as presidential elections that brought opposition candidates into office in both the United States and Brazil; the September 11 terrorist attacks; and the ensuing wars in Afghanistan and Iraq.

I also had the exceptional experience of accompanying, at close quarters, a lengthy period of relations between Brazilian and US administrations representing two presidents (Cardoso and Lula) who were pursuing very different lines of foreign policy, occasionally leading to breakdowns in mutual understanding between the two countries.

Despite our good relations with the United States on political and diplomatic issues, dialogue with the American government was almost exclusively limited to issues of a bilateral nature, as well as certain regional and a handful of global problems and occasional matters of specific interest to Washington. At that time, Brazil had some involvement in the broader issues of international politics of the day, but its role in these was of less significance.

It would hardly be news to say that a diplomatic mission at a post like the United States is laden with challenges. It was essential, from the very beginning, to open up a direct and unimpeded line of communication with the local authorities and opinion shapers and to find new ways to champion Brazilian interests in the capital of the world's most powerful nation.

On one hand, it was gratifying to pursue that goal and to see, at the same time, the extent to which local interest in knowing Brazil's thinking and position on global issues of the highest relevance was steadily growing. On the other hand, it was frustrating to note that Brazil still carried little weight in international decision-making forums, unlike other BRIC nations—Russia, India and China—which historical and geographical circumstances have placed at the heart of regional conflicts, and whose nuclear arsenals mean they command considerable attention in US foreign policy.

From my near-daily contact with fellow ambassadors and the reports that came back to me of discussions with US authorities during visits by Heads of State or ministers, it was clear just how far removed Brazil still was from the hub of global decision making. In informal conversations with the ambassadors of many of the United States's key allies, such as the United Kingdom, France, Germany and Japan, or even its main rivals, like China, I could see that the international political issues and themes they discussed with the American government were of an order as yet inaccessible to Brazil. The coming chapters will evince the limitations Brazil still faces on the international scene, despite the visible increase in sway it now enjoys in Latin America.

That said, mounting external exposure had begun to show that Brazil had enormous potential, not only in a supporting role, but as a major player in the Latin American field and on economic and political issues of international scope.

In virtue of Brazil's growing involvement in global issues, the embassy stepped up its participation in matters of our interest, such as trade, energy, the environment, climate change, agriculture and regional integration, themes that are at the top of the international agenda. Today, more and more, Brazil's voice is being heard and respected.

As a result of all these experiences, having spent nearly five years in Washington, I am convinced that our most important bilateral relationship remains the one we share with the United States. Views that contend otherwise belong to the domain of rhetoric and prevent us from maximizing the benefits Brazil could draw from a solid relationship with this country.

Of course, the importance of the United States does not exclude the necessity and validity of strengthening our ties with other countries, much less sideline the defense of national interests.

The Washington Dissensus struck me as a fitting title for this book.

The idea was to provide an overview of the political conflicts cleaving American society and to describe the many divergences between the United States and Brazil in particular and Latin America in general during the period in which I served as ambassador.

I would like to close this introduction by acknowledging the contributions of those who helped me develop this book. At the outset, I was able to count on the support of Maria Antonieta Mello, who read my papers and notes and transcribed and organized my recordings. Later, Magda Maciel Montenegro edited the text, removing much of the jargon that might have confounded the lay reader.

My wife, Maria Ignez, journalist and author, was responsible for the transition from diplomatic-speak to a more readable blend of prose. Her perceptive and rigorous appraisal of my text contributed greatly to the clarity of the ideas expressed in this book. For all of this I am deeply grateful.

I was also able to draw upon a valuable haul of suggestions, comments, and criticisms from my former colleagues in Washington, the Ambassadors Marcos Galvão, Evandro Didonet, and Minister Paulo Roberto de Almeida. I thank these friends and colleagues for their support and advice.

It goes without saying that responsibility for the contents of this book is solely my own.

São Paulo, May 1, 2011

CHAPTER 1

Brazil and the United States

Brazil–United States Relations under FHC and Lula

When I arrived in Washington in June 1999, President Bill Clinton had only a year left in his term of office and President Fernando Henrique Cardoso, three. Assuming the embassy in Washington after five and a half years as ambassador in London was the biggest challenge I faced in my career. In the American capital, I witnessed the elections of Presidents George W. Bush, in 2000, and Luiz Inácio Lula da Silva, in 2002, and helped in the democratic transfer of power to the Partido dos Trabalhadores (The Workers' Party), as President Cardoso wished.

I lived in Washington during a time I consider to be one of the most significant in the history of Brazil–US relations. It was a period in which Brazil's international visibility had clearly extended beyond Latin America. The tone and content of our bilateral relations would never be the same again.

Relations with the United States during the eight-year presidency of FHC had been pivotal in terms of Brazilian foreign policy. Brazil was reeling from a succession of four international financial crises (Mexico, Asia, Russia and Argentina) and the restoration of financial stability depended on US support, both directly and through the International Monetary Fund (IMF), as occurred during the crisis of 1998–1999.

At Clinton's invitation, FHC had visited Washington in the early months of his first term of office and formed a personal rapport with the US president, and this greatly facilitated communication on both sides. At a time of such major internal change in Brazil, the general understanding was that it was important to maintain a constructive relationship with the United States if we were to benefit from our bilateral relations.

A convergence of interests and values did not prevent certain fundamental differences from arising between the two countries, as became evident with regard to the issues of the Mercosur and Free Trade Area of the Americas (FTAA) and the involvement of the military in the war on drugs. Nevertheless, you could say that these matters were resolved without much ado, and with the Brazilian government always upholding the national interest.

When I arrived in Washington, Brazil was in economic turmoil, much worse than 2011 would turn out to be. The Brazilian government was struggling to stabilize the economy and restore the country's credibility as an investment hotspot. I continued the effort to keep the bureaucratic channels open for the exploration of Brazilian interests, which were concentrated in the financial area at the time. The order was to boost trade-flows and strengthen the already highly diversified ties between Brazil and the United States.

Another aim was to consolidate Brazil's position as the United States's main interlocutor in South America. Washington responded to our foreign policy actions and maintained a positive relationship with Brazil, respecting our characteristics and interests.

In the first year of the Lula administration, Brazil's approach to the United States remained the same as it had been under FHC, as the positive results of the visits both presidents made to Washington in 2002 and 2003 attest.

During his first visit to the United States, on December 10, 2002, Lula, then president-elect, publically stated: "I come to Washington with a message of friendship from Brazil and the aim of beginning four years of frank, constructive, and mutually beneficial relations between our two countries."

After drawing a parallel between Brazil and the United States, the incumbent president declared: "History shows that we failed, at times, to avail ourselves of opportunities to build a wider partnership. We might have derived more benefit from the impetus that came of our shared fight against Nazism in Europe to create, in times of peace, a degree of cooperation worthy of our nations. However, I am convinced our bond can grow, if our societies get to know each other better . . . if we shake off our stereotypes and prejudices . . . if we learn to value the affinities and respect the differences that exist between us."

On the same visit, during a meeting with Bush, Lula said that he wanted to take relations with the United States to a new level. He proposed that the countries draft a common agenda involving their respective presidents, ministers, diplomatic corps, and commercial sectors, in order to create a much ampler political, diplomatic, and commercial framework for action. It was a move that gave rise to the ensuing slew of comparisons with FHC.

On one hand, Lula genuinely seemed to want to continue with the outgoing government's policy and cement a more mature phase in Brazil–US relations, one geared toward Brazil's traditional target fronts of economic growth, technology transfer and, in the wake of his election, human development and social promotion—"Zero Hunger" was the mantra at the time. Throughout the FHC years and during Lula's first two visits to Washington, our relationship was flourishing. However, while the centrality of bilateral relations between Brazil and the US was initially recognized by the incoming administration, the reality that followed bore little resemblance to the picture President Lula had painted on those first visits.

From 2003 on, Brazil's foreign policy priorities underwent changes that had negative consequences for our relations with the United States. The worldview of the Lula government started to pit the developing countries against the developed world.

The priority placed on South–South relations, with Brazil stepping up its actions in South America, Africa, and the Middle East in terms of politics and trade, and its active pursuit of partnerships with emerging nations, consigned the developed world to the background.

From 2004, the more affirmative foreign policies of the Lula government, such as Brazil's intensified presence on the world stage and its support for the creation of South American institutions that excluded the United States, expanded the areas of friction between the two countries and led to a clash of policy and opinion on themes that extended beyond South America.

In the months preceding my return from Washington in April 2004, there were signs of anti-Americanism in certain sectors of the Lula government, the result of the growing influence the Partido dos Trabalhadores was bringing to bear on foreign policy. The situation had grown increasingly complex in the wake of September 11, as Washington became less tolerant of dissonance.

On the other hand, the convergence of interests and values between Brasília and Washington—such as the protection of democracy and human rights, free trade and the fight against terrorism and narcotics—ensured frank and positive dialogue with the US authorities, despite occasional differences.

I always endeavored to carry out the precise instructions I received from Presidents Fernando Henrique Cardoso and Luiz Inácio Lula da Silva to broaden bilateral relations with the US, reducing the differences and exploring new perspectives for cooperation. "If the US want to play, then we'll play," President Lula told me when I first visited him at the Planalto on January 3, 2003, for a briefing on what he would say in Washington on his first official US visit that March.

With the exception of a US lobby to oust ambassador José Maurício Bustani as director-general of the Organization for the Prohibition of Chemical Weapons (OPCW) during the FHC administration, when Celso Lafer was foreign minister, at no time did the Americans act in a manner that betrayed the principle of mutual respect, the bedrock of any bilateral relationship. And even during the lamentable episode involving Bustani, a clear expression of the arrogant unilateralism of US foreign policy under Bush, the United States understood that the bilateral relationship was never in question, so much so that Brazil was offered the opportunity to nominate another Brazilian to the same international post.

My contact with the US government, particularly with the State Department, was always fruitful. It is interesting that, during my years in Washington, the Bureau of Western Hemisphere Affairs, which covers the Americas in general, was always chaired by secretaries of state of Cuban or Mexican origin.

In a sense, events in Cuba and Mexico determined how the United States handled their interests in Latin America, which was seen as a single bloc. In practice, the State Department did not have separate policies for Central America, the Caribbean, and South America.

In the routine examination of subjects of Brazilian interest, I always tried to show the secretaries of state—Peter Romero, Otto Reich, and Roger Noriega—and those responsible for the region under the White House National Security Council that the specificities of Brazil and the economic and commercial interests it shared with the US precluded it from being handled in the same generic way as the rest of the region.

Throughout my ambassadorship, the open and frank dialogue with our main US interlocutors extended to the other agencies of the administration, which started to view the Brazilian embassy as an informed interlocutor with strong support in Brasília.

Of the many examples I could cite to indicate the degree of credibility and trust we had obtained with Washington, one involves John Maisto, who was in charge of Latin American relations on the National Security Council. Maisto called me one night from the Situation Room in the White House and asked me to consult with FHC about the possibility of his trying to convince President Hugo Chávez of Venezuela to support the application of the Inter-American Treaty of Reciprocal Assistance at an upcoming vote at the Organization of American States (OAS). The treaty had been invoked by Brazil after September 11. I spoke to President Fernando Henrique and explained the urgency and importance of his interjection. "Contrary to American belief, I don't have that kind of influence over Chávez," he joked. Even so, he agreed to speak with the Venezuelan president. When FHC called me back, he said the conversation with Chávez had been positive and that he'd agreed to give the matter some thought. The following morning, when I went to meet Minister Celso Lafer at the airport to accompany him to the OAS meeting, I met the Venezuelan ambassador, who was also there to pick up his chancellor. He told me that Chávez had changed his mind and that he would not be causing any trouble at the conference of American nations.

On another occasion, aware of an impending visit to Brazil by President Jiang Zemin of China, President Bush called FHC to ask him to intercede on his behalf to secure the release of the crew of an America fighter plane that had gone down in China some time before. It was a situation the Americans had been unable to resolve. After talking to Zemin, FHC contacted Bush to say that the crew would be released, but not straight away, and that a Chinese response to the American President would take some time to arrive. Such telephone exchanges between the two presidents became a frequent occurrence, with the embassy normally being informed and mediating proceedings.

In nearly all of my conversations with the State Department and National Security Council, my interlocutors only ever discussed political and economic matters of interest to both countries or concerning South America in general.

In the 1990s, the main themes of US relations with the region, largely financial and economic in nature, were, given the economic difficulties of many South American countries at the time—Brazil included—followed most closely by the US Treasury. As a result, this was a period during which visits by secretaries and high-level Treasury Department officials were more numerous than those from any other area of the US government. The Department of State was the key diplomatic interlocutor, but the Treasury, Federal Reserve Board (FED), US Central Bank, and even the Defense Department were effectively those who formulated and implemented foreign policy for South America.

As it was pursuing negotiations on the creation of the FTAA, the United States changed its stance on Mercosur in the latter half of the 1990s and became more overtly critical of the group. However, contrary to speculations at the time, these objections did not turn into restrictions upon Brazil's initiatives in relation to Mercosur and other matters of regional integration, at least not during my time in Washington.

As an illustration of the absence of any such restrictions, I might mention the meetings I had with Under Secretary of State for Political Affairs Thomas Pickering, at which he wanted to know the outcome of the first summit of South American presidents convened by FHC in 2000 and asked me to extend the US government's congratulations to the Brazilian president on the success of this historic gathering.

During the usually bi-annual meetings between Brazilian foreign ministers (Luiz Felipe Lampreia and Celso Lafer during the FHC administration and Celso Amorim under Lula) and their US counterparts, the embassy prepared the groundwork for an agenda that might vary depending on the conjuncture, but remained structurally unchanged: bilateral relations, with emphasis on economic and trade issues (the FTAA, protectionist disputes, intellectual property); hemispheric relations (Cuba, Peru, Argentina, Colombia, Venezuela, and Bolivia); global themes (energy and the environment) and occasional matters of international politics, such as the conflict in the Middle East and relations with Russia, China, and India.

During the FHC government, these meetings did not always make the headlines, but they did invariably serve to broaden dialogue and strengthen the bond of mutual trust.

The diplomatic agenda between the two countries was, however, ample and diversified, and it is certainly worth mentioning some examples of how the embassy acted in relation to the main themes under discussion.

COLOMBIA

In the early 1990s, the peace process in Colombia was a recurrent theme. Toward the end of the decade, the United States began negotiations with the Colombian government on Plan Colombia, a financial and military aid package designed to help tackle narcotics and contain the guerrilla insurgency led by the Revolutionary Armed Forces of Colombia (FARC), a situation the US authorities claimed was being sensationalized in the international press. Washington wanted to keep Brazil abreast of US–Colombian understandings and wanted to know if we would be willing to help with the peace process. In 1997, Minister Lampreia informed Secretary of State Madeleine Albright that Brazil had already expressed its support for the peace process, but that it had its reservations regarding the US military component of the plan.

According to Minister Lampreia, in 1999 Marco Aurélio Garcia, then secretary of foreign affairs for the Partido dos Trabalhadores (PT), approached him to offer PT's mediation should the Brazilian government choose to make contact with the FARC. Given its ties with the FARC, Garcia claimed PT would be able to make the necessary connection. Years later, when these overtures came to light on the eve of the Brazilian presidential election of 2010, Marco Aurélio Garcia issued an official note in which he denied any such offer and claimed to have been invited to Lampreia's cabinet to discuss the matter of Brazil's support for President of Peru Alberto Fujimori. At no time, the note states, did Marco Aurélio offer assistance, personal or on behalf of the party, in negotiations with the FARC, because "there are, and never have been, any such ties between the party and that organization."

In August 1999, I sent a draft containing suggested elements for a Brazilian policy on the mounting tensions in Colombia to policymakers in Brasília. In this document I offered to help arrange a visit to Brazil by Barry R. McCaffrey, the man in charge of US counternarcotics policy and therefore a relevant interlocutor on Plan Colombia. With my frequent contacts with McCaffrey, I was able to understand the complexity of the issue and the level of the US government's involvement. However, I always discouraged any attempt to engage Brazil.

According to the Argentinean newspaper *El Clarín*, the Colombian president Andrés Pastrana had declared that Brazil was "the only country that did not support Plan Colombia." Brazil's misgivings on the issue stemmed not only from the instability that the escalating military conflict with the FARC was causing along our borders, but from the US military presence in Colombia, where US military advisors and bases were located uncomfortably close to Brazilian territory.

VENEZUELA

Another recurrent theme in my conversations was the situation in Venezuela, especially the verbal attacks on the United States by President Hugo Chávez. I recall one senior staffer at the Department of State telling me that "we don't need any more crazy presidents in South America" and that Chávez, in the light of his "international responsibility" as a head of state, ought to be more careful in his declarations. As this diplomat saw it, the hike in oil prices at the time was not due to economic factors of increased demand alone, but was also due to Chávez' irresponsibility, especially in his incendiary speeches to the Organization of Petroleum Exporting Countries (OPEC).

Greater importance was attributed to Chávez back then. Today, despite his constant and tedious anti-American tirades, the Venezuelan president's rhetoric is taken much less seriously by the United States.

GUIANA AND SURINAME

In the early 2000s, relations were strained between Guiana and Suriname. FHC brokered bilateral talks between their respective heads of state in Brasília. In September, Under Secretary of State Thomas Pickering approached me to ask whether there was room for reconciliation and if Brazil or the OAS might be able to mediate. The level of trust and understanding on regional issues showed the extent to which the United States had come to attribute greater importance to Brazil within South America.

PARAGUAY

Given the assassination of Vice-President Luiz Mária Argaña, the resignation of President Raúl Cubas, and his succession by the president of the legislature, Luiz Macchi, 1999 was a year of political turmoil and fragility in Paraguay. It was clear that the United States had adopted a policy of non-involvement and Brazil's responsible handling of the situation reinforced the perception that it could assume the role of moderator in South America.

PERU

In Peru, in the second half of the 2000s, when Alberto Fujimori won a hotly contested third term of office, Brazil followed the situation closely. Brazilian policy had given Fujimori the benefit of the doubt, but not a blank check. Information and analyses collected by the Brazilian government were requested and appreciated by Washington, which was also carefully following events there.

TERRORISM

The terrorist attacks of September 11, 2001, and their profound impact on the government and on the North American people made relations with the US even more difficult and complex for the majority of nations.

September 11 was a watershed in American history and politics, altering not only the country's priorities, but the manner of its diplomacy. The foreign agenda today is very different from that pre-September 11. Security and terrorism are now leading issues.

Once the initial stupefaction began to fade, the world's nations sought to adapt as well as possible to the new reality, and to glean some benefit in the process. Countries like India, China, and, particularly, Russia knew just what to do to open new spaces of cooperation with the United States, such as on the war on terror, and this enabled them to further their own interests, despite some political burden on the home front.

In a sense, though without making concessions on its sovereignty, Brazil did the same. Understanding the new conjuncture, the Brazilian government went about addressing the various aspects of its bilateral relationship and protecting its interests.

In the wake of September 11, it became even more difficult to find a balance between the defense of the bedrock principles of our foreign policy—such as multilateralism, the peaceful resolution of conflicts, non-intervention in internal matters and equality among states—and concrete interests with immediate repercussions on Brazil's economic and social development, such as access to the North American market, direct investment in Brazil, financial aid, technology transfer, and tourist flows. Conflict between these dimensions was not necessarily inevitable, but the threat was ever-present during the Bush administration.

From a political and strategic point of view, the already scant attention paid to Latin America in US policy dwindled further after September 11.

With regard to Brazil's interests, the fact that the United States began to focus on other regions of the globe post-9/11 turned out to be more positive than negative, as it gave Brazil more room in which to maneuver, especially in South America.

That said, from my vantage point in Washington, I was able to note and assess just how important it was in terms of a positive image worldwide, and among our South American neighbors, to have a sound relationship with the United States. It is and will remain crucial that our regional partners see Brazil as having good relations with the United States, not only so that we can protect our own interests, but also those of the region as a whole.

Any hint of strained relations between Brazil and the United States would have dire consequences for our broader aim of South American integration. The Lula government's idea of positioning Brazil as an alternative to the United States made no sense at all, as the majority of our neighbors would never take that option.

In October 2002, the new worldview and international conduct of the Bush administration, as set forth in the National Security Strategy of the United States—the Republican government's most important foreign policy document—incited the perception of growing differences between Brazil and the United States.

While it recognized Brazil's presence on the international scene, especially economically, the document did not list Brazil among the emerging powers, as it did Russia, India, and China, much less include the country among the United States's traditional allies, largely due to certain independent positions taken by the Brazilian government. This and other existing economic-commercial differences at the World Trade Organization (WTO) and on the ill-fated FTAA idea added new fronts of discord and strain in the political sphere as well, especially on a multilateral level.

Washington had come to see Brazil as a reluctant partner. At a meeting at the Department of State, two direct collaborators of mine, the then-ministers Roberto Jaguaribe and Marcos Galvão, heard US officials observe that Brazil was "out there to save the world from the United States." That was how the US government viewed Brazil as far back as the FHC administration.

Corroborating this perception of Brazil, in April 2002, President FHC reiterated our traditional concerns about the crisis in the Middle East. At that time, the violence of the Palestinians, including suicide bombings and missile attacks on cities in Israel, was just as worrying a prospect as an invasion of Palestinian territory and destruction of infrastructure by the Israeli forces. Responding to Brazilian public opinion, FHC sent a letter to President Bush in which he condemned both the unacceptable acts of terrorism by the Palestinian organization Hamas and the actions of the Israeli army. The letter ended with an appeal to President Bush to use his influence with the Israelis and with Yasser Arafat to broker an immediate ceasefire and return to peace talks.

The importance placed on public opinion in both countries was a new factor in determining the nuances and directions of bilateral relations. In Brazil, surveys showed that the majority was against US occupation in Iraq, and this led certain sectors of the Brazilian government to make that anti-American sentiment known. One could expect nothing else, seeing as repudiation toward the US reached record levels worldwide under President Bush.

ECONOMY AND TRADE

During my time in Washington, the main focus of Brazil–US relations was on the economy and trade. This is hardly surprising, however, given that the commercial area was the only ambit of the bilateral relationship in which discord and attrition was ever-present on both sides.

The way these divergences—natural whenever there is a large volume of trade—are handled has progressed greatly over the last twenty years. In the same manner as occurred between the United States and Europe or Japan, or even Canada and Mexico, trade disputes between the US and Brazil were "de-ideologized" and no longer contaminated other areas of the bilateral relationship, such as policy and diplomacy, as had occurred back in the mid-1980s when Brazilian protectionism on IT sparked a crisis.

Reflecting the changes in the Brazilian economy and its potential for North American companies, Brazil was listed by the Trade Department in 2002 as one of the United States's six biggest commercial partners, alongside China, India, Mexico, Canada, and Turkey. This had positive effects, such as more extensive trade with the US, and negative implications too, with heightened Brazilian concerns about US protectionism and fears of non-compliance with intellectual property norms. That year the world's major economic power surpassed the European Union as Brazil's biggest trading partner.

Gradually, economic, financial, and commercial agents and governmental agencies in the United States recognized the importance of the interests at stake and Brazil's relevance as a partner and consumer.

In 2000, with the aim of creating a closer working relationship with the US Treasury Department and Internal Revenue Service, the Brazilian government decided to create the post of tax attaché to Washington. The first Brazilian IRS official to hold this position at the embassy, as of May 2001, was Luiz Henrique Casemiro, with whom I established a close professional relationship.

Though there was no clear policy for promoting trade with Brazil in the United States, in the hope of boosting exports to the world's largest import market, the US continued to be the preferred trading partner and target market for Brazilian products. In 2000, after six years of deficit, Brazil began to post a trade surplus with the United States.

Given the dynamism of the two economies and their respective private sectors, there was every reason to predict that bilateral trade could even double over the next ten years, with or without the FTAA. The global economic crisis, slowed import and export growth on both sides, as well as Brazil's relegation in terms of US foreign trade strategy, might account for why that failed to materialize.

In this regard, we will take a brief look at the FTAA negotiations, dealt with more thoroughly in Chapter 4. The negotiations for the creation of the Free Trade Area of the Americas were foremost in Brazilian relations with the US throughout my time in Washington.

During the years in which I participated directly or indirectly in these negotiations, as under secretary for Integration, the Economy and Foreign Trade in Brasília and, later, as ambassador in Washington, internally I defended a change of direction in the talks in order to redress lost balance. As such, in substance, I agreed with the position adopted by the Lula government in 2003, which sought to bring the agenda back on track through concrete proposals or, if that failed to work, to break off negotiations entirely, which was what happened.

While following the diversified agenda between the two countries and trying to broaden it, I clearly saw an improvement in the quality of the bilateral relationship, despite the mixed signals that occasionally issued from either side, and the difficulties that arose on the political and economic fronts, which were not always easy to read.

The density of these relations owed more to the intensity of reciprocal flows in the economic area (which has a lot more to do with the private sector) than to an active approach from either government. Be that as it may, the Brazilian public sector, especially the Finance Ministry, used to pay more attention to the United States than it does now. It should be recognized that, given our historical trade balance difficulties, Brazil was much more dependent on the United States in the past, both bilaterally and in terms of American control over multilateral institutions.

CHANGE OF PERCEPTIONS
Due to Brazil's growing influence in South America and on the international stage, and for reasons of an internal political nature, I always set Brazil apart from the Latin American and South American context in my conversations with governmental counterparts and in public presentations.

Despite occasional difficulties in various areas, the United States was showing signs that it was beginning to see our country differently. Our effectiveness and the potential leadership role we were playing in South America was important to the formation of this new perception of Brazil.

This shift first became evident in the financial sphere, through uni- and multilateral support for the Brazilian government's efforts to normalize relations by renegotiating its foreign debt in the early 1990s, and, later, in its actions to avoid an economic downturn during the crises of the late 1990s (Mexico, Asia, Russia) and early 2000s (Argentina).

In the southern hemisphere, Brazil alone has been able to eke out a diplomatic space of its own and to ensure some degree of autonomy for itself as a regional power. However, with a solid dose of realism, I understood that this singularity was limited to the context of the Americas.

From the US perspective, the Latin American picture at the turn of the century was bleak indeed. Only Chile, Mexico, and Colombia had any real affinity with Washington. Brazil, as one of the United States's few interlocutors in the region, was treated in a positive light, and within this context the presidential diplomacies of FHC and Lula, differences in motivation aside, played an important role.

Were that treatment to be extended to the wider sphere of international relations, the American attitude might change concerning Brazil's incorporation into the G8 and acceptance onto the United Nations Security Council as a permanent member.

A later example of this change in attitude toward Brazil by US decision makers, now during the Lula government, is the document "Global Trends 2020," organized by the National Intelligence Council, a research institute with ties to the Central Intelligence Agency (CIA). This document proved very influential in shaping US foreign policy and it envisioned Brazil as one of the main global economic powerhouses over the next fifteen years.

This fledgling recognition of Brazil's potential gave rise to positive readings that stressed the stabilizing and constructive side to the country's international relations, but also detected, not entirely without reason, a Brazilian desire to challenge US projection on the continent.

If I had to single out the high points of the bilateral relationship during my time in Washington, I would not hesitate to pick the support Brazil received from the United States government in obtaining a loan from the IMF during the 2000–2002 financial crisis, without which we would have been forced into default and therefore moratorium. Later, in 2002, US leadership, in defense of the financial package—gainsaying Europe once again—averted a major crisis during the presidential elections. US engagement in favor of Brazil at that time contrasted starkly with the indifference it had displayed toward similar problems in Argentina some months earlier.

Another important moment was when Brazil convened the signatories to the Inter-American Treaty of Reciprocal Assistance in the wake of the September 11 terrorist attacks. However rhetorical the gesture may have been, it was recognized and appreciated by the US government. Also relevant was an official visit by President Lula in June 2003, when the two governments decided to redefine priorities and draw up a positive agenda for the years ahead that emphasized, among other aspects, public and private cooperation on energy.

I left Washington at the end of March 2004, right in the middle of President Bush's re-election campaign. The nation was divided and a win by the Democrat John Kerry was not yet off the table, though the prevailing view was that the Republicans would scrape through again, as indeed they did.

Had Kerry been elected, it is unlikely that the bilateral relationship would have changed in essence. Presumably, there might have been greater openness toward more intense coordination of positions on international matters and the consideration of points of view emanating from other countries, but the US stance on national security and the war on terror, the foreign policy staples of the Bush administration, would not have altered substantially. With trade, however, there was a real danger of increased protectionism, a tendency that was gaining an upper hand at Congress due to pressure from pro-Democrat unions.

Bush's re-election, on the other hand, would have meant little or no change to the internal political situation of the United States, so it was inadvisable for representatives of the Brazilian government to express, however indirectly, any preference with regard to the electoral outcome. Brazil had nothing to gain from a show of support for either candidate— and much to lose, especially in the area of trade barriers. For example, had Brazil supported the democratic candidate and had Bush won the election, Lula's good relationship with the Republican would likely have suffered.

My experience in Washington taught me not to harbor any illusions as to the cost-benefit of a government's decisions in relation to the United States. Even those considered of little importance end up affecting day-to-day relations.

In the case of Brazil, the bar was set that much higher than for most of the United States's other Latin American partners, even if, toward the end of Bush's first term of office, one could already sense that the foreign policy unilateralism accentuated by September 11 was beginning to wane.

Of course, these observations should not be construed as suggesting that we should have strayed from our traditional policy of adopting autonomous positions, but we did have to be aware of the need to be careful in weighing the costs and benefits of our actions abroad and in establishing objective criteria for determining priorities.

Opening or broadening areas of discord or conflict with the United States when there are no objective reasons to do so, or clear gains to be obtained, seems questionable at the very least.

In broad strokes, after everything I experienced in Washington, I would describe our bilateral relationship at the time in the following terms: the United States, like ourselves, prioritized economic/commercial relations and displayed a mixture of affinities, suspicions, and reservations toward us in the political-diplomatic arena. The US was beginning to look at Brazil as a player in its own right, but always within regional bounds.

A Difficult Period in Bilateral Relations

My final months in Washington were the most complex and delicate I faced during my five-year tenure. The tensions that had been mounting since late 2003, with the collapse of FTAA negotiations, intensified in the wake of rippling minor incidents that betrayed an undercurrent of anti-American feeling on the part of the Brazilian government.

A short time later, in early November, in parallel with a meeting of the Group of Friends called by the secretary-general of the OAS to discuss Venezuela, Minister Celso Amorim met with American Secretary of State Colin Powell. The routine agenda covered South American themes—such as the situation in Venezuela, Argentina, and Colombia—and bilateral issues, such as the progress of the working groups created during Lula's visit the previous June and the so-called 'shootdown' policy, the possibility of Brazil downing suspect aircraft in national airspace that fail to respond to orders for immediate landing. I do not believe that Minister Amorim's visit to Washington had anything to do with the overtures Marco Aurélio Garcia had made to US authorities some weeks earlier.

As discussed in greater detail in the chapter on the FTAA, against all expectations—on the part of the media and most of the countries present—the meeting in Miami in November 2003 saw Brazil and the United States, co-chairs of the negotiating process, reach an agreement that kept the possibility of the FTAA alive. The two governments agreed to keep talks going on a two-track basis, with different levels of commitment. However, opposition from Mexico, Chile, Costa Rica, and Canada forced the US to backtrack, restoring the general impasse.

It was the end of FTAA negotiations, which, in the final analysis, represented a victory for those in the Brazilian government who had taken a stance against a free-trade agreement with the United States.

From what I could gather from my interlocutors, by reading between the lines rather than through any direct comments, there were clear signs of concern in the Administration for the future of our relationship.

The government in Washington seemed to understand and accept the rationale of our assertive policy in relation to Cuba and our neighboring region, as well as the economic and commercial reasons behind our differences at the WTO and on the FTAA.

However, certain more recent actions and attitudes by our government had made the US uncomfortable about Brazil, with various acts of Brazilian diplomacy being met with reservations by US authorities—with the exception of our reaction to the war in Iraq, in which we were not alone, as we shall see later.

In December 2003, Lula plowed ahead with his presidential diplomacy by making an official tour of the Middle East, including Libya and Syria, countries about which the US was particularly sensitive. Syria in particular was accused of arming anti-US rebels in Iraq and of providing them with a porous border.

Lula's meetings with the leaders of these two countries, especially his tête-à-tête with Muammar Kadafi in Tripoli, proved disastrous. Lula's calling the Libyan leader "his friend and brother" caused resoundingly negative repercussions in Brazil. Our president's declarations in support of the Libyan dictator and his calls for deeper relations between the two countries threw fuel on the fire of US misgivings. This Brazilian posturing was considered a direct confrontation with Washington, particularly given the mounting difficulties the US was facing in Iraq and its general sensitivity toward the Middle East.

These presidential visits (not to mention successive gestures of extreme sympathy with Hugo Chávez and Venezuela), Brazil's camaraderie and leniency toward the Castro regime, and the constant friction on the FTAA and within the WTO revealed a Brazilian foreign policy that was, in official parlance, becoming increasingly shrill and active.

Back from his trips to Lebanon, Libya, Syria, the United Arab Emirates, and Egypt, Lula organized the first summit of South American and Arab countries for May 2005. The United States did not understand the reasons for Lula's Syrian visit or his refusal to invite Israel to the summit, despite insistent lobbying by the US embassy in Brasília.

According to a US Embassy cable released by WikiLeaks in 2008, "Brazil's initiatives on the Middle East are bungling at best, and the Brazilian government's declarations on key issues for the region just hamper the negotiations." The document goes on to say that "Itamaraty underestimated the sensitivities aroused by its somewhat ham-handed diplomacy, yet [is] unwilling to acknowledge that the Summit . . . could undermine the Middle East peace process at a delicate and promising moment. . . . The cliché-laden bromides of Brazilian officials are also indicative of a lack of real understanding of the Middle East . . . and just add to the anti-Israel choir."

At much the same time, Brazil registered its disapproval of the condemnatory resolutions the United Nations Security Council passed on Iraq and, in return, met with a more trenchant US stand on the renewal of the Non-proliferation Treaty and additional inspection measures that might have led to divergences on nuclear non-proliferation and the development of sensitive technologies.

Perhaps because we had failed to gauge the level of insecurity and vulnerability the terrorist attacks of 2001 had instilled in the United States, Brazil went too far in its protests against the restrictive measures adopted by immigration in US airports. I recall one particular case in which Brazil, alleging reciprocity, started having US citizens fingerprinted and photographed upon entry into the country.

On the Brazilian side, there was growing irritation at US insistence on making unsubstantiated allegations of terrorist activities along the Triple Border; the mounting trade disputes concerning barriers against Brazilian steel and shrimp; the continuation of cotton subsidies; and the increasing consular and immigration problems faced by the Brazilian community in the United States.

In mid-December 2003, the White House asked the Brazilian Embassy in Washington to schedule a telephone conversation between Presidents Bush and Lula, ostensibly on the Americas Summit to be held in Monterrey, Mexico, although the visits to Syria and Libya were also broached.

When pressed on the reasons for the Brazilian visit to the Middle East, Minister Celso Amorim declared that he would not swap a policy of principle for one of product—a contention he was caught contradicting on various occasions, especially with regard to Brazilian accords with certain African nations that showed plain disregard for democracy and human rights.

The escalation of these events might have caused an even greater impact on bilateral relations were it not for the growing importance Washington attributed to Brazil as a stabilizing and moderating influence in Latin America.

In the months that followed, smaller trials were heaped on those larger tribulations: the treatment given to Brazilian tourists and the delays they faced in being issued visas to the United States; the identification of US tourists upon arrival in Brazil; the deportation of Brazilians with expired visas; the difficulties in negotiating the final declaration of the Special Summit of the Americas in Monterrey, scheduled for mid-January; and the US suspension of Brazilian processed meat imports due to mad cow disease.

Against this backdrop of multiplying points of divergence and without having received any information or guidance from Itamaraty, I called the US ambassador in Brasília, Donna Hrinak, to find out how her conversation had gone with Ambassador Vera Pedrosa, then under-secretary of policy at the Brazilian chancellery. My reason for doing this was that, shortly beforehand, the economic secretary at the US Department of State, Allan Larson, had signaled his concerns to me about how this meeting had unfolded. Larson had learned that when the American ambassador voiced her fears that stalled negotiations on these issues would not be good for bilateral relations, Vera Pedrosa's retort was that: "We don't really care about the US–Brazil relationship."

Donna Hrinak confirmed the meeting with the under-secretary and said that she had found her extremely negative. However, she added that she'd had the chance to discuss the same issues the following day with Minister Celso Amorim and that he had been much more constructive and had taken onboard many of her points concerning the Summit declaration. From the perspective of the State Department, this was a matter of relevance and a lack of give-and-take on either side might have resulted in unnecessary attrition. According to the ambassador, the chancellor Celso Amorim had said that the US government should not underestimate Brazil's capacity to contribute to consensus building on this and other matters.

In a conversation I had with Vera Pedrosa in October 2010, the former under secretary said that she had never told—and would never tell—a diplomatic representative from any nation with which we maintained bilateral relations that they did not interest us. To do so, she said, would be a contradiction in terms. Pedrosa also claimed that the "negativity" Ambassador Donna Hrinak had detected was an interpretive leap on her part or perhaps a reflection of her disappointment with the response to her request to include Israel in the Arab and South American Summit.

Interpretations aside, what Donna Hrinak confided to me in January 2004 was that the Department of State's concerns over Brazil were growing.

According to Hrinak, Secretary of State Colin Powell had made a negative assessment of US relations with Latin America in general and with Brazil in particular during a coordination meeting with American ambassadors to Latin America in December 2003. Powell said that relations between the two countries had deteriorated since the highly positive meeting between Presidents Bush and Lula in June that year, with November having been a particularly low point. Although the concept of the BRICs as an organized group had yet to arise, Donna added that Powell had analyzed Brazil, Russia, India, and China at length and observed that Brazil was the country showing the greatest uncertainty in its moves. When asked by one of the ambassadors what might be done to secure these nations' support, Powell replied that it was no easy task, as Brazil's reactions were the most unpredictable of the group, and its positions the least clear.

It is undeniable that Brazil is less decided than China, Russia, and India with regard to what it wants from its relationship with the United States. And it is also a fact that while these three often pursue lines of policy that are antagonistic to the US, their actions and reactions are much easier to predict.

However, Powell's observations at the time may have derived from disinformation or the usual old stereotypes, as it was not exactly the case that Brazil did not know where its interests lay, but rather that the United States was beginning to feel the effects of the worldview held by the political party now pulling the foreign policy strings at Itamaraty.

It was now early 2004, two months before my departure, and bilateral relations remained tense, with these minor incidents causing unnecessary friction. In terms of domestic politics, our government had no interest in changing the situation, as anti-American feeling was swelling in the face of the war in Iraq and the adverse effects US protectionist measures were having—and continue to have—on our foreign trade.

From my privileged vantage point in Washington, I could see little prospect of a reversal of fortunes in the foreseeable future, despite the fact that, in light of our more global interests, it was hard to justify certain attitudes of near-provocation toward the US.

However, one of the hottest flashpoints had been resolved: the issue of the deportation of Brazilians detained in US territory for irregularities with their resident visas. Our government was against deportation, to be paid for by the US, and responded by creating obstacles in relation to entry documents, place of arrival, and the number of passengers on the flights. After some weeks of uncertainty, Itamaraty finally had the good sense to change its position and accept the arrival of specially chartered flights carrying our compatriots.

Another minor dispute, the product of diplomatic filigrees, concerned the granting of *agrément* to the new US ambassador in Brasília, John Danilovich. In retaliation for the four weeks or so it took for the United States to approve the name of the new Brazilian ambassador Roberto Abdenur in 2004, the Brazilian government decided to sit on the Danilovich request. The new ambassador, with whom I had become friends while in London, was a businessman and White House insider, had served as US ambassador to Costa Rica under Bush and was now being given a second posting during the same administration, unusual for a political ambassador.

Though Washington complained and asked for the process to be accelerated, Danilovich was only granted *agrément* after the acceptance of Roberto Abdenur.

At the same time as these bureaucratic skirmishes, there was another administrative incident that very nearly escalated into something more serious. The US consul in Brasília publicly criticized Brazil's record with regard to the falsification of passports and visas. Minister Celso Amorim threatened to request the diplomat's recall, but settled for summoning Ambassador Donna Hrinak in order to formalize his dissatisfaction.

It is important to note that my regular contact with US government officials, the White House, the Department of State, the United States Trade Representative (USTR), Treasury and Agriculture Departments, and, most importantly, the public declarations these made, left me of the opinion that the US authorities, particularly the Department of State and Treasury Department, deliberately minimized conflict with Brazil in order to keep a positive bearing on Brazil–US relations.

It is hardly surprising that the most affirmative declarations about continuing to support the favorable results being posted by the Brazilian economy came from the US Treasury. Maintaining a smooth understanding with the largest country in South America was always going to be advantageous for Washington, especially because the US government wanted to be sure that its fundamental interests would not be affected by Brazilian positions or initiatives already marked our autonomy from Washington.

A political decision had evidently been made to avoid friction with Brazil and to accommodate clearly divergent visions, perceptions, interests, and goals concerning current affairs. Brazilian opinions and positions were absorbed for the sake of a mature and stable long-term relationship. The desire to preserve and develop bilateral contact spoke louder than the occasional disgruntlement.

In retrospect (up to 2004), this good will can be explained on various grounds: the respect and good chemistry between the heads of state Fernando Henrique Cardoso and Bill Clinton, first, and later between Luiz Inácio Lula da Silva and George W. Bush. While the affinity between the former pair was genuine and based on shared interests and similar philosophies, the chemistry between the latter pair was staged and utilitarian, seeing that Lula never stopped firing criticisms at Bush.

Mistaken Perceptions of Brazil and Latin America in the United States

During my time in Washington I was able to confirm that US policy toward Brazil is still based on blurred visions, myths, stereotypes, and distortions of reality.

The US lacks a deeper knowledge of our political, economic, social and cultural reality. As a result of this misinformed perception, what spills over is a combination of low priority, a sometimes superficial and shortsighted political reasoning, and concrete economic and commercial interests that fall short of our developmental potential.

The same is true on the Brazilian side. As stated earlier, among the major emerging nations, Brazil is the only country that does not have a clear strategy toward the Washington powerbrokers, perhaps because the Brazilian government does not have a clear notion of what to extract from its relationship with the United States. This might be because Brazil—whether as a nation or government—does not pay sufficient attention to the potential of the relationship with the United States, as does China, for example.

Prior to my arrival in Washington, Itamaraty commissioned a survey from the University of Chicago's National Opinion Research Center to gauge how Americans viewed Brazil. The analysis covered various segments of American society: Congress, politicians, businesspeople, the media, society in general, and the everyday man-in-the-street.

I did not have to wait for the survey results to see that the average US citizen's knowledge of Brazil was very poor. While the general impression was positive, the age-old stereotypes prevailed.

Brazil was not even recognized as a coffee producer. For the Americans, coffee came from Colombia, or so they had been programmed to think after a twenty-year advertising campaign. The aircraft produced by Embraer, which had bitten off a sizable chunk of the regional American market, were not actually considered to have been *Made in Brazil*.

The results of the University of Chicago survey proved the need for urgent action toward a better, more focused promotion of Brazil abroad. It reinforced my conviction of the importance of creating centers for Brazilian studies, making more frequent contact with the American media and participating more intensely in seminars and discussion forums, such as the local think tanks. What had struck me as necessary from my very arrival there had become imperative. The economic crises of the early 2000s and the uncertainty stirred by the approaching election in the latter half of 2002, with the real possibility of a PT victory, were making the government in Washington and US investors increasingly jittery about the course Brazil would take. It was therefore of the utmost importance that the embassy redouble its efforts to supply information about and analyses of the situation in Brazil. It was essential that we allay the stakeholder's fears about the direction in which Brazil would move under a leftist government led by a former factory-floor worker and union leader.

In my presentations I always highlighted that, despite the progress made and the continuation of the country's economic policy, Brazil was still on "permanent probation," that is, its explanations were always accepted with reservations by the international financial community. The expression was adopted by Minister Pedro Malan in parrying the misgivings of our interlocutors.

Public diplomacy became one of the main work fronts of the Brazilian mission in the United States. After almost five years of intense contact and observation, I considered myself reasonably knowledgeable about how the US government operated in its relations with the region. I had begun to understand the inner workings of the Washington bureaucrats' decision-making process on Latin America and Brazil.

At the many Washington think tanks I was involved in, I took part in countless debates on US–Latin American relations, and my comments frequently covered the following points:

- Neither the region nor Brazil ranked among the United States's main global interests. We simply weren't on Washington's radar.
- The US government did not have adequate information processing or knowledge about the region's recent development, perhaps because we posed no threat politically (militarily, financially, economically or diplomatically) and because we were not viewed in the US as politically relevant or important to the economy.
- This information processing was inadequate because the governmental organizations that directly accompanied relations with Brazil (the Department of State, the Treasury, Departments of Trade and Defense, the USTR) lacked a staff that was qualified or knowledgeable enough to help shape policy.
- In 2002, the Department of State's bureau for western hemisphere affairs was left practically acephalous, with not a single specialist on Brazil. No one spoke Portuguese there, or had the slightest understanding of reactions in Brasília.
- The Treasury—the agency with the best knowledge and most accurate analysis of the real political, economic, and financial situation in Latin America—was cut off from the rest of the US government.
- Despite always viewing us in the negative light of disputes and distrust, the Department of Trade and the USTR were, by necessity, our most frequent interlocutors.
- The White House, National Security Council, and Economic Council, which, based on presidential rhetoric about Latin America as a priority, might have drafted new foreign policy, remained too engaged with American problems elsewhere in the world to do so. Furthermore, those responsible for Latin America did not have the political weight to make a positive impact and even had to receive inadequate contributions and suggestions from other, less qualified sources.
- Some so-called Brazilianists and experts in Latin America suffered the same deficiencies. They thought they understood

Brazil, but they held true to the same equivocal perceptions of old.

- At the American Congress, ignorance about Brazil was even worse, given the overall lack of general knowledge about what went on elsewhere in the world. Brazil simply did not inhabit the minds of this important source of power in Washington.
- The information in the hands of the American businesspeople, which was largely positive and accurate, had no official channel of communication through which to inform governmental decision making.
- Over the last thirty or forty years, in the absence of a coherent policy, a clear definition of priorities, and a positive agenda, a certain ill will toward Brazil had taken root and permeated the middle tier of department staffs—exactly where there is the least change over time.
- This ill will toward Brazil stemmed not only from decades-long trade disputes, but also from the perception nurtured by the local bureaucrats that Brazil behaved differently from the rest of the region. By adopting public attitudes and positions that diverged from or clashed with those defended by the US, while putting its own interests first, Brazil set itself apart from its regional neighbors.

This was the backdrop that explained the US government's discourse and general attitude toward Brazil. The memory of an erratic economy, default on foreign debt, military authoritarianism, and human rights abuses had helped sear this negative perception into North American minds.

This negative disposition and wrongheaded perception of Brazil were made evident by the way the US government received the speeches President FHC delivered in France in October 2001, in which he critically addressed the US government's behavior in the war on terrorism, its declarations about the Triple Border, the US policy of withholding aid from Argentina—despite Brazil's appeals—and about US reactions to Brazil's stance on the FTAA. Various public statements from high-ranking members of the US government, including President Bush himself, revealed the level of discontent with Brazil at that time.

Knowledge and understanding of the Brazilian reality, a clearer notion of our relative international importance, and a more concrete perception of US interests in Brazil are the prerequisites for a change of attitude toward the country in the United States and for the definition of a positive bilateral relationship. If this were to happen, Brasília would certainly enjoy more favorable winds in Washington.

I had the opportunity to collaborate on the first policy document to present Brazil in this clearer light, drafted in January 2001 by the New York Council on Foreign Relations and sent to the incumbent President Bush and his chiefs of staff.

CHAPTER 2

Panoramic View from the Embassy in Washington

The Election of George W. Bush

My term began in June 1999, sixteen months before the elections returned the Republicans to the White House. I was able to follow Bill Clinton's last term at close quarters, and to watch the electoral process that would confirm George W. Bush as the forty-third President of the United States at the end of 2000.

Some consider the American presidential elections to be the "greatest show on earth." I watched proceedings as an external observer from the primaries through to the party conventions, and it certainly is a unique experience.

Invited, along with other ambassadors, to attend mega-rallies and meetings with candidates from both parties, I was able to witness firsthand the victories of Al Gore at the Democratic Party Convention and of George W. Bush at that of the Republicans. As in most countries, during the months leading up to an election, those who work for the government are more interested in organizing their futures and finding some academic or private-sector post, making diplomatic work and contact with government staffers all the harder.

Throughout the electoral campaign, I maintained contact on both sides, attending meetings with advisors to the candidates, some of whom ended up filling posts in the new government.

I took the initiative of drafting a memorandum for candidates Bush and Gore explaining the relevance of my country within Latin America and underscoring the importance of US relations with Brazil. The Republican candidate replied through his campaign coordinator, the future chief of staff Joshua Bolten, saying that he had read the material and forwarded it to the advisor in charge of Latin American affairs, Robert Zoellick, with whom I had established a good rapport prior to the elections. Zoellick went on to become the US trade representative during the Bush administration, and we maintained close contact. During the electoral period, I also met Paula Dobriansky, representative of the Council for Foreign Relations in Washington and undersecretary for multilateral affairs in the Bush administration. She would go on to play a key role in negotiations on human rights and the environment.

After Bush's inauguration, the contacts made during the campaign meant that the embassy was already an interlocutor of the new government, which greatly facilitated our access to the administration.

The whole electoral process of 2000 made it clear that the United States was still split down the middle politically. Over the last twenty years, presidential and congressional elections, with two victories for Clinton and two for Bush, showed that the country was divided along geographical lines: the Republicans and conservatives held the midlands while the Democrats and liberals prevailed on the east and west coasts.

The electoral system of the world's largest democracy is decentralized and, compared with the Brazilian process, frankly outmoded. In the absence of a centralized electoral court like we have in Brazil, each state is left to set its own rules. The presidential election itself is indirect, with the popular vote converted into an electoral college consisting of a contingent of party electors for each of the fifty states. In 2000, the voting systems used in various states were antiquated, with some still using paper ballots and punch cards, which increased the likelihood of fraud, as occurred in Chicago in 1961 when John F. Kennedy was elected, and in Florida when George W. Bush received his first mandate.

In the latter case, the irregularities evinced not only the precarious manner in which the votes were collected and counted, but also the obstacles posed to African American voters, many of whom were barred from polling stations on the most varied pretexts. To make matters worse, the state of Florida was governed at the time by candidate Bush's brother, Jeb Bush, who controlled the electoral maneuvers through one of his protégées, the general coordinator of the state's canvassing board. In light of such patent irregularities in the American presidential vote, it is impossible not to speculate on how the media and international organizations that monitor electoral probity would have reacted had this occurred in a country like Brazil.

The Democratic candidate Al Gore won the popular vote, but lost Florida by a tiny margin, a result that might have been reversed had the recount not been so contaminated by political influences. The Democratic Party appealed and tried to have the Florida vote overturned.

After weeks of recounts that calculated only minor corrections to the original tally, the Democratic Party took the matter to the Supreme Court, where most of the judges had been appointed by Republican governments. Weeks after the election, by a total of five votes to four, the Supreme Court declared George W. Bush the winner, silencing Democratic protests and demonstrations. Though contestable, the Florida count proved decisive to the end result, as the state's electors swung the Electoral College tally in Bush's favor, making the Republican candidate the president-elect.

The media covered the presidential election in meticulous detail. Many newspapers and television news programs highlighted the deficiencies of the electoral system and the need for reform. The whole debacle was followed closely and hotly debated by American society. But once the Supreme Court passed its ruling, the establishment emerged and exerted its considerable influence. Three hours after the announcement of the Judiciary's decision, candidate Al Gore went on television to recognize Bush's victory and put himself at the incumbent's disposal. With that, the United States showed once again that, contrary to what occurs in many other countries, you just don't argue with the rule of law.

As is praxis, FHC sent a message of congratulations to the new US head of state. Like other diplomatic representatives, I also congratulated Bush, reminded him of his promise to prioritize Latin America and expressed my hope that relations between the US and Brazil would grow stronger and closer, despite our occasionally conflicting interests and perceptions.

For an external observer, it is fascinating to see how effectively democratic institutions and mechanisms actually work in the United States. After the Supreme Court ruled to uphold the outcome in Florida, the party-political dispute immediately ceased, as if by magic. The political powerbrokers and the media accepted the decision without question. The press stopped picking through the failings of the electoral system and society in general, regardless of party preferences, and recognized the legitimacy of George W. Bush. According to political tradition in the United States, the president-elect is considered the new leader and commander-in-chief of the armed forces, and, as such, warrants the support of one and all. The strength of the institutions prevailed over all other interests, party-political or otherwise, rightly considered less important than the permanent values of democracy.

On the economic level, President Bush received the country in a stable condition, running an internal surplus and enjoying high rates of growth. During the previous eight years under Clinton, the United States had grown at 3 percent per annum on average, which, at the time, meant an increase of the US GDP equivalent to the whole Brazilian GDP every two years. American society was brimming with self-confidence and opinion polls revealed a high degree of consumer satisfaction. However, current account deficits and the trade balance were beginning to cause concern both internally and externally.

In June 1999, on the crest of an economic boom, the United States was in the grips of euphoria. This was when the "real-estate bubble" began to inflate, and consumer excess was clear for all to see. With savings down to near zero, people were buying up homes, boats, cars, consumer goods of all kinds, spending almost without limit. The result was imbalance, creating market conditions that snowballed into a financial and economic crisis that would shake the very foundations of the global financial system in late 2008 and 2009, with devastating consequences for economies worldwide.

George W. Bush arrived at the White House with entrenched ideological principles that would greatly influence government actions throughout his mandate. In order to secure election, Bush had sealed alliances with far-right conservative cliques and with the religious right. It was an option that had always framed the Republican leadership's vision on issues of politics, economics, and civil rights from the very start.

The election of George W. Bush therefore represented a change of direction. On the economic front, the government introduced ideologically motivated tax cuts that mostly benefited big business and the richer tiers of the population, at a time when the financial burden was being ratcheted up after September 11.

In terms of domestic policy, right-wing sectors allied with religious fundamentalists came to the fore with disastrous effect, basking in the prestige afforded by a born-again Christian president. Bush radicalized the government's already conservative positions on civil rights, abortion, gay marriage, stem-cell research, and even Darwinism, among other issues.

Under George W. Bush, US foreign policy became arrogant and unilateral, in stark contrast to the position adopted by the previous government.

The first months of the new administration saw the resurrection of an action plan originally formulated back in 1991 but shelved after Bush

Senior's defeat and the ensuing eight-year tenure of Bill Clinton. Entitled the "Project for the New American Century," this was a strategy for reaffirming US international dominance in the economic, political, financial and military spheres. The plan was drafted by a neo-con think tank that included Dick Cheney, Donald Rumsfeld, Richard Perle, and Paul Wolfowitz, all of whom held influential posts in Bush Sr.'s government.

This project created conditions for strengthening the US presidency and, externally, its bedrock was the National Security Doctrine and a series of presidential resolutions and laws, such as the Patriot Act, which led to serial infringements upon civil liberties and encouraged the use of torture as a means of fighting terrorism. The national interests of the United States were now to be defended by the military through the use of force, buoyed by the theories of preemptive strikes and regime change. For the Department of State, all that was left was to conduct foreign relations in accordance with the doctrine.

While Bush was still trying to assert himself before the world and the American people and prove that he was a fitting occupant of the White House, the nation was rocked by a series of terrorist attacks that changed US history and the course of the presidency.

With the change of atmosphere in New York and Washington after September 11, I watched the new domestic political context take shape. The Republican Party was strengthened by the dramatic impact of these terrorist actions, expanding its majority in the House of Representatives, winning control of the Senate in the congressional elections of 2002, and electing the highest number of governors.

What ensued was a period of total neo-conservative dominance over domestic politics and foreign policymaking.

September 11

Accepting an invitation made the previous week, I was due to have lunch with Under Secretary Rogelio Pardo-Maurer at the Pentagon at noon on September 11, 2001. I could never have imagined that on that very day the headquarters of the US Department of Defense would be partially destroyed by an airliner hijacked by terrorists on a suicide mission.

On the morning of the 11, at around nine a.m., I was getting ready to leave the residence for the chancery when I received a phone call from Minister Marcos Galvão telling me to turn on the TV to see what was happening in New York: a plane had just crashed into the World Trade Center. I switched on the television and saw a plane plow into one of the towers. Like many others, I thought what I saw was a replay, when in fact it was a second plane and a second tower. I went straight to the chancery, where I took a series of calls from other ambassadors, all concerned about the news coming in from New York and the possibility of similar attacks on Washington.

At that moment, I was keenly aware that we were witnessing an event of extreme gravity, something unprecedented that would have a major impact on the United States and therefore also on the world.

Unconfirmed rumors reached us of other hijacked planes and explosions in various parts of the city, such as the State Department building, as well as information about a third kamikaze plane, said to have crashed into the Pentagon.

For security reasons, all planes were ordered to land, which meant air traffic controllers had to bring 4,500 aircraft safely to ground, all at once. Washington was seized by panic and tension, with public buildings being evacuated and hordes of people rushing to get home.

Many ambassadors decided to close their diplomatic missions in order to prevent panic from spreading through their staffs, but I decided to stay at the chancery with the diplomats and administrative personnel, and tried to contact FHC.

With the national communications system jammed, I only managed to get hold of the president an hour after the attacks. In a world of instantaneous communication, the intention was not to inform Brasília of what was going on, but to brief the president on the situation in Washington and transmit my first impressions as to the reaction to the tragedy in the American capital.

I remember telling the president that these events would certainly have deep-running repercussions on internal and external US policy. For the first time in two hundred years, the United States of America was being attacked on home soil. The last time had been during the Anglo-Franco-American war, in 1814, when the British set fire to the White House.

My initial impression—that the United States would never be the same after those attacks—turned out to be true, as I was able to witness for myself over my remaining time in Washington.

On the day after the tragedy, I was eager for news of Under-Secretary Maurer, with whom I was supposed to have lunched at the Pentagon on that Tuesday. I called him up and, to my surprise, he insisted that we meet for lunch the following day so I could see the damage in loco. In true American style, lunch was a sandwich with Coca-Cola, and then we strolled through the Pentagon interior and along some corridors directly facing the crash site. Maurer told me that the impact had left a thick blanket of ash on the ground, and that the walls were all smoke stained. You could still smell the cinders and engine fuel in the sector where the Secretary of Defense has his cabinet. We then went outside, where I could see the full extent of the damage, which only wasn't greater because a wing had hit the ground with thirty or forty meters to impact and because the concrete façade and windows were designed to withstand the force of a four hundred and fifty-pound bomb. When we reached the destroyed part of the building, which had been in renovations at the time of the attack and was therefore only partially occupied, Maurer said to me: "You're luckier than you imagine." He went on to explain that if his transfer to a new office had not been held up by red tape, our meeting on September 11 would have taken place in precisely the area where the plane hit, killing one hundred twenty people.

The impact destroyed a segment of the building, but I did not see any plane wreckage. It is peculiar that there was no sign of the engines, fuselage, or parts of the wings, a fact that gave rise to countless conspiracy theories insinuating that the compound had not been hit by a plane at all, though it seems very unlikely to me that a bomb or truckload of explosives could have caused that kind of damage.

My conversation with Maurer concentrated on the Pentagon's perceptions of terrorism and on its possible existence within Latin America and Brazil. I took the opportunity to advance the Brazilian government's position—which I was scheduled to outline later at a meeting with Western Hemisphere Mission leaders at the State Department—on the multilateral support for the United States in our region and, specifically, the invocation of the Inter-American Reciprocal Assistance Treaty (IARA). Maurer expressed American gratitude for the Brazilian government's support and solidarity, and stressed that the destruction of the World Trade Center would not affect the US alone, but various countries worldwide, Brazil included, as there were a great many foreigners among the dead.

September 14th was declared a national day of mourning. Stars and stripes could be seen all over the city. A religious service was held at the Washington Cathedral, with President Bush, the government, and the entire diplomatic corps in attendance. In the first row sat former Presidents Carter, Clinton, and George Bush, Sr., who discreetly congratulated his son after his brief speech. Amidst the emotion and outpourings of patriotism, there were no signs of unease within the government ranks, despite Bush's dismissive handling of the episode.

On the day of the attacks, the President disappeared for hours, spirited away to secret bases while the security agencies, with Vice-President Dick Cheney at the helm, tried to reassert control. In New York and Washington, public gatherings, the media, and the mass for the dead in the attacks were awash with demonstrations of patriotism and national sentiment stirred by renditions of traditional songs and anthems. The general perception was that the country was at war and each citizen had to do his or her part to defend the nation. The atmosphere in Washington remained tense for a long time, and the behavior of the US government and American people came to display an unmistakable current of insecurity and fear.

From its first statements, the government in Washington attributed the attacks to Al-Qaeda and its leader, Bin Laden, who publically assumed responsibility the day after the tragedy.

To garner further information about the possible political and economic fallout from the terrorist attacks on Washington and New York, I spent the following week in conversation with colleagues, including the ambassadors from the UK and Russia.

The British ambassador, Christopher Meyer, told me that the United States was preparing its reaction, though without haste. I asked him if he thought we might expect a US response in the short term, and he replied that the government was proceeding with care and weighing its military options. On that same day, Bush gathered his cabinet around him at Camp David and announced, for the first time: "We are at war." International solidarity was already assured (through NATO, the UN, ANZUS and the OAS reciprocal assistance treaty). In Bush's words, it was now that the US would really see who its friends were. The British ambassador confirmed that Powell had had tough words with the Pakistani ambassador in Washington and given him a checklist of concrete actions the government expected Islamabad to take. He observed that Bin Laden was US enemy number one and that the challenge to its leadership role would be to maintain sustainable multilateral support.

Straight off, Yuri Ushakov, the Russian ambassador to the US, said that internal pressure would force Bush to retaliate heavily. He added that the Russian President Vladimir Putin had already spoken to Bush more than once and that Russia would support the US. Ushakov reck-

oned this would considerably improve the two countries' bilateral relations. He also said that Russia and the US would be discussing the main
issues on the international scene, such as Libya and North Korea.

Tension was rife and rising in Washington. I recall, on October 12th,
a month and a day after the attacks, I was at a meeting at the Department of State when the bomb alarm sounded, to general consternation.
Many of those in attendance were scared and wanted to leave, but, convinced that further terrorist attacks were unlikely, I was among those
who remained calm and continued with the meeting. In the end, there
was no need to evacuate. As the FBI informed the Department later, it
was all just another hoax.

The Capitol, the White House, ministries, and other public buildings
were all barricaded behind concrete blocks that cut them off from the
surrounding public and traffic. Countless checkpoints were set up and
Washington began to resemble a city under siege.

A week after September 11, fears grew of a proliferation of terrorist
attacks using anthrax, a lethal chemical substance that was found in letters addressed to individuals and institutions in the government, Congress and the press. Five people who had handled these envelopes had
died, and the general suspicion was that Islamic terrorists were to blame.
However, after intense investigations, in early 2002 the FBI managed to
identify the culprit. Much to American disappointment, the man behind the lethal letters was not a foreign enemy, but one Bruce E. Ivins,
an American biodefense specialist who worked in a military lab near
Washington. Ivins committed suicide in 2008. At its flag-waving best,
the press was very low-key in its handling of this news. It was only in
2010, eight years after the attacks, that the scientist was formally accused
by the FBI of perpetrating the anthrax crimes.

At the height of the anxiety caused by these events, the administrative head of the Brazilian embassy informed me that he had called the
FBI because a suspect envelope had just arrived in the mail. Part of the
chancery had to be sealed off to prevent possible contamination, but
thankfully it was all a false alarm. According to the specialists who analyzed the envelope, all it contained was talc and a newspaper clipping.
We discovered that the sender, who was never identified, had tried to
create some intrigue by sending me a news story about a visit that the
Brazilian consul general to New York had made to a town in New Jersey,
where he presented himself not as consul general, but as the Brazilian
ambassador to the US.

I forwarded the talc-sprinkled envelope to the consul general Flavio Perri in New York, and he rang me to say that he had never passed himself off as Brazilian ambassador to the United States, and he sent me his visiting card as proof. Luckily for all of us, the whole story ended in laughter rather than tears.

There are ten Brazilian consulates general in the US. However, despite the nomenclature and their purely consular duties, the fact that they are often referred to as ambassadors can cause no end of confusion.

AMERICAN SOCIETY AFTER SEPTEMBER 11

The terrorists had shown frightening precision in targeting the archsymbols of American power: financial, represented by the Twin Towers in New York; military, represented by the Pentagon; and political, represented by the White House or Capitol.

Whoever planned the attacks had shown real ingenuity. After all, four planes were hijacked almost simultaneously, despite the security and logistical obstacles, and three of these hit their designated targets.

To better understand the reaction of the US government and society in general, it is important to remember that September 11 occurred at the height of American power and affluence and affected American hearts and minds so deeply because no one could have imagined, or could now accept, that the country was as vulnerable as the attacks proved it to be.

September 11 and the two wars that ensued, in Afghanistan and Iraq, were a watershed in US history, and they radically changed international relations and the way the US saw itself and was seen by others. In terms of foreign policy, the agenda was completely redrawn. Security and terrorism became priority, and all dealings with the US became more complex, sensitive, and delicate. Internally, the preventive measures adopted offended certain time-honored principles of the constitution, mainly those concerning individual freedoms.

Initially, American society viewed the terrorist attacks more as kamikaze suicides than as ideologically-driven acts that materialized deep resentment toward the United States, even though Bin Laden's video claiming responsibility had left no doubt about this. In the months that followed, rarely did I see or hear any analyses in the US that attempted to explain the causes and real motivations of those who took part in the attacks on New York and Washington. The desire for retaliation stifled any moves toward a deeper understanding of what had happened.

The strikes against the World Trade Center and Pentagon made me think of Jean-Christophe Rufin's book *L'empire et les nouveaux barbares* (*The Empire and the New Barbarians*), published in 1991, in which he argues that the reasons for terrorism can best be found among those who are excluded from everything the Empire represents. The "barbarians" or "new barbarians" who rebel are precisely those who do not partake in the prosperity that the empire affords. Islamic fundamentalism, largely peripheral, has managed to hold out, at least to some extent, against many aspects of globalization, and this creates political instability and threatens the dominant economic and social system.

On the other hand, the arrogance of the United States's unrivalled power, evinced by its political parading of military might, its alliance with Israel, and its military presence in Saudi Arabia, stoked disputes with many Muslim countries.

The fact is, insofar as they were considered a direct aggression against the very essence of the American way of life, the September 11 attacks were seen by the United States as justifying an immediate and unilateral "good versus evil" counterstrike.

Two governments later, in December 2009, when Barack Obama was awarded the Nobel Peace Prize, the new US president surprisingly returned to the idea of a "just war" in his acceptance speech, referring to the contradiction inherent in a leader embroiled in two wars being given such an award. On May 1, 2011, the US was sent into paroxysms of nationalist euphoria by the successful operation in Pakistan to track down and kill Bin Laden, the arch enemy of the American people and government.

The network of support from other countries that grew up around the US in the wake of the attacks was not so much asked for by Washington as expected as a natural act of solidarity. George W. Bush's declarations in this regard—"if you're not with us, you're against us"—were the best translation of that expectation. In the war against terror, a faceless enemy, those countries not allied with the United States could only be on the side of the terrorists.

The atmosphere was heavy in Washington, redolent of the McCarthy period, the communist witch hunt of the 1950s. In a city that lives and breathes politics, no one had the animus to subject the different aspects of what was happening to deeper scrutiny. There were questions, certainly, but they were not asked in public.

Regularly, Maria Ignez and I organized or attended private dinners with intellectuals, politicians, and journalists, dinners like those held at the homes of Bill Haseltine and Gale Hayman, both well-known businesspeople and good friends I made in Washington. For six or seven months after September 11, the word "war" was practically taboo at these informal gatherings. If it was mentioned or discussed, it was with the utmost caution.

Known as a champion of freedom of expression and for the presumption of innocence pending proof of guilt, the US had suddenly changed its ingrained behaviors, railroaded by the ideological radicalism of Bush.

After the attacks, anyone could be detained on suspicion of committing terrorism or of harboring terrorists, without the possibility of habeas corpus. People started weighing their words in public and avoiding value judgments on acts of government related to terrorism or to Afghanistan.

September 11 changed routines. President Bush authorized the air force to shoot down any aircraft under terrorist control, even those carrying civilians. Airports and train and subway stations were given reinforced security, with successive body and baggage searches and a whole new set of rules. The inconvenience to travelers was immense, and it took a lot of patience to tolerate the obvious excesses committed by often inadequately trained security agents. Check-in for international flights was now four hours ahead of flight time, three for domestic flights. Metal detectors and x-ray screenings of baggage became routine, not to mention the inconvenience of having to remove one's shoes, belt, and jacket. On arrival, there was obligatory fingerprinting for all travelers not from developed countries allied with the US.

As I mentioned previously, alleging reciprocity, Brazil introduced finger-printing for US citizens, much to American and international surprise. The measure, taken out of retaliation rather than necessity, was soon abolished by the Brazilian government.

The paranoia engendered by this atmosphere of good-versus-evil spread to airports the world over, in response to demands from the US and its allies, the UK and Spain, which had also suffered terrorist attacks against their bus and train systems.

Stirred by the measures being adopted by the government, which declared war on terrorism, a certain ill-feeling toward foreigners began to arise in US society. The worst hit were Arabs in general, as the September 11 hijackers had all been of Islamic origin. President Bush hitched a ride on this exacerbated patriotism to push through draconian legal measures in homeland security.

The Patriot Act was hastily signed into law to provide legal cover for the government's actions. Given the state of exception it ushered in, I often drew parallels between this package and Institutional Act n° 5, issued by the Brazilian dictatorship in 1968. The big difference between the two measures was the strength of the institutions and democracy in the US, which, to an extent, curbed the excesses of such authoritarian legislation.

Even so, civil liberties were gravely affected. The Patriot Act authorized the invasion of privacy of American citizens and foreigners and the detention of "enemy combatants" in such places as Guantanamo, something that was often done arbitrarily and illegally, without access to habeas corpus or any contact with lawyers or family.

At the height of the war on terror, President Bush asked Alberto Gonzáles, the Attorney General, to draw up a framework specifying what the authorities could and could not do to extract confessions from detainees—a euphemism for torture. Taking his ideological convictions to an extreme, González produced a secret memo in January 2002 that determined what non-fatal psychological and physical tactics could be used without constituting torture. On the strength of this memo, signed into law by presidential decree, the United States officially started to ignore the Geneva Convention in its handling of enemy combatant detainees. Individuals accused of participation in terrorism held at Abu Graib, Iraq, and at the military base in Guantanamo Bay were subjected to acts of torture sanctioned by González' memo. The worst cases of torture, carried out by soldiers and documented in graphic photos circulated worldwide online, were never punished to the extent they deserved.

Everything the United States had always defended in relation to human rights was forgotten in the name of national security, justified on the grounds of defense against further terrorist attacks.

From that point on, neo-con radicalism prevailed and the "New American Century" project, drafted back in 1991, could be put into practice. The United States was at war not with another state, but with an intangible enemy.

Some counter-terrorism measures implemented by Vice-President Dick Cheney remained secret until May 2009. It is now known, for example, that the Washington government, at the height of its radicalism, hired the security company Blackwater—known for its controversial operations in Iraq—to eliminate Al-Qaeda and Taliban leaders, in contravention of US law, which states that actions of this nature must be approved by Congress.

In conversation with US authorities, I was able to follow at close quarters US opposition to the International Criminal Court (ICC), a permanent institution created under the Rome Statute of 1998. The ICC came into force in 2004 with powers to prosecute civilians and non-civilians accused of war crimes, genocide, and other crimes against humanity. The stance in Washington became more trenchant under Bush, who made the unprecedented move of withdrawing as a party to the Rome Statute. There were various attempts to undermine the ICC, especially through the negotiation of bilateral immunity agreements (BIAs) on article 98 of the statute that would shield US military personnel from the jurisdiction of the ICC. Legislation passed by the Bush government in 2002 prohibited the provision of military assistance to countries that refused to sign BIAs, Brazil included. This prohibition, however, could be suspended at will by the White House.

These internal defense measures had a huge impact on a number of sectors. In terms of foreign trade, there were significant modifications to the regulations that, given the juxtapositions of demands and controls, changed the relatively deregulated environment within which the US had built its economy in recent decades and positioned itself as the driving force behind foreign trade and globalization.

The main instruments Washington employed were the Bioterrorism Law, Maritime Transportation Security Act, the Trade Law of 2002 and the Container Security Initiative and the Prior Notice of Imported Cargo, which introduced myriad new demands that caused considerable impact and additional costs for US trade partners.

The Bioterrorism Act, sanctioned as law in June 2002, and still in force today, imposes strict rules on the importation and distribution of foods for consumption on the US market, including the registration of domestic and foreign food facilities with the Food and Drug Administration (FDA) and prior notice of imported foods being shipped into the country. The law also obliges domestic and foreign companies to keep detailed records of who supplies and receives the goods they produce, pack, hold, or distribute, and introduces new rules for the administrative detention of products considered suspect or as constituting a "threat."

In 2002, the Brazilian government created an inter-ministerial work group, coordinated by Itamaraty, to examine the impact this legislation would have and to help prepare the Brazilian private sector for its application. The Brazilian government adopted measures to adjust to the new rules, but even today this adaptation is not complete. The scanning of containers as a prerequisite for unobstructed exportation to the United States is a case in point.

The international order did not change post-September 11, but the global political agenda did, not so much due to the action of terrorists as due to the saber rattling of the world's sole "hyperpower," as French Foreign Minister Hubert Vedrine liked to classify the United States.

BRAZIL AND SEPTEMBER 11

On the morning of September 11, 2001, FHC sent a message to Bush and made a public statement expressing the Brazilian government's condemnation and repudiation of the terrorist acts against Washington and New York, and our wholehearted solidarity with the American people in the face of so many civilian deaths. He underscored Brazil's tradition of peacefulness, inscribed in our Constitution, and voiced our comprehension of the generalized insecurity that had gripped the United States. The president also referred to information that I had supplied to him and said that he perfectly understood the gravity of the situation in all its aspects, including security. He understood, therefore, the defensive measures the US government had taken (rigid control of ports and airports) to prevent further atrocities.

The US chargé d'affaires in Brasília was invited to the Presidential Palace so that FHC could transmit, in person, his message to the government in Washington.

The Brazilian government's main concern at the time was with the economic consequences, given the global repercussions of the crisis and their effect on our economy, which was starting to recover. The Central Bank took some precautions to avoid speculation and continued to convey to the market a sense of confidence and tranquility. There was also concern about the negative impact the terrorist attacks would have on the progress of trade negotiations, especially the Doha Round, as we shall see later on.

The Brazilian government reacted swiftly, not only in manifesting its solidarity and in the precautionary measures it adopted in the economic area, but also in its decision to invoke the Inter-American Reciprocal Assistance Treaty, signed in Petrópolis in 1947. The treaty provided for hemispheric defense should one of its member states be attacked. The Rio Pact, as it is sometimes called, was the precursor of, and substantive and formal inspiration for, the Washington Treaty of 1949, which created the North Atlantic Treaty Organization (NATO) in response to rising tensions between the former USSR and the western allies at the start of the Cold War.

Brazil immediately accepted the counter-terrorism resolutions passed by the United Nations Security Council and played its part in the informal mechanisms created under the anti-terrorism effort, including the control of financial flows that might be irrigating organized crime networks. The Brazilian Treasury imposed stricter controls on financial movements and the security organs reinforced coordination measures with the United States.

In the days that followed, I maintained close contact with Brasília and with the US authorities concerning the Rio Pact. Shortly after the attacks, and during the discussions that preceded the OAS ministerial summit on the matter, I was called to the Department of State by Secretary Peter Romero, who wanted to know what Brazil's position was on the Rio pact, the application of which we had supported from the outset.

A week before September 11, during a presidential visit by Vicente Fox to Washington, Mexico had called for the extinction of the treaty on the grounds that it was a Cold War relic, and exercised no small amount of pressure to prevent the hemispheric defense mechanism from being invoked. Argentina, which was undecided, ended up adopting a position that ultimately favored the Mexican stance.

In light of all this, my reply to Romero was thus: "You know what Brazil's position is, and it hasn't changed; I would like to know America's position on this. Do you or do you not want the Rio Pact to be applied? Brazil proposed its application, and we know that Mexico and Argentina are against it. Have you changed your position? If so, tell me, because I have to inform the Brazilian government." Surprised by my incisive attitude, Romero affirmed that the United States was holding to its decision to invoke the treaty and recognized Brazil's strong support.

Through our Embassy, the Washington government thanked Brazil for its show of solidarity, particularly our resolute position on the Rio Pact and the hemisphere-wide response to the September 11 attacks.

The issue of terrorism was a major challenge to the immediate objectives of the United States in the post-9/11 context and began to influence the US agenda with Brazil on bilateral, regional, and multilateral levels.

If, on one hand, the tragedy shunted the Brazilian priorities onto the backburner; on the other, with regard to the thematic emphasis on security, it rescued relevant aspects of our foreign policy that, while not making the daily headlines, were nonetheless important to our country's defense. Brazil, whose territory borders on so many turbulent regions, such as the Colombian Amazon, could not continue to neglect the issue of internal and external security.

On the domestic and international agenda, the issue of security assumed a greater weight than it had in the past, though this did not mean that our priorities—economic and social development, stability, reduction of inequalities, trade, more open markets—were being neglected by the Brazilian government.

The binary atmosphere of a "fight of good against evil" created by the United States posed a serious political challenge to Brazil, starting with the very concept of such a dichotomous and dangerous arrangement, resulting from a superpower's sorting of nations into "friends and enemies."

Brazil ranked among the former and assumed its responsibilities in adopting preventive measures against transnational terrorism and organized crime. That said, Brazil never lost sight of its own immediate interests.

If no country in South America played or plays a major role in the fight against global terrorism, they did and do make a contribution, shoring up their own national security, ensuring the region's democratic stability, and collaborating on what we might call a "global program" to contain terrorism and other threats.

Direct action against terrorism also led to the discussion of preventive and repressive measures in ampler fora, both regional and universal, such as the UN, the IMF, and the general conferences of non-proliferation agencies, particularly the International Atomic Energy Agency (IAEA) and the Organization for the Prohibition of Chemical Weapons (OPCW).

As the initial shock caused by the attacks began to wane, a process got underway to create foreign policy syntony among nations concerning the new priorities and the assertiveness of the US government.

In this readjustment process in the face of the new behaviors of a wounded superpower, each country angled for the best possible position it could obtain within parameters that, having changed to a greater or lesser extent, would never be the same again.

Due to its continental proximity and the fact that the US is Brazil's largest economic and financial partner, the country was never immune to oscillations in US foreign policy, or at least not until recently.

Amidst these post-September 11 rearrangements, Brazil and the United States sought to find some common ground and overcome specific differences.

Brazil was seen as a stabilizing influence and keen interlocutor in the region, factors that increased its influence on the international stage. Our active presence on the South American continent in the areas of policy/diplomacy, trade, finance and economy, and defense and security was becoming increasingly guided by closer common regional interests, the opening of markets to our South American partners on preferential terms, and the defense of democracy, collective security, economic growth and social justice. However, Brazil's leadership role on the continent was hampered somewhat by changes on the political and economic scene, with the emergence of social movements with a clearly ethnic component and of neighboring governments with actively anti-American leanings. On the other hand, US unilateralism, especially in the wake of September 11, reinforced the perception in Washington that stronger multilateralism would result, directly or indirectly, in decreasing the degree of freedom of the US. With the arrogance that goes with being a major power, the US was only willing to accept international law so long as it did not affect its national interests. This stance directly conflicted with Brazil's policy of fortifying multilateral agencies and of respecting the United Nations's line with regard to peace and security.

From the point of view of Brazilian interests in the international agenda, September 11 shifted the focus away from the issues to which our national attention was traditionally devoted—such as trade and development—and toward those of security and terrorism.

The terrorist attacks heightened the accumulated frustrations with the protectionist machinations of the American administration, which, in practice, worked against the principle of free trade, one of the deepest-set pillars of globalization.

This situation made the already complex commercial negotiations even more difficult regionally (FTAA and sectorial agreements) and multilaterally (Doha Round, at the WTO), as it underscored the unilateralism of US foreign policy and relegated all issues not directly or indirectly tied in with the new priorities to a lesser rank. It is not surprising that, in a bid to secure congressional approval for commercial negotiations, the US government sought to associate them with the fight against terror.

Brazil suffered concrete losses in its attempts to further the Doha talks, the main priority of the Lula government's trade agenda, and to secure access to the US market for Brazilian produce. We might recall, for example, the difficulties surrounding congressional approval of the Trade Promotion Authority (TPA) and the imposition of protections for the steel sector, which revealed the gulf that existed between the rhetoric of free trade and the hard reality of US protectionism.

On the regional and bilateral levels, there were bountiful examples of US efforts to achieve a sort of "painless free trade." Only those sectors in which the United States was most competitive were subject to negotiation and market-access agreements.

However, while it is true that explicitly and abusively protectionist practices and subsidizations harmful to the interests of countries like Brazil did not start with the Bush government, it is also true that the events of September 11 led Congress, already a staunch defender of so-called "special interests," to commit more fully to protecting less competitive sectors historically shielded against lines of foreign supply.

A few weeks after the terrorist attacks, I was invited to deliver a lecture at Harvard. I spoke about the current situation in the United States, September 11, the war in Afghanistan, and US unilateralism. I said that the United States's actions and attitude could be seen as those of an "Empire," far more powerful than that of ancient Rome or of "Perfidious Albion." The expression "Perfidious Albion," coined by the French poet the Marquis de Ximenes in 1793, has never been quite so apt. For Ximenes, Britain (Albion, to the Romans) was the perfect example of a kingdom in which you said one thing and did the exact opposite.

After the conference, a Harvard professor came up to me and said: "I enjoyed your lecture, despite your saying that the United States is an empire. That is not how Americans see their country; no one here views the nation in that manner." This was an academic reaction expressed immediately after the attacks. With time, and the consolidation of the unilateral Bush doctrine, the concept of "empire" was not only absorbed by the academic community, but by American society in general, and with a certain patriotic pride. Many books that interpret and defend the imperial antics of the United States were published in the years that followed, and they made quite a splash.

In October 2001, at the height of US sensitivity regarding the actions and measures being taken by the Bush government in response to the terrorist attacks, President FHC made a speech at the National Assembly in Paris, France, widely covered in the American press, in which he criticized US authoritarianism and its unilateral use of force. Two points assumed particular resonance in the media: his definition of terrorism as barbarity, and of barbarity as a unilateral imposition upon the wishes of the international community; and his observation that US protectionism was even greater than that of France. In diplomatic terms, the speech was harsh toward Washington and so, for precisely that reason, received a standing ovation from the French legislators, who were ostensibly critical of US policy.

I think it pertinent to reproduce part of the speech in which FHC notes a shift in public opinion against the United States and voices the Brazilian government's views on the unilateralism at the heart of foreign policy in Washington.

> In the wake of the September 11 attacks, the fanaticism of the terrorists seems to find echo in the nefarious desire to stir up trouble between religions and cultures. We tenaciously oppose the view that there is a clash of civilizations: with the Judeo-Christian "West" on one side and the Muslim world on the other. . . . As heterogeneous as these two traditions are, barbarism and authoritarianism can unfortunately take root in both, but also warrant repudiation by the more lucid-minded segments of each. I recall Albert Camus and his idea that *pour faire triompher un principe c'est un principle qu'il faut abattre* (upholding principles is a principle we need to break). I hope we can do as the great writer suggests. Against fear and irrationality, we must make dialogue and cooperation prosper; values we know all civilizations to share. . . . The danger of a new recessive cycle is all too present for us to waste the chance to resume multilateral trade negotiations in Doha. It is also time to control the instability of financial flows. If the market is the most efficient in-

strument for the generation of wealth, it is essential that we curb its distortions and abuses. . . . We must dare, if necessary, to tax capital flows in order to ensure the liquidity of emerging economies and the resources needed to tackle poverty, hunger and illness in the neediest nations. . . . The institutions of international governance were created for a Cold War world. The time has come to bring these institutions up to speed with the circumstances of the twenty-first century. . . . As this century begins, we find ourselves facing new opposition between barbarism and civilization. Barbarism is not only the cowardliness of terrorism, but also the intolerance and imposition of unilateral policies on a global scale. We cannot allow the logic of fear to replace the logic of freedom, participation and rationality. . . . Nor can the new order neglect to shore up human rights.

As was to be expected, FHC's speech was attacked in the press and in the US Congress. The Bush government chose not to respond officially to the harsh wording FHC used, but I did hear some negative feedback from the Department of State, though not in the form of protest or complaint.

In the end, security fears led to restrictive measures, such as increasingly stringent controls in airports. The manner in which these controls were introduced caused diplomatic problems with Russia, Chile, and Brazil. I recall two episodes in particular.

In January 2002, upon arrival in Miami, the minister for foreign affairs, Celso Lafer, was searched by airport security and forced to remove his shoes. The Chilean foreign minister received similar treatment, as did the Russian deputy foreign minister, in Washington. These unpleasant episodes could have caused diplomatic fallout, but they were played down. The press and PT went to town on the incident. With the change of government, the incumbent foreign minister was Celso Amorim, and whenever he had to visit the United States, he would tell the embassy in Washington and the American ambassador in Brazil, Donna Hrinak, that he would not, under any circumstances, remove his shoes for airport security; they could arrest him if they liked, but he would return to Brazil with his shoes firmly on his feet.

Though President Lula said on more than one occasion that he would not keep any minister in his cabinet who removed his shoes or belt for US authorities, several ministers and high-ranking officials did submit to these demands and allowed themselves to be searched by immigration agents in US airports.

In early April 2002, the embassy was preparing a visit by Ruth Cardoso, who was not traveling as first lady, an expression she did not like, but as a private citizen. We were concerned about possible complications upon arrival, particularly with a possible search at the airport in Washington. The Department of State washed its hands of the matter, as the airports were in charge of internal security. Nevertheless, Ruth was spared all inconvenience and disembarked without any problems.

The Attack on Afghanistan

The outbreak of war in Afghanistan, in October 2001, with attacks on the Taliban regime and Al-Qaeda training camps, was the first chapter in the counteroffensive orchestrated by the powerful neo-conservative group so influential in the Bush administration.

As in earlier conflicts, in response to an attack upon an ally, such as occurred in the Gulf War of 1991 after the invasion of Kuwait, the bellicose endeavors of the United States were legitimized by strategic alliances with other countries or resolutions passed by multilateral entities.

The suspicion that Osama Bin Laden was in hiding somewhere along the Afghan/Pakistani border justified the intensification of the search to capture the terrorist leader "dead or alive," as President Bush declared loud and clear.

This military operation was considered by many to be the first war of the twenty-first century and it brought to mind Samuel Huntington's prognosis of a "clash of civilizations" between the West and the Islamic world. In the heat of the aftermath of September 11, President Bush went so far as to speak of a crusade against Islamism, an explosive turn of phrase soon dropped from the official rhetoric by the more reasonable members of his inner circle.

Still reeling from the shock of the brutality of the 9/11 attacks, the international community showed solidarity with the United States in its military actions in Afghanistan. Various countries, especially NATO member states, joined the fray in what was to become the organization's first military operation outside of Europe.

In November 2001, at a meeting with President George W. Bush, FHC said that as part of the international humanitarian mission to Afghanistan, Brazil would be willing to receive a number of Afghan refugees. Bush expressed his gratitude for the gesture.

The initial aim of capturing Bin Laden and destroying or severely limiting Al-Qaeda's operational capacity was soon diluted by the growing difficulties US troops encountered as they negotiated the mountainous terrain and the diversity of Afghan tribal interests.

Such was the complexity of the war in Afghanistan that as late as 2009, now under President Obama, the US had to commit still more troops in a bid to get the situation under control. In the second half of 2010, the president announced that the US military would start withdrawing troops from Afghanistan within the year, leaving the local government in charge of national defense and security. Against his will, the new American leader found himself associated with a war, started by his predecessor, that would probably have tainted his presidency as Vietnam had that of Lyndon Johnson, had it not been for the successful elimination of Bin Laden.

The Invasion of Iraq

Shortly before the invasion of Iraq, President Lula strongly criticized the imminent military strike against Saddam Hussein on the grounds that it "disrespects the United Nations and disregards the opinion of the rest of the world."

After the terrorist attacks of 2001, and proceeding with the "Project for the New American Century" resurrected after the election of George W. Bush, the government started priming public opinion in the US for war against Iraq, which began in 2003.

Throughout 2001, the Bush government made various attempts to associate the Iraqi regime with the September 11 tragedy and stepped up its accusations against Saddam Hussein and his supposed development of weapons of mass destruction, both nuclear and chemical, which, it was claimed, posed a direct threat to US security. However, these allegations did not hold up under investigation by the International Atomic Energy Agency and other independent observers.

It was later proven that all these suspicions were false and had the objective of legitimizing a US attack against Saddam Hussein. Be that as it may, public opinion was fully behind the war on terror, first in Afghanistan and later in Iraq. *A Nation at War* was the oft-repeated mantra.

The attacks on the World Trade Center and Pentagon had changed the way the United States viewed the world. In his State of the Union address in 2002, President Bush made his first use of the expression "axis of evil," referring to North Korea, Iran, and Iraq, Washington's prime targets in the war on terror.

Gradually, all the political capital the United States had amassed after September 11 was squandered and lost.

The atmosphere in Washington grew increasingly tense. In 2003, on the eve of the invasion of Iraq, the situation internally was still fraught with difficulties. In terms of foreign policy, the radicals in the Bush administration were strengthening their ties with Tel Aviv, then under the command of Prime Minister Ariel Sharon, while the religious right in the US was tightening its bonds with the more orthodox groups in Israel.

In Brazil, the Lula government, which came to power in January 2003, largely followed the movement that would invariably lead to an attack on Iraq through information supplied by the embassy in Washington.

On February 25, 2003, weeks before the invasion, I was called to a meeting at the State Department. Secretary of State Condoleezza Rice had invited all the Latin American and Caribbean ambassadors in order to ask for their support and financial backing for the Iraqi reconstruction effort. As many of the attending countries were publically against military action in Iraq, it is hardly surprising that this curious meeting bore no concrete results.

The foreign ministers of France, Germany, and Russia—Dominique Villepin, Joschka Fischer, and Sergei Ivanov, respectively—stood as a bloc against the war. France said that it would veto any UN resolution that demanded the removal of Saddam Hussein, and so it migrated overnight into the "hostile" column of the US government's atlas. The atmosphere was tense and there was no longer any doubt that war was now in its final phase of preparation.

I spoke to President Lula and Minister Celso Amorim on the telephone and conveyed to them the general outlook in Washington. Pragmatically, I counseled moderation in the Brazilian government's reaction, which everyone knew would be totally against armed conflict in Iraq.

The state of the Brazilian economy during the first two or three months of the new government was brittle and unlikely to stabilize any time soon, as indicators such as inflation and the so-called "Brazil risk premium" remained high. War at this juncture could have created an unfavorable international environment for the Brazilian economy and affected the US Treasury Department's positive attitude toward Brazil. I stressed that the moment called for caution and prudence in all public statements.

On March 7, Bush called a press conference to prepare the American people for the imminent attack on Iraq. These were extraordinary days in Washington, not just because of the pall of war and supposed terrorist threats, but because the US government was unable to form a political coalition to support the attack. Europe, led by the French and Germans, was against military conflict. Old US–French rivalry flared up, and there was general animosity toward all the naysayers on Bush's bellicose policies. To vent their anger and displeasure with the French government's stance, many American citizens took to smashing or throwing out bottles of French wines.

Unlike on September 11, 2001, when national trauma and pain eclipsed the debate on the causes and consequences of the terrorist attacks, the discussion of the invasion of Iraq was open and wide-ranging. American society and the Congress were divided on the issue, and there were open demonstrations for and against the war.

Many sensible voices in Congress, the media, and academia warned of the political and economic difficulties that the United States would face after the attack. The events that unfolded before our eyes were like something out of a new chapter to Barbara Tuchman's *The March of Folly*. In her book, the American historian observes that, from the Trojan War to Vietnam, when major decisions had to be made, political leaders tended to ignore prudent advice and to embark foolishly on the course of disaster.

When the invasion of Iraq started to figure on the horizon as a real possibility, public opinion changed, both inside and outside the United States. After September 11, the United States was given carte blanche to attack Afghanistan, but as war loomed in Iraq, that positive will began to wane, both domestically and internationally, amid spiraling criticism. In the American press, isolated voices against the war could still be heard, though the propaganda bombardment gave the impression that the vast majority was behind it.

On the international stage, US pressure for regime change in Bagdad divided the west into those for and those against the war. The arguments posed by the Bush government were inconsistent, even blatantly false, as would be proven later. The United States did not seem to gauge the level of resistance there was worldwide to Washington's unilateral policies, much less how the invasion of Iraq was fast transforming solidarity and support for the US into repudiation in the majority of nations.

The decision to attack Iraq had been made even before September 11. I received information to the effect that at a meeting at the Pentagon in 2002 it was disclosed that the decision had been made and that invasion was only a matter of time. The Brazilian government, through its embassy in Washington, therefore knew of the plan a year in advance.

The main source of criticism against the invasion was that the United States was embarking on an Iraqi adventure that had become, for various reasons, a geopolitical obsession of its civilian leadership.

The foremost of these reasons was control of the region's oil, something Alan Greenspan, who presided over the US Federal Reserve for eighteen years, would later recognize in his book *The Age of Turbulence*. Control over Iraq's oil reserves was crucially important to the US, which feared increasing instability in the Middle East caused by the Palestinian-Israeli conflict. Moreover, the serious problems with terrorism emanating from Iran and Yemen further aggravated the situation. The solution was for the United States to increase its presence in the region, something it started doing after September 11 by setting up military bases in the Middle East, especially Saudi Arabia, a solid and traditional ally. Nineteen of the terrorists who took part in the September 11 atrocities were Saudis, and Bin Laden, in his first public declarations, identified the presence of infidel soldiers in Mecca, the Islamic holy land, as one of the main reasons for the attacks.

Another justification Washington presented for the occupation of Iraq was the threat Saddam Hussein posed to US security. Members of the Bush administration insisted on the thesis that the Iraqi dictator had weapons of mass destruction and connections with Al-Qaeda, allegations that both proved to be false.

A third motivation was of a personal and psychological nature and concerned the "completion" of the war George H. Bush had waged against Saddam. During the first Gulf War, in 1991, Colin Powell, then chair of the Joint Chiefs of Staff, was of the opinion that the US army did not have sufficient military superiority to enter Bagdad and topple Saddam Hussein, as originally planned by the neocons. The same ultra-conservative group that had staffed Bush Sr.'s government returned under the son's administration and was keen to pursue some unfinished business. One must also remember that Bush Sr., on a post-presidential visit to Kuwait, suffered an assassination attempt attributed to Saddam Hussein. This family vendetta was further motivation for regime change in Iraq.

In a frank conversation that I had with Huda Farouki, a Jordanian friend of mine and a man with a strong interest in Iraq and a deep knowledge of the region, I was told, quite frankly, that the conflict would be over in a matter of days, as there would be little resistance from the Iraqi military, not even Saddam's elite Republican Guard. According to Farouki, the Iraqi military was not equipped to withstand a US offensive. The US would take Bagdad within a week, Saddam would be overthrown, and the population would welcome the invaders as their liberators. However, after a month or so, once the Iraqis had time to realize that the Americans were in for the long haul, they would quickly go from being seen as liberators and friends to being viewed as an occupying foreign force, and gratitude would turn to hostility. Over the course of its four thousand-year history, Iraq—the former Mesopotamia—had suffered serial aggressions, and this would be just one more. For Huda, the Iraqi people, who had seen so many invaders before, would act no differently now.

All this was foreseeable, except for the bungling manner in which the US handled the period immediately following Saddam's ouster. The conviction that this would be a brief war, as the administration's hawks believed, was soon contradicted. What's more, the inefficiency of the first administrator of the coalition provisional authority of Iraq, Paul Bremer, and the level of corruption in which the reconstruction effort was mired, both in the areas of oil and infrastructure, became a nightmare for the government. Bush's failure to secure a coalition of forces to support the invasion was glaring and embarrassing.

The ill feeling between Europe and the United States grew after the invasion. A concrete example of this occurred at the embassy residence at the height of the crisis.

When I hosted a farewell dinner for the Italian ambassador, Ferdinando Salleo, who had become a close friend of ours, I took his advice and invited Secretary of Defense Donald Rumsfeld, as well as other Washington personalities, ambassadors, and politicians. When I received the French ambassador, who had just arrived in Washington, I made a point of introducing the two guests. He presented himself to

Rumsfeld as an ambassador from "Old Europe," a reference to the defense secretary's distinction between pro-war "New Europe" and the "Old" variant represented by France. The introduction was formal in tone, and Rumsfeld simply smiled. I learned later that when the German ambassador went over to greet Rumsfeld, the secretary turned his back on him. Tempers were clearly still flaring. The country was at war with terrorism, and no excuses would be taken. Those who had not sided with the United States were seen as having sided against it.

From August 2002, US pressure on Iraq mounted. There was a wartime atmosphere on TV, in the newspapers, and in Congress. At the United Nations General Assembly that September, Bush made a belligerent speech against Iraq. Soon thereafter, the White House issued its National Security Strategy, which outlined the doctrine of pre-emptive strikes and regime change as means of protecting US interests. In the intense patriotism of the hour, these rarely used expressions entered clamorously into the post-9/11 lexicon as the buzzwords of nationalist manifestations that clearly suggested the imminence of an attack on Iraq, with or without United Nations Security Council endorsement. It became common in society to hear comments against the United Nations, suggesting that it was an outmoded organization.

Toward the end of January, amid preparations for a visit that President Lula was to make to Washington, and for the meeting of the Group of Friends called by the secretary-general of the OAS to discuss the situation in Venezuela, Minister Celso Amorim spoke to Secretary of State Colin Powell. During their conversation, Amorim conveyed Brazil's concerns about the effects a possible war might have on Brazil, particularly the negative economic impact. He also referred to the Brazilian government's position that all possible avenues toward a peaceful resolution should be explored before any use of force, and then only under the auspices of a Security Council resolution. The secretary of state replied that no executive decision had yet been made on the use of force, but that all options were on the table. He also indicated that, if it did come to war, the United States would engage the enemy and emerge victorious.

The anxiety mounted, and preparations for war intensified. On March 16, in the Azores, President Bush and Prime Ministers Tony Blair of Britain and José Maria Aznar of Spain, Washington's greatest allies at the time, prepared the groundwork for invasion and announced that they would present a new resolution to the UN condemning Saddam Hussein. In order to avoid the drastic consequences the resolution would entail, the allies gave Saddam a window of opportunity to go into exile prior to the Security Council vote. It was a day of extreme tension. Bush went on national television to highlight the threat Saddam Hussein represented to US security.

At the United Nations headquarters, in the presence of the UN Secretary-General Kofi Annan and representatives of the Security Council member states, all visibly uncomfortable, Secretary of State Colin Powell—looking no less awkward—went over the evidence, forged by the CIA, supporting the case for military action. Powell, who would later publically lament his performance at that plenary session, left his government post at the end of Bush's first term.

There was no doubt that the United States had made the unilateral decision to invade Iraq. The rejection of the ultimatum of resignation made to Saddam Hussein was Washington's final justification for going to war.

On March 19, 2003, the invasion finally began. With awe and horror we watched the spectacular TV images of long-range missiles raining down on Iraq. This demonstration of the arrogance of war during the first few days, depressing to most of us, was, however, cause for glee to many Americans. After a few days, there was no doubt that the outcome of the war would be favorable to the United States, but, contrary to Washington's expectations, the number of US casualties kept on rising. The difficulties the military was facing in securing and controlling the territory became increasingly evident.

In my communication with Itamaraty, I reported that President George W. Bush had made a live address from the Oval Office in which he confirmed that the attack on Iraq had begun. Disregarding the United Nations, and accompanied only by Britain, the United States had gone to war.

It was the first explicit act of an American empire. It was the first time the United States had taken the initiative to wage war without having first been attacked by the invaded nation. It was also the rollout of the nascent national security doctrine, with its principle of pre-emptive action. It was, however, the nineteenth time in a century that the United States was forcing regime change in another state—all under historically distinct circumstances, it is true—though, in the last analysis, democracy prevailed in only five of those countries: Germany, Japan, Italy, Panama, and Granada.

I conveyed the fact that, after the attack against Iraq, nations and citizens would now be living in a world in which an imperial superpower had elected to sweep aside multilateralism and international law and take it upon itself to prescribe and impose situations and rules that would affect us all. Future events, however, soon showed that US unilateralism would not last very long.

Brazil and the Invasion of Iraq

When the Iraq war began on March 19, 2003, Lula had been President for a little over three months. I spoke to the President over the phone on more than one occasion and prepared a report on the country's position on the invasion and its political, diplomatic, economic, and social implications for Brazil. I suggested that whatever criticisms were made should be political, not personal, so as to preserve good relations between the heads of state. In early February, I advanced some analyses on the possible global effects of war against Iraq, many of which were confirmed by later events.

On the day the offensive was launched, I briefed the President over the phone. He said that he remained convinced that the developed nations should be fighting starvation and poverty, not waging wars, and added that he would meet with foreign minister Celso Amorim and make a statement—without any anti-American declarations.

Nevertheless, in the heat of the moment, Lula leveled severe criticism against the United States on the day of the attack. For my part, I was worried about the repercussions his comments would have and also about the public statements other members of the Brazilian government might be moved to make.

In the heavily charged atmosphere of Washington, where the prevalent perception was that if you weren't with the United States, you were against it, I knew that the way we handled the war issue would have a direct bearing on US–Brazilian relations.

At that time, any activism on our part in relation to the invasion could have rebounded negatively on Brazilian interests. Earlier statements by high-ranking authorities in the Brazilian government, from the president and foreign minister to other ministers, had already been felt by the Department of State, to the point of its making informal inquiries about our nation's position on the war.

Minister Antonio Palocci, with whom I was in constant contact, was sensitive to these problems. I also spoke to the president of the BNDES, the Brazilian development bank, Guido Mantega, and with the vice-president, José Alencar, about the oil issue, barrel price trends on the international market, and possible problems for Brazil. I insisted on the need for people to be aware of the price that would have to be paid for certain positions taken and the Brazilian government's initial reactions. It was important to remember that we might end up isolated—like France, Russia, China, and Germany—in a very uncomfortable position, especially if the national economy were to be broadsided by the crisis. That said, there was no reason to think that a critical position, devoid of militancy, should contaminate our relations with the United States.

True to its word, Brazil voted against the invasion of Iraq at the UN. During that delicate moment, the Brazilian press published news reports saying that Brazil might accept Saddam Hussein as an exile, a rumor later debunked by Minister Celso Amorim.

Some months later, at the height of the attacks on Baghdad, Brazil found itself directly involved in the war in the most tragic manner: the death of the diplomat Sérgio Vieira de Mello, the top UN envoy in Iraq, who was killed in an Al-Qaeda bomb attack on the UN headquarters in Baghdad on August 19, 2003.

Through President Bush and Secretary of State Colin Powell, the US government extended its condolences to President Lula and Minister Celso Amorim. The repercussions in the US were enormous. I spent the whole day giving interviews to Brazilian and American TV and radio stations.

Sérgio Vieira was the United Nations representative par excellence, a man capable of putting his own life at risk to defend the organization. His determination, courage, and dedication were characteristics that pervaded his efforts to maintain order, peace, and global security.

Elections in Brazil

The campaign for the presidential elections held in October 2002, fought by José Serra (PSDB) and Luiz Inácio Lula da Silva (PT), was followed closely by the US authorities. The prospect of victory by Lula, a leftist leader from a party that did not disguise its critical view of the United States, was cause for concern among segments of Bush's conservative administration, which held positions diametrically opposed to those of the Partido do Trabalhadores. Much of the insecurity stemmed from the fact that a PT victory would be further confirmation of what many in the administration saw as a socialist shift in South America, and also from the fact that the Brazilian economy, which had been recovering well since the late 1990s, began to deteriorate before the election of 2002, showing increased instability as a consequence of the perceived risk a leftist government in Brasília might pose.

The general atmosphere of uncertainty hanging over the Brazilian elections was already being observed with apprehension on Wall Street, with Brazil figuring more heavily in think tanks and the media. In this context I received various invitations to comment on developments in Brazilian politics and outline what we might expect from a future Lula government.

The possibility of a financial crisis caused by the return of inflation and instability in the wake of an incumbent opposition government was raising fears in the United States that Brazil might become another "problem country" in South America. External indicators, such as the so-called "Brazil risk premium," were responsible for the alarm bells. Another contributing factor was that PT had always campaigned for sovereign default on foreign debt and against negotiations on the FTAA, largely due to a blatantly anti-American attitude.

Shortly before the elections, a group of twelve US congressmen sent a letter to President Bush expressing concerns over certain declarations made by leaders of PT and candidate Lula regarding the Nuclear Non-Proliferation Treaty (NPT). These statements had apparently touched upon some sensitive issues and raised doubts about the Brazilian government's future policy on the nuclear topic. The letter requested that a report be drawn up by the Department of State to assess the threat to US national security. The congressmen also mentioned the close ties between PT and the São Paulo Forum and the party's connections with FARC and Fidel Castro.

Deputy José Dirceu, Lula's campaign coordinator, sent a letter to the US ambassador, Donna Hrinak, explaining that the candidate's position was precisely the opposite of that circulating in the press. He reminded her that PT had voted in favor of the Brazilian government signing the treaty in 1997, during the FHC administration, and that Lula was personally in agreement with the party's position on the matter.

The Brazilian embassy in Washington started to receive requests for information on potential changes of political and economic direction in the event of a Lula victory. I gave lectures and attended think tanks to clear up whatever doubts existed about possible changes of tack under the new government.

As the elections drew closer, I spoke to President FHC about how the embassy should respond to requests for assistance in organizing visits to Washington on behalf of the candidates. I was given carte blanche to provide whatever assistance was required, including arrangements for official meetings. The embassy was to do whatever was necessary to ensure that the US Congress, government, and business community had every opportunity to know the programs of any candidate interested in presenting them.

However, only one presidential candidate, Ciro Gomes, decided to visit Washington. Accompanied by Professor Mangabeira Unger, Gomes asked for my assistance to arrange a series of meetings with the government and union milieu.

One of the embassy's most important lines of activity leading up to and following the elections was to get information across to both government and economic agencies and the US media.

In February 2002, I was informed that candidate Lula planned to make a visit to Washington. I drew up a suggested program and submitted it to Itamaraty for appraisal. However, in June I received word from Stanley Gacek, a director of the AFL-CIO, a powerful national trade union in the US, that Lula would no longer be traveling and that José Dirceu, his main advisor and campaign leader, would be heading to Washington in his stead to meet with US authorities.

In Brazil, José Dirceu had been in contact with the businessman Mario Garnero, who knew Bush Sr., and with Gacek, a Harvard-trained lawyer and self-proclaimed friend and advisor to Lula since helping secure his release from prison during the dictatorship. According to Gacek—or Stan, as he is known to his friends in PT—when Bill Clinton was elected in 1992, he arranged Lula's first meeting with the democratic administration, an audience with the then-Deputy Secretary for the Treasury, Larry Summers.

Dirceu arrived in Washington with Marcos Troyjo, a diplomat on leave from the corps who worked for Garnero, and was immediately met by Gacek and other AFL-CIO representatives.

Following the orientation I had received from Brasília—a tradition in our diplomacy, which sees Itamaraty as serving the state above any government—I did what I could to make the requested contacts. I scheduled meetings at the White House with the chief economic adviser Lawrence Lindsey and, at the Department of State, with the western hemisphere secretary, Roger Noriega. These meetings dealt with the prospects of a Lula victory and his plans for the economy. The tensest of these was at the White House, when José Dirceu, speaking on behalf of Lula, sought to put the US authorities at ease concerning the positions the future government would assume. He introduced Lula as a moderate left-wing politician and presented a copy of his "Letter to the Brazilian People," in which Lula pledged to respect all contracts entered into during the FHC government, to pursue a policy of economic stability, to keep inflation under control, and to observe the law of fiscal responsibility. In other words, if elected, Lula would not default on foreign debt, as his party had long said it would. All of this was stated in a categorical manner so as to leave no doubt about the PT candidate's intentions.

Having accompanied José Dirceu on all of these meetings, I believed it was clear that here was someone in Lula's trust, bound to occupy a key position in the PT government.

Dirceu's American interlocutors were impressed by this appeasing message. The information sent by Donna Hrinak, US ambassador in Brasília, and the good rapport she and Dirceu established, helped the embassy in Washington in its task of setting up meetings with high-ranking officials in the US government.

Some time later I learned that José Dirceu had written a letter to Vice-President Dick Cheney indicating that the PT wanted to open channels of communication with the Republican Party and that Lula would soon be making a visit to the United States. Similar correspondence was sent to Donald Evans, then-secretary of trade, and to Lindsey, the economic advisor.

A lot was said of Mario Garnero's recommendations to the Bush family and Ambassador Donna Hrinak. Garnero had put José Dirceu in contact with Lindsey and this led to an open channel of communication between Dirceu and the White House, with the US embassy as an intermediary. The high point of this articulation was when Lula, still president-elect, was received in Washington by President Bush.

However, the widespread version that the credit for establishing this conduit between the PT—and José Dirceu in particular—and the White House lay exclusively with Mario Garnero and the US embassy in Brazil paints a distorted picture of the facts. Nor does it do PT credit. I have no doubt that Donna Hrinak and Mario Garnero had a lot to do with the success of José Dirceu's Washington mission, and I witnessed some of it myself, but this view ignores a lot of hard work by the Brazilian embassy in Washington, not only in preparing José Dirceu's visit, but throughout the electoral campaign and period of transition—a fact that does not seem hard to explain today, given the PT government's insistence on ignoring anything positive the previous government may have done.

The candidate José Serra did not visit the United States during the campaign, nor did he send a representative to establish contact with the US authorities.

In the face of the bleak economic and financial outlook worldwide and the growing prospects of war with Iraq, the impending presidential election in Brazil, held on October 6, 2002, was cause for further concern, especially with regard to certain historical positions defended by PT.

From May to October, I was called to give a great many lectures and seminars about Brazil, explaining Serra and Lula's electoral platforms and always mentioning the "Letter to the Brazilian People."

On the day of the Brazilian elections, for the first time ever, our electronic polls were put at the disposal of Brazilian citizens in the United States. Some 27,000 registered voters were able to cast their votes across eight electoral districts at consulates and at the embassy's chancery. In Washington, of the 2,600 registered voters, 1,500 turned up to vote, with a slight advantage in Lula's favor.

The following day, the Brazilian embassy in Washington received a note from the Department of State and the White House praising the calm, democratic atmosphere that had prevailed throughout the election and reiterating the American government's hopes of resuming a working relationship with whomever was chosen to lead Brazil. I transmitted the message to candidates Lula and Serra, who reacted immediately and positively. I was instructed by Itamaraty to extend the nation's thanks to the Department of State and to the White House.

A radical shift in government in Brazil no longer seemed to be such cause for concern. George W. Bush was the first head of state to call to congratulate the president-elect, soon after the electoral outcome was announced, despite the fact that there had been some doubts as to whether he would. Bush said to Lula: "Congratulations on your victory. You ran a fantastic campaign, which we followed closely. We were really impressed by the huge majority you won. If you'd be interested in visiting me in Washington, it would be my pleasure to meet you." Lula accepted the invitation, saying: "Mr. President, I hope we can meet by the end of the year. We have a lot to talk about."

Bush's gesture was the result of a lot of patient work by Ambassador

Donna Hrinak, who, like me, was aware of the significance of that telephone call.

However, a lack of confidence still continued on Wall Street. The price of Brazilian bonds plummeted in October, during the elections, and the market was still underestimating Brazil's economic outlook. The volatility of the financial market persisted until the third quarter of 2003, despite the assurances of economic responsibility from the Finance Minister, Antonio Palocci.

DEMOCRATIC TRANSITION

The election of Lula and departure of FHC marked the setting of an exemplary precedent in Brazilian politics, one we hope to see replicated in future transfers of the presidential sash: a democratic and civilized transition of power. For the first time in our political history, a president who was ending his mandate without having elected a successor determined that the transition be organized down to the details so as to ensure a smooth hand-over to the opposition party. In this case, that party was PT, which was about to occupy the Planalto Palace for the first time in its history.

I was instructed to prepare a program of visits to the White House for the chief of staff, Minister Pedro Parente, who was to be in charge of coordinating contact with the incumbent PT government. I recall that valuable information on transferring power to an opposition party was exchanged at a White House meeting with George W. Bush's chief of staff, Joshua Bolten, and over dinner at the residence. After all, only a few months earlier, the Republican Bush had defeated the Democrat Gore, the candidate supported by outgoing president, Bill Clinton.

In Brazil, on the express orders of FHC, the Presidency of the Republic had prepared the ground and drawn up a detailed manual for the exchange of power. In conversations with the White House, Pedro Parente explained how the situation was being handled in Brasília to ensure the smooth flow of information to the opposition, especially in the field of the economy and foreign policy. The manual, which had been developed by FHC's aides, was shown to Bush's chief of staff.

As Minister Pedro Parente explained the various provisions recommended for the transition, the White House official went to fetch a similarly robust volume. It was the US equivalent of the manual, which, upon comparison, revealed extensive procedural similarities.

In a democracy, it is hard to invent novelties in this regard. The full and unrestricted transfer of information from the outgoing government to its successor is the rule, not the exception.

TEAMWORK

During the nearly five years I spent in Washington, I maintained a close working relationship with my US counterparts, Ambassadors Donna Hrinak and Anthony Harrington, who represented the United States in Brazil during that period. In establishing this coordination, I was able to draw on my successful experience in London.

During the electoral campaign and the first year of the Lula government, this understanding greatly facilitated my work. I was impressed by Donna Hrinak, a career diplomat and liberal in a Republican government, who, during the ceremony at the Department of State appointing her to her Brazilian post and in the presence of Colin Powell, had the courage to criticize US interventions in Latin America, particularly in Chile during the crisis that led to the fall of President Salvador Allende. After the ceremony, I went to congratulate her and mentioned how surprised we all were at her words. Donna smiled and glanced over at the secretary of state, who, like herself, was far more open-minded than the rest of the Bush administration.

As the presidential race went into the home stretch, Hrinak forged ties with both PT and the PSDB candidate, José Serra. She was in contact with Lula on numerous occasions and had established a direct line of communication with José Dirceu even before the future chief of staff's visit to Washington in May 2002. The information and recommendations issued by the US ambassador helped dispel a lot of doubts about the new government and ensured that the Department of State properly understood some of the initial measures that were taken in Brasília.

We worked together to have the US government receive Lula in Washington before his inauguration, while still president-elect. Normally, presidents-elect who request meetings with the US government are received by the Department of State. The US president only meets with foreign leaders at the White House after they have been sworn into office.

To lend weight to this bold idea, I prepared some information for the western hemisphere secretary, Otto Reich, and approached the Brazil–US Caucus at Congress to underscore the importance of the United States making a show of support for a democratically-elected center-left leader in the region.

The invitation was finally made and Lula, not yet inaugurated for his first term, was received in Washington by the US president. I have no doubt that Donna Hrinak was instrumental in having the decision made. In a conversation with President Lula, Hrinak described the situation in Washington and alerted him to the real possibility of some hostile coverage in the press. The president-elect left no room for doubt: "There'll be no surprises. My government will not be ideological."

This was one of the few times a US head of state had received a president-elect in the Oval Office, and it was the first-ever meeting between a Brazilian president from a leftist, union background and an ultra-conservative American counterpart.

Despite the two leaders' ideological differences and worldviews, they were able to develop a relationship that was more dynamic and direct than that between Bush and FHC. During the previous government, Fernando Henrique Cardoso and Bill Clinton had enjoyed political affinity and reciprocal respect. It is known that Bill Clinton spoke very highly of FHC's intellectual prowess to Bush, and this may have intimidated the new American president in relation to Cardoso. The fact is, there was no immediate empathy between them, and their relations, though cordial, never deepened—partly because of the increasingly radical positions President Bush kept adopting. I had my doubts about how things would flow between Lula and Bush, but it was apparent from the very first meeting that the two leaders took an immediate shine to each other.

Bush's lack of knowledge about, if not disinterest in, foreign policy issues in general, and western hemispheric issues in particular, meant that the amount of contact he maintained with Lula declined considerably as his term wore on. On the Brazilian side, ideologically fuelled resistance from PT and the restrictions it imposed upon the development of a closer relationship with the United States were becoming increasingly palpable, though these did not diminish the quality of contact at the Presidential level.

CHAPTER 3

Presidents FHC and Lula in Washington

PRESIDENTIAL DIPLOMACY, BY FHC and Lula, was instrumental in Brazil's growing projection abroad. With different styles and backgrounds, they had their own ways of relating to other leaders. The four presidential visits I followed in Washington left no doubt as to the relevance of personal contact between the US and Brazilian heads of state. Personal affinities, to a greater or lesser degree, helped establish a relationship that fostered solutions for issues in the national interests of both nations.

Brazil Comes First

Despite the close contact between FHC and Bill Clinton, no presidential visit was made to Washington during the final year of the Democrat's term of office, my first year at the Embassy. I did, however, accompany two visits by FHC and two by Lula during the first term of George W. Bush.

At the meetings I sat in on, Bush always came across as nice, friendly, and down to business. He never used notes during his conversations with the Brazilian leaders and seemed well informed about the subjects on the agenda.

FHC met with Bush twice, once in March 2001, shortly after the US President took office, and again in November, less than two months after the September 11 terrorist attacks.

When President Bush came to power, he called President FHC to express his interest in maintaining the same good relations the Brazilian had always had with Clinton.

I suggested that FHC visit Washington sooner rather than later in order to establish direct contact with the new leader, so a meeting was arranged through the diplomatic channels for the end of March, a few weeks before the FTAA talks at the Summit of the Americas in Quebec.

In March 2001, not long before FHC's visit, the embassy's telephone lines began to present interference and a discernible loss of call quality. I ordered that the chancery be swept for bugs and we detected what appeared to be a direct telephone line between the building and the Defense Department. After a recheck, I informed Brasília that the chancery's phones had been wiretapped and notified the Department of State. The technicians who assisted us told us that the same had happened at other embassies, usually on the eve of presidential visits.

During our preparations for the visit, the wording of the communiqué that was to be released after the meeting of Presidents Fernando Henrique Cardoso and George W. Bush was discussed with the US authorities. Confirming the strong ideological bias of the new government, my interlocutors took issue with my suggested use of the expressions "economic and social development," "reduction of inequalities," and "social inclusion," which they considered either too vague or counter to the convictions of the Bush administration. According to the staffers at the State Department, social inclusion is a direct result of economic growth, so there was no need to mention it in its own right. I did not bother to respond to the crash course in economic orthodoxy being administered to me by John Maisto, as I knew that pretty soon I would have to disagree on something more essential—the calendar and co-chairmanship of the FTAA.

The meeting between the two presidents went smoothly. Firstly, at FHC's request, the heads of state had a private twenty-minute conversation in the Oval Office. As such discussions are not recorded, the note takers were Condoleezza Rice and the ambassador Eduardo Santos, the Brazilian President's diplomatic aide. The broader discussions, in the company of the full delegation, lasted for over an hour.

At all of the presidential meetings I attended, the subjects to which the most time was devoted were the economic situations of both countries; their bilateral relations, with emphasis on commercial exchange and possible obstructions thereto; and the examination of the political and economic juncture in South America. Every now and then a global theme would arise, usually the environment, energy, human rights, or global warming, or some matter of international politics, such as conflict in the Middle East.

The first meeting between the two presidents was no different. During their private conversation, FHC spoke about the significance of the countries' bilateral relations and the importance of expanding them, given the relevance of the United States to foreign trade and to the restoration of Brazil's economic stability. When the talk turned to the global situation and the role the United States was playing within it, the Brazilian president, having sensed the direction the Bush administration was taking, said that it was important that Washington not monopolize the global decision-making power, but try to strengthen multilateralism and broaden the participation of the international community in the way the larger world issues were handled.

In a surprising response to FHC's comments, President Bush signaled the possibility of Brazil's being invited into the G7. When asked whether Brazil would be interested in joining the group of the world's largest economies, Fernando Henrique said that it would, although he had no illusions as to the real possibility of that happening at that moment.

While they were on the subject of international governance, FHC brought up the matter of UN Security Council reform and Brazil's interest in obtaining a permanent seat. President Bush's reaction was as expected, and he refused to commit to endorsing either call.

Another subject given surprising treatment at this presidential meeting was the FTAA negotiations, still in-course at the time. FHC said that he had followed the discussions and that he had a clear picture of the political and economic panorama in the hemisphere, but that one thing was certain: "For me, Brazil comes first"—a paraphrasing of Bush's own words to the then-German Chancellor, Gerhard Schröder: "To me, America comes first."

I had prepared an outline for the president to use in his conversation with Bush and a briefing on the advantages and disadvantages of Brazil proposing negotiations on a trade agreement, something I will go into in more detail in the chapter on the FTAA.

The proposal was that the agreement should adopt a 4+1 format, that is, the four Mercosur nations and the United States. It was an innovative suggestion, because it opened up a parallel route to that originally envisioned for the FTAA, i.e., the inclusion of every country in the hemisphere, except for Cuba. President FHC, who had accepted the idea, presented it to Bush during their private meeting. It was the perfect time and place for Brazil to suggest establishing new bases for the bilateral relationship. Washington's constant changes of position had made it increasingly difficult for Brazil to engage with the United States.

Bush received the suggestion well, but just when he seemed willing to accept it, his national security advisor, Condoleezza Rice, interjected, saying that Robert Zoellick, the man in charge of trade negotiations at the USTR, should be he heard before any decision was made. Bush acquiesced and FHC was informed that the US government would consider the proposal and give him an answer after the Quebec summit.

Condoleezza Rice told me in private, with a certain air of condescension, that our proposal had caught her off-guard: "I was surprised by your move. Congratulations."

Used to requests for loans and aid from Latin American leaders, the US government had rarely received a proposal as serious and ambitious as the one FHC put to them at that meeting.

Had it been accepted, it would certainly have been a step forward in US–Brazilian trade negotiations, with profound implications for both sides.

Present at the group talks in the Oval Office were Colin Powell, Condoleezza Rice, Peter Romero from the Department of State, Robert Zoellick of the USTR, John Maisto from the National Security Council, and Andrew Card, Bush's chief of staff. On the Brazilian side were Minister Celso Lafer and myself.

The meeting was relaxed and cordial, with frank and direct discussion on the main issues on the agenda, such as energy and the situation in Latin America, especially in Venezuela, Argentina, Colombia, and Ecuador.

The US President seemed to be well briefed on these countries, but the tone and superficiality of his comments betrayed his disinterest in the region. He was clearly more concerned with more crucial issues on other continents.

Mindful of the impending summit in Quebec, to be held just weeks later, and all too familiar with the inconvenient outbursts of Hugo Chávez, the American President went straight to the point: "I don't want him poking me in the eye. I hope he's not going to embarrass me and my nation in public." He also expressed his concern with the situation in Colombia, where the battle with the FARC was escalating in equal measure to the amount of financial and military resources the US deployed, and with Argentina, because of the economic policy measures being taken there. Ecuador was another problem, given its political instability and threatened democracy.

FHC asked the United States to back an IMF loan to Argentina, which was going through severe economic and financial turmoil, but as Bush did not agree with the economic measures being taken by the

Argentinean government, he refused Brazil's request for backing. At the end of an exchange of information on Latin America, FHC introduced the subject of Paraguay, but the American cut him off with his customary mischievousness and said: "Paraguay is your backyard; it's your problem, not mine."

Environmental issues were discussed in depth. At a certain moment, Bush smiled disconsolately and said: "I can't really talk, as I'm seen as the world's biggest polluter." Reiterating one of his government's priorities, George W. Bush said he was anxious to reduce American reliance on oil. He stressed his interest in developing new energy sources, such as biomass and hydrogen, and, to that end, suggested close cooperation between the US and Brazil.

Between one matter and another, and sort of gratuitously, Bush asked whether there were many black people in Brazil. Before FHC could reply, Condoleezza Rice interjected with detailed and accurate information about the country's Afro-descendant population.

At the end of the meeting, a cordial Bush repeated that he was very pleased to have finally met Cardoso in person. He said that he would study the proposed trade agreement between Mercosur and the United States and that we would come back to it in further discussions.

Although we had been told a response would be given after Quebec, none came, and the Brazilian proposal was forgotten. The US government was already preoccupied with the future unfolding of the crisis in Iraq and with a protectionist urge that was beginning to well up in Congress.

The Bush–FHC meeting was widely covered in the press, with repeated references to the "Brazil comes first" remark.

Back in Brazil, in a telephone conversation with Hugo Chávez, FHC passed on the US President's concerns about having his authority publicly flouted at the summit. Chávez promised FHC that he would "behave himself" and told him that, for fear of losing the run of himself at OPEC meetings, he had arranged a warning signal with the Saudi-Arabian Prime Minister, who would place his hands on his chest, as if in prayer, every time Chávez looked like he was about to go off the rails. He asked the Brazilian president if he wouldn't mind doing the same. At the summit meeting in Quebec, Fernando Henrique was invited to give the opening address and made such an affirmative and tough defense of Brazil's positions before the American heads of state that his speech caused quite a stir. Afterwards, when FHC returned to his seat, Chávez got up and went over to him with his hands cupped on his chest, as if to say "it wasn't me who crossed the line this time. . . ."

The presidential visit in March 2001, with George W. Bush only recently sworn into his first term of office, took place at a time of internal political change and concerns for the US economy. Given the new president's connections with the most conservative sections of society, the Republican victory represented a major change in the role the State would play in the economy and in the steering of internal politics.

If the meeting had taken place during the Lula administration, and not in 2001 under FHC, it would certainly have been touted by the Planalto as the beginning of a dynamic phase in US–Brazil relations. It would not be an inapt description for that encounter between Fernando Henrique and George W. Bush, but not for the reasons so often invoked by the official propaganda machine of the PT government. What made it a watershed were the deep transformations that took place in Brazil and the ensuing gradual recalibration of our country's relations with the United States.

With a strengthened economy and society built upon solid democratic foundations, Brazil had come to be seen as an increasingly influential player on the regional level and in the international sphere.

From the perspective of business and strategic interests, Brazil was now perhaps more important to the United States than most European countries, even if few had actually realized it yet.

However, the preparations for the arrival of the Brazilian head of state in Washington showed that, on a technical level, the USTR, the Department of State, and the White House National Security Council still had a lot to learn about Brazil.

In terms of public perceptions and the private preparatory conversations, President FHC's visit was marked by the affirmation of our position on the FTAA negotiations and the future Mercosur–US relationship. As a result, within the government, the press, and various private sectors of American society there was a slow-building but clear interest in better understanding Brazil and its particularities.

US insistence on fast-tracking negotiations on the FTAA—a theme of major interest to the USTR—and the inconsistency, if not the crudeness, of the arguments employed in the attempt to co-opt us, revealed that the US had misjudged the firmness of our stance and the complexity of the reasons that underpinned our rejection of the American proposal.

There was no reason for us to expect a change of approach from the United States, as the Washington government continued to suppose that Brazil would display the same erratic behavior as the majority of our Latin American neighbors.

To judge from the way our local interlocutors had conducted themselves during the buildup to the Brazilian president's visit, you could say they were still in kindergarten when it came to Brazilian studies. The Department of State's ignorance about Brazil was made all too evident in a lamentable declaration by Secretary Peter Romero, who, criticizing Brazilian policy on Colombia, publicly questioned the wisdom of the presidential visit. At that time, the US Department of State's bureau for western hemisphere affairs did not have a single diplomat on its staff who had lived in Brazil or could have been considered an expert on Brazilian affairs.

This was perhaps the biggest obstacle I had to overcome during my time in Washington: trying to disabuse the Department of State of the perception that Brazilian foreign policy during the FHC government had an anti-American edge to it, when all we were trying to do was defend our national interests.

When the Brazilian presidential plane landed at Andrews Air Force Base, there were two alternative scenarios: President Bush would either raise the prospect of bringing forward the FTAA deadline, in which case it would dominate the discussion, or, in the face of the technical deadlock, he would try to keep the issue from coming up at all. On this first encounter between the two leaders, the last thing we wanted was for the dialogue to get bogged down in specific issues and perhaps turn sour, and the fact that Bush opted not to broach the FTAA deadline signaled that the US was serious about building a constructive relationship with Brazil.

During the presidential meeting and in all his public declarations throughout the visit, President FHC kept the right balance between divergences and convergences, between reciprocal concessions and a refusal to yield, and, most importantly, scorned the possibility of using the firmness of his position to score cheap political points back home, and all this showed President Bush and his team just how mature and independent Brazil had become.

The visit was a success in terms of the cordiality it established between the two presidents, and this was reflected in their positive declarations to the press.

We could also say that this first meeting between the Brazilian and US presidents went exceptionally smoothly if we consider that, during those first few weeks of the Bush administration, the United States had just refused to sign the Kyoto Protocol and was already flexing what would become a key trait of its foreign policy: an urge to retaliate against the slightest sign of opposition to American interests.

It was interesting to analyze the coverage given to the meeting between FHC and Bush in the US and Brazilian press.

On the days before and after the visit, all the main newspapers in the United States published at least one extensive piece of analysis on the meeting. Invariably, these articles underscored the positive aspects of Brazil's rapid economic growth, the development of our political milieu and, most importantly, the country's increasing international clout. Though limited in volume, this coverage still outweighed and qualitatively outdid that for previous presidential visits. In relative terms, it also went beyond the treatment the press usually extended to visitors from countries not currently in focus on the international scene or high up on the list of national strategic priorities.

Of course, greater visibility for Brazil in the American press was not—nor could have been—a goal in itself, but it did serve as an indicator of our country's increased relevance on the international scene.

FHC's visit helped open the eyes of American leaders and public opinion to the true measure of Brazil and the reality that steered and determined its positions. The need for the United States to treat the country in a manner more befitting of its importance and specificities had been made clear.

While the place Brazil occupies within the hemisphere and in the comity of nations derives from its own attributes and the reach and range of its economic, political, and financial interests both internally and externally, the quality and intensity of its relations with the United States are determinant factors upon our regional leadership and, consequently, our standing on the global stage. So the importance of the signs Washington emitted in this regard could not be overstated.

Brazil's growing visibility in the eyes of Washington is clearly perceived by our neighbors, the international community, and the Americans themselves. So while we want to be recognized as good partners to the US, it is also important that they see us as preserving a certain distance and independence. Among other objectives, President FHC's visit to Washington and his meeting with George W. Bush helped to reinforce this perception.

Priority for the War on Terror

Fernando Henrique Cardoso's second visit to Bush, between November 7 and 9, 2001, was related to the September 11 terrorist attacks. FHC wanted to deliver, in person, a message of solidarity from the Brazilian people to the government and nation of the United States. The Brazilian government had already made a public statement about the attacks and had made clear its decision to take whatever measures were necessary to support the US within the Organization of American States (OAS).

The presidential meeting focused on three issues: the terrorist threat to the American territory; the economic situation in Brazil and South America; and the FTAA negotiations.

President Bush stressed the measures being taken internally to reduce the risk of further terrorist attacks and outlined his perception of the threat that the Al-Qaeda network and the Taliban posed to the American people. Even then, Bush identified Saddam Hussein as a security threat to the United States, an early indication of his will to resuscitate the plan devised by the neoconservatives back in the 1990s.

The US president made an impassioned and emphatic defense of the hard line the United States was taking against the terrorists.

On this issue, an enflamed president Bush demanded Brazil's support for his increasingly affirmative stance on Iraq, already defending the thesis that Baghdad had had a hand in the September 11 atrocities. These were the first signs that the wheels of war were grinding into motion and that the US would find some excuse for carrying through on its plan to oust Saddam Hussein.

President FHC reaffirmed the Brazilian position that all peaceful political and diplomatic means should be exhausted before any drastic action were taken that might have a profoundly destabilizing effect on the Middle East and the international oil market.

After the meeting with Bush, FHC, while still in Washington, spoke briefly about the positive development of the Brazilian economy and discussed the situation in Argentina at a breakfast meeting with the executive director of the IMF, Horst Köhler, and the Fund's director, Stanley Fischer. On the Argentinean issue, FHC put the same request for aid to Kohler, but to no avail. The Fund had severe reservations about the policies Buenos Aires was pursuing to restore confidence in its enfeebled economy.

Before returning home, President FHC went to New York to visit the World Trade Center site, symbolically re-named Ground Zero, after the Pentagon's central patio, the supposed target for Soviet long-range missile strikes during the Cold War. I accompanied him on this visit and, as one would expect, we were both moved and shocked at the magnitude of the devastation. We strolled along the walkway created for visiting authorities, which took us out among the debris, but we could not see where the towers themselves had stood, as the site was buried under a mountain of wreckage and rubble from the charred and ruined surroundings.

INITIATIVE TOWARD INSTITUTIONALIZING RELATIONS

During my time in charge of the embassy in Washington, I tried to encourage moves toward institutionalization, in other words, making the existing mechanisms and others still in the pipeline permanent in order to promote the expansion of our bilateral relations. During the Clinton administration, I sent a concrete suggestion to the Brazilian Foreign Ministry recommending how we should broach the theme, to be discussed and pursued with the Department of State at a later date.

While preparing FHC's visit in November 2001, I started discussing the matter with the Department of State and National Security Council at the White House.

If accepted by Washington, this institutionalization proposal would crown the relationship Presidents Clinton and FHC had built together, provide long-term prospects for expanding bilateral relations, and avoid any change of attitude on the part of the United States in the event of a PT victory in the 2002 elections.

The reasons for making this proposal were:

- We had excellent bilateral relations and the opportunity to strengthen them further by including new themes and sensitive issues on the agenda of talks between authorities from the two nations;

- The role of presidential diplomacy, given the trust and respect that had developed out of the personal relationship between FHC and Clinton;
- The trust and respect Minister Luiz Felipe Lampreia had built with Secretary of State Madeleine Albright, USTR chief Charlene Barshefsky, and Trade Secretary William Daley, among other high-ranking members of the US government;
- The importance of not letting the contacts made during the FHC government get lost amid the 2002 elections;
- Interest in consolidating the channels that had been opened and in transforming these into regular lines of communication for future administrations.

With these premises accepted, presidents Clinton and FHC would then be able to approve an agreement, at a meeting in Washington or Brasília, consolidating all the initiatives taken on either side during the two presidents' mandates, raising Brazil to a whole new level among the United States's partners.

To achieve this, a handbook—*Brazil–US Framework for a Strategic Partnership*—would be drawn up to cover all aspects of relations between the two countries.

An institutional framework for a constructive partnership between Brazil and the United States would cover the following:

1. High-level consultations:
   - presidential meetings every two years;
   - annual meetings between foreign ministers;
   - regular ministerial meetings in priority areas
2. Sector-based consultations:
   - politics
   - economics
   - political planning
   - agriculture
   - foreign trade
   - security and defense
   - finances
   - education
   - the environment

- justice
- energy
- science and technology
3. Hemispheric and regional integration:
    - South America and US foreign policy
    - Mercosur
    - FTAA
4. Macroeconomic and structural consultations:
    - G20
5. Cooperation on global themes:
    - the environment
    - drugs
    - terrorism
    - corruption
    - human rights
6. Relationship between the two Congresses through periodical meetings.

The proposal the embassy had submitted for Itamaraty's consideration and had begun to examine with the Department of State and National Security Council distinguished Brazil from the hemispheric context and presented a level of prominence that had never been obtained before.

However, the discussions that began in the second semester of 2001 did not bear fruit. The lukewarm personal relationship between presidents FHC and George W. Bush, the electoral campaigns in both countries, and the change in government in the United States all contributed to shelving the proposal before FHC's administration had even come to an end. Naturally, after some political calculations, the United States decided to offer something similar, although less ambitious, on the occasion of President Lula's visit to Washington in June 2003.

THE POLITICAL CONTEXT

The September 11 terrorist attacks completely dominated the political and social scene in the United States during this presidential visit. The tragic events had rekindled interest in foreign policy in an administration that, in its first months, had shown a marked and worrying tendency toward unilateralism. Washington came to define its foreign policy toward other nations in terms of their strategic importance; in other words, how they reacted to, and to what extent they engaged with, the "war on terror." Though it was a way of gauging US relations with the international community, it was a distorted one at best.

With nerves frayed, priorities were re-evaluated, and themes and nations came to the fore or fell by the wayside depending on their usefulness and relevance to this fight against an abstract enemy. Hence the energy and insistence channeled into establishing and maintaining a multiform and diffuse Coalition of the Willing in the war against terrorism in Afghanistan and the invasion of Iraq.

The presidential meeting in Washington was held two months after the 9/11 attacks, and the military campaign in Afghanistan was less than a month old. The prevailing atmosphere was thus one of tension and frustration.

The US government's confrontational attitude was causing mounting discomfort, especially in Europe. Internally, criticism was beginning to well against the military operation in Afghanistan, which was failing to deliver on its promise to capture Bin Laden, and also against the way the public was being browbeaten on a supposed bioterrorist threat.

American society, which had rallied behind Bush after September 11, was showing signs of impatience and doubt, though none of this seemed to have affected the president's approval ratings. With each passing day, xenophobia seemed to grow stronger, peddled as patriotism in speeches laced with bloated rhetoric that distorted the reality.

US susceptibility and the temptation to interpret as betrayal the slightest dissonance on the subject of the "just and patriotic war" also grew by the day.

Pressed by public opinion, the government, once so confident that the military operations would yield near-immediate results, was now forced to admit that the war against terror would be long and hard, as the facts have since borne out.

Internally, the dissatisfaction with the way the government was handling the terrorist threat was becoming increasingly evident. Attempts by certain politicians, mostly Republicans, to exploit the situation in order to push through personal projects and protect the interests of big industry, particularly mining and petroleum operations, were roundly condemned.

As for the military campaign itself, information was sparse and not always positive. Few results were emerging from the theater of war and a troubling number of tragic episodes, such as the bombing of Red Cross warehouses and civilian homes, were just adding to the overall embarrassment. While the government tried to keep images of American casualties out of the media, devastating footage and photos of dead and mutilated soldiers began to emerge. Reports of "collateral damage" were becoming more and more common in Afghanistan, as they would later in Iraq, with news of women and children among those killed by air strikes and shelling, despite the military's declarations that it was doing everything possible to keep civilian casualties to a minimum.

It was also proving difficult to form a post-Taliban government. There were too many unanswered questions and interminable discussions about nation building. People were starting to question the viability and competence of the Northern Alliance, the so-called United Front. Another open question was the role of the United Nations, which the US wanted to see being more active. But that would take convincing the other member states and securing the support of Secretary-General Kofi Annan and his special envoy to Afghanistan.

The failure of American diplomacy to reduce anti-Americanism among Muslim populations was another target for criticism. In places like the Middle East and Kashmir, the Bush government was beginning to realize that simply working to contain complex problems that caused deep-running divides was not enough.

Although officially the US would not accept the validity of any grievances or sense of retaliation that might explain the terrorist attacks, the government was showing signs that it was aware of the need to find a way to get the Israeli/Palestinian peace process back on track, despite Bush having said, upon coming to office, that the problem had to be resolved by the parties involved, without American interference. Relations with India and Pakistan were being handled with kid gloves by the Department of State, given the precarious nature of the Islamabad regime.

The United States had become a hostage to September 11. In addition to the material damage, American self-esteem had been rocked. It was becoming increasingly clear that the nation had changed, literally overnight. Still reeling from the impact, foreign policy priorities had to be revised, projects suspended, expectations lowered, and new fronts of action opened. In the aftermath of the attacks, the Bush government succumbed to pressure from the more radical sectors, which insisted on applying unilateral policies regardless of the reaction from the international community. Multilateral action continued, although in a much reduced form, as dialogue with the Europeans was important in order to shore up support for the war on terrorism. But the United States was in no mood for compromise or consensus building.

Under these new circumstances, the NATO allies began to receive special attention: Russia, the former Soviet republics of Central Asia, the so-called moderate Arab regimes, and even China. In the opposite direction, Latin America lost ground (including Vicente Fox's Mexico), and the only themes that seemed to register with the US were those of security and defense, terrorism, narco-trafficking, money laundering, and other transnational crimes.

As a result of this new unilaterally driven approach to foreign policy, the United States began to lose prestige and credibility worldwide, a decline that would continue throughout the Bush administration.

THE ECONOMIC CONTEXT

The tragic events of September 11 aggravated the economic slowdown that began in the second half of 2000. A 0.4 percent fall in GDP in September 2002 put an end to eight years of continuous growth and signaled the onset of recession.

The discussion on the possible initiatives the Bush government could take to stimulate the economy and rescue the sectors that had been hit the hardest indicated a change, however short-lived, in the country's prevailing philosophy. Led by President Bush, the opponents of the tax-and-spend liberals, as some liked to call the Democrats, found in this worsening economic crisis strong grounds on which to go against their most deeply engrained Capitalist principles and do what—at that moment anyway—was considered "best for the United States."

In a Senate with a Democrat majority, attention initially turned to a bill proposed by the Bush administration, and approved by the Republican-held House of Representatives, that provided for a tax cut to the order of US$99.5 billion in 2002 and US$159 billion over the next ten years. The aim was to stimulate economic growth. The approval of the bill by 216 to 214 votes reflected the traditional Republican–Democrat divide on the issue.

The four main elements of the bill approved by the House of Representatives were: tax rebates for those who had not yet received the benefit that year; annulment of the alternative minimum tax applied to corporations; an increase in spending write-offs on capital assets for the business sector, which had previously been cut; and an accelerated reduction of the 27 percent income tax rate scheduled for the following four years under the existing legislation. Other important issues tackled by the bill were: decreased rates on long-term capital gains for most taxpayers; the controversial refunds to major corporations of any alternative minimum tax paid since 1986; and the right to deduct operating losses carried back from 1996. The main problem the Democrats had with the bill was the protection it extended to big corporations to the detriment of the workers they had let go, and the threat it posed to budgetary balance, an important achievement of the Clinton administration.

As for the external economic and financial agenda, the war against terrorism and its financial support became a priority, as can be seen from the attention paid to it from that time on by the IMF and G20.

Problems both internal—such as the risk of new terrorist attacks and the counterproductive results of the Senate stimulus package—and external—such as the impact of Argentina's foreign debt default and the dubious results of the military incursions in Afghanistan—painted an outlook of economic recession that was fast shaking the confidence of market analysts and agencies.

The capital markets in the US began to slip as a result of a combination of risk factors and the behavior of the key economic indicators, such as reduced consumption, higher unemployment figures, and a slump in industrial production.

Lula Presents Himself in Washington

Lula's first stay in Washington, still as president-elect, on December 10 and 11, 2002, was basically a working visit. There was a lot of curiosity about the man who would be sworn in as president of Brazil just a few days later.

During the electoral process, the prospects of Lula and PT (The Workers' Party) getting into power had caused a great deal of uncertainty in the United States, especially with regard to which way he would steer economic and foreign policy.

In a sense, this first visit was designed to put market and government minds at ease as to how the Lula administration would handle these important issues.

INTENSE PREPARATIONS

In Brazil, in November of that year, I had a meeting with some of the main coordinators of Lula's campaign, such as José Dirceu, Antonio

Palocci, and Luiz Dulci, with whom I was to go over the program to identify areas of interest and priority themes. In these preparatory conversations, I underscored the special meaning of this first visit to Washington by a Workers' Party president and the visibility it would generate.

In November 2002, I met with Lula at the PT headquarters in São Paulo to discuss the Washington trip. During our conversation, he told me of his plans to create a foreign trade department to promote Brazilian products abroad. As the president-elect saw it, the ambassadors should function as traveling salesmen committed to increasing and diversifying Brazilian exports. I observed that there was no need to create yet another official organ in order to boost exports, but merely to increase the budget to Itamaraty so that it could give the embassies the means they required to do just that. I reminded him that under its present budget, the Washington embassy had less than five thousand dollars with which to assist Brazilian companies that wanted to break into the US market.

Given his interest in the subject, I took the opportunity to leave with the president-elect a copy of a project I had recently developed for the creation of just such a foreign trade department, though one whose authority included not only the promotion of export growth, but also the expansion of the internal coordination of the decision-making process and a unified command of the foreign trade actions then scattered across some twenty ministries and governmental agencies. After this conversation with Lula, I realized that a foreign trade department in the model I had imagined would be a long time coming. Unfortunately, my impressions were correct. The Brazilian Agency for the Promotion of Exports and Investments (APEX), created at the beginning of Lula's first term under the jurisdiction of the Ministry for Development, Industry, and Foreign Trade, began to compete with and overlap the Foreign Office in its efforts to promote Brazilian products abroad.

In November, before the visit, Secretary for Western Hemisphere Affairs Otto Reich came to São Paulo to meet the president-elect and the key figures in PT. Lula, Mercadante, Palocci, and Dirceu sought to placate their interlocutors by adopting a far more moderate tone than usual. Their interest in strengthening ties with the United States was obvious, while critical observations on the São Paulo Forum—a Latin American and Caribbean group of leftist political parties and nongovernmental organizations created with the support of PT, FARC and

Hugo Chávez—flowed free and easy, much to the American delegation's surprise, as the WikiLeaks cables would later reveal.

According to the US embassy cables, Lula was anxious to meet President George W. Bush. "Two politicians like us will understand each other when we meet face to face," said the confident president-elect. Again to the surprise of the US officials, the PT circle raised the possibility of Brazil signing a free trade agreement with the US, something they said the Lula government could propose after consultations with its Mercosur partners.

President Lula arrived in Washington on December 9th, alongside Antonio Palocci, Marta Suplicy, Aloizio Mercadante, and André Singer.

The few days I spent with the president and his party, all hosted at the embassy residence, passed in a simple and informal manner, affording long and relaxed conversations. The preparatory work for the meetings was easygoing and straightforward.

This close contact with Lula leading up to his inauguration showed me his modus operandi and capacity for leadership. I was struck by the sharp intuition and perspicacity of his observations, always direct and objective, about the new world that was opening up before him. There was no doubt as to his skill as a communicator, something we would see so successfully applied throughout his two mandates, whether to magnify his government's achievements or to evade thorny issues.

As was only to be expected, there was a lot of concern about the success of the visit and its media impact. The president-elect's support crew worked tirelessly. The team gathered over breakfast, prepared the papers for the meetings, especially those with President Bush, and for the first press conference at the National Press Association (NPA), a platform often used by world leaders to get their message across to the American people and to the international community. As this was Lula's first international press conference, the embassy had prepared a long list of questions and suggested responses, covering sensitive themes that might come up during the Q&A. This homework proved extremely useful, as it was discussed and expanded by the presidential aides and put to good use at the NPA.

At the Press Association, after a crowded lunch with congressmen and journalists, the future president made his address and took questions from the floor. The charisma and frankness Lula displayed at this event were key to its success and impact in the media.

On this, his first presentation on the world stage, Lula reaffirmed the democratic character of his future government and its commitment to economic policies to curb inflation and bring down Brazil's risk premium. In many of his answers, Lula made it clear that he would not be a radical leftist leader, as many Republican conservatives had feared he would.

I spoke at length with the president-elect on the opportunities that were opening up in terms of foreign trade, science and technology, and energy, given the interest President Bush had shown in that sector.

In my private conversations with Lula, much was said about the formation of his ministerial cabinet and about the Brazilian Foreign Office, Itamaraty. President FHC had already told me that Lula would mention Celso Amorim as a possible chancellor.

I found out later that the first choice for foreign minister had actually been José Viegas, who had declined the invitation, and that Celso Amorim had emerged from talks between Samuel Pinheiro Guimarães and Marco Aurélio Garcia as the likely appointee. The diplomat, who was ambassador to London and had not yet met the incumbent president, had called José Dirceu and asked for a meeting with Lula. During the campaign, Celso Amorim is known to have maintained close contact with José Serra and supposedly even made contributions to his government program. His previous work as ambassador to the WTO, on the launch of the Doha Round and in drafting a document on intellectual property had impressed the former minister for health, Lula's rival candidate for the presidency.

In Washington, President Lula was surprised to see the stars-and-stripes flapping freely not only atop public buildings, but on many private residences too, reflecting the nationalist, patriotic spirit ignited by the September 11 attacks and the invasion of Iraq. I remarked that, contrary to the way the national flag is used in Brazil, in American society it was seen as a symbol of the nation, its union, and vigor—something that had also impressed me upon my arrival there. During his first term of office, perhaps influenced by what he saw on his Washington visit, President Lula made it obligatory for the flag to be flown at schools, a provision that was passed into law but which, like so many other good initiatives, fell by the wayside.

"I LIKE THIS GUY"
On December 10th, Lula had a fifty-minute meeting with President Bush in the Oval Office.

The two men clicked immediately and the conversation flowed. The perfect simultaneous translation by the competent Brazilian interpreter Sérgio Xavier avoided any wasted time and ensured the dynamic nature of the meeting.

On the Brazilian side, present at the encounter were Antonio Palocci, the future finance minister; Marta Suplicy, then mayor of São Paulo; Aloizio Mercadente, senator-elect; André Singer, the president's spokesman; and myself. On the US side were Secretary of State Colin Powell; National Security Adviser Condoleezza Rice; Robert Zoellick, the United States trade representative; Donna Hrinak, US ambassador to Brazil; the international secretary from the Treasury Department, John Taylor; and the Latin American director of the National Security Council, John Maisto.

Bush broke the ice with a long introduction in which he thanked the president-elect for having accepted his invitation to visit the United States in such a tense political environment and while in the middle of forming his own cabinet. He said that he considered this to be an important meeting in terms of their working together to broaden and deepen Brazil–US relations. He noted that the encounter had sparked a great deal of interest and added, with good humor: "Everyone wants to know how a Texan like me is going to get along with a guy like you, and this meeting will prove to them all that we can understand each other just fine." He observed that he had been paying close attention to the president-elect's declarations, especially those on the possibility of engaging Brazilian society in volunteer programs, the need to apply solid fiscal policies (on which he congratulated Lula), and on foreign trade. All of this had helped abate uncertainties and prepare the ground for a partnership with the United States. Bush thanked the president-elect for having met with Zoellick and underscored the need for Brazil and the US to work together at the WTO and on the FTAA, despite the difficulties ("it won't be easy").

In the most substantial part of his opening comments, Bush proposed that the countries examine a framework for the bilateral relationship, starting with a summit meeting (presidents and ministers) in March or April 2003, when they could work out directives and begin this new phase on a solid basis.

In response, Lula outlined his personal and political biography ("I was born in one of the poorest regions of Brazil, where a child who lived past its first year could make it all the way to the Presidency"). He said that his victory signaled a desire for change in Brazil and that his election was the result of over twenty years of hard work. He mentioned the ample support he had received from the most varied sectors of society, including the business community, represented by his vice-president-elect, José Alencar. Lula said that he was aware of his responsibilities to Brazil and that his government would strive to restore the economy to the path of development, but with social justice. He also stated that for many years he and his party had suffered from unfair and prejudiced accusations based on distorted perceptions and that he wanted to thank Bush and the US government for not interfering in the recent elections, unlike previous administrations in earlier campaigns. In relation to the Workers' Party, Lula said that prejudices and distortions continued to exist, but noted that, had it not been for the role PT had played in Brazilian politics, the country might have found itself in a situation not unlike that of Colombia, which was then in the throes of a violent conflict with the FARC.

As for his government's foreign policy, the president-elect underscored the following three points:

- Foreign policy would be bolder. The intention was to deepen bilateral relations, intensifying political, economic, and cultural exchange between Brazil and the US, its most important partner;
- Brazil would begin to exercise a leadership role in South America. His government would help further continent-wide development, consolidating democracies and peace and stepping up the fight against narco-trafficking. To symbolize this, Lula's first foreign visit had been to Argentina. The president-elect said that he was positive he would be able to count on US support in this effort;
- His government would work toward South American recovery and would do what it could to help Argentina.

Lula said he was aware that he would have no room for error, unlike his predecessors, who had always had the benefit of the doubt, because if his government did not deliver as promised, the frustration would be immense. In this sense, Lula announced that the first measure he planned to adopt would be a program to tackle hunger, for which he would have widespread support from the Brazilian state and society. He said that he had the budget for social expenditure and that under his government Brazil would experience the awakening of a socially driven agenda.

As the Fome Zero (Zero Hunger) program was still a flagship project at the beginning of Lula's term of office, he outlined his ideas for it and spoke of the policies he would adopt to reduce social inequalities in Brazil, and the effort his government would channel into eradicating poverty. Leaving aside the political clichés that always exalt responsibility and social justice, Lula stated his objectives with frank simplicity: "My aim is that, by the end of my term of office, every single Brazilian will be able to have three meals a day, 'breakfast, lunch and dinner.'"

Lastly, he said he was convinced that the Workers' Party would play an important role in influencing leftist parties throughout the region to take the democratic path toward achieving their goals.

After hearing the president-elect's opinions on issues internal and external, especially on the need for the ampler involvement of society as a whole, not just the government, in solving problems, President Bush declared that the two men shared the same vision and that he could easily have described the Brazilian incumbent as a "Bushite republican."

After this comment, Lula observed that Brazil would fight to defend its interests and that the country's line on trade negotiations would be tougher. He added, however, that once an agreement was reached, they would stick to it. Hearing this, Bush encouraged Lula to negotiate hard, but "within reason," and said that he would be willing to work closely with Brazil to defend their common interests.

In the most highly charged part of the meeting, President Bush laid out his ideas on the issue of US security. Pointing over to the Oval Office desk, he said that every morning he sat down there to find CIA reports red-flagging up to forty possible terrorist threats against US territory. "In this seat, in which sat Roosevelt, Kennedy, and Lyndon Johnson, I receive threat after threat. I'm here to defend the safety of the American people and I will do whatever it takes to protect my country."

He said that his main objective was to defend the United States and its people: "We are a country at war against those who would threaten us." The president observed that he would take whatever risk was necessary to secure peace and homeland security. For Bush, since September 11, "the strategic vision of the United States has changed." He was determined to keep all his options on the table. He said that while he hoped, for the sake of peace, that he did not have to use force, he would not allow "some crazy dictator" to threaten the United States with weapons of mass destruction.

Following that, he argued that friendly nations had mutual obligations and wanted to know what the Brazilian position was, adding immediately that he did not expect an answer straight away. "I will not yield," he said. He claimed that he had suffered severe criticism and become one of the most misunderstood leaders in the world for having taken a supposedly unilateral route. Lastly, he said that he and Colin Powell had been working strenuously with the international community and had received its go-ahead, as reflected in the UN Security Council resolution on terrorism, passed by unanimous vote.

Lula replied that all nations had a duty to fight for peace, that the September 11 attacks had been a deplorable act of madness and that combating terrorism was a fight that belonged to all the countries of the world. He said that Brazil would be a US ally in carrying through any UN resolution and that Iraq would be called upon not only to disarm, but to comply in full with the terms of the standing Security Council resolutions.

Bringing to a close his comments on Iraq and terrorism, President Bush said, "I am convinced that the United States will be attacked again and when that happens we will react vigorously."

To complete the meeting, the American president raised two further subjects. Reminded by Colin Powell, Bush asked the president-elect for his support on a mini-summit of the Americas proposed by Canada, signaling that the encounter would not be to discuss the FTAA alone, but also corruption, governance, hunger, and drugs. The Venezuela issue was the second item. Bush asked for Brazil's help in finding a way to resolve the political crisis in Venezuela, perhaps through a referendum or early elections. Lula said that he knew Chávez well and that he had spoken to him on many occasions to get him to tone things down and realign with reality. He said that, in his opinion, the Venezuelan president had difficulty understanding the political game, as his was effectively a soldier's view of problems, but he said he would speak to him further.

One of the reasons why Lula was able to win Bush's respect so quickly was the direct and straightforward way he expressed his ideas and perceptions, which gelled well with the American's to-the-point and far from intellectual style.

According to some high-level American officials, what had most impressed Bush was Lula's comment about the people having three meals a day, as it brought home a situation that would have been unthinkable in a rich country like the United States, which had yet to pass through the economic crisis of 2008–2009, and the rampant unemployment it caused. After the meeting at the Oval Office, Bush is reported to have said: "I like this guy."

As they left the White House, the Brazilian committee expressed its concerns with Bush's bellicose attitude. The delegation emerged from the meeting with the distinct impression that the American president was, to put it lightly, a radical, near-fanatic who would march the US all the way to war on Iraq.

During the customary post-meeting press conference in the White House gardens, the president-elect ran through the most important points of the discussion with President Bush before announcing—to the surprise of everyone, including the delegation itself—Antonio Palocci as the future Minister of Finance and Marina Silva as Minister for the Environment. The impact of the announcement, made in the middle of an official visit, was enormous.

THE TRADE CHAPTER

At the meeting between the president-elect and the United States trade representative, Robert Zoellick, the latter took the opportunity to reiterate his government's message of support for the new Brazilian administration. Right at the beginning he said that he felt that the meeting with Bush had been highly beneficial and that the US president was very satisfied with how things had gone.

Zoellick thanked Lula for having taken time out from forming his cabinet to go to Washington and present his ideas for his future government, especially his concerns with social inequality and poverty. He said that on his last visit to Brazil he had encountered a vibrant and dynamic economy, but had also noted that a large chunk of the population seemed to have been left behind by the development process. For Zoellick, faced with that reality, the government's focus on resolving social problems was correctly placed. He also praised the leadership role PT had assumed among the left-wing parties of Latin America, especially in attempting to usher them onto the democratic path and to shed their anachronisms.

Lula said that President Bush had been a pleasant surprise, concluding that you really can't judge people from what is said about them on TV, because, contrary to the image conveyed of him, the US president had come across as a very nice guy. The president-elect said he was convinced the visit to the United States had laid the bedrock for an excellent, frank, transparent, and productive relationship between the two countries.

At the meeting held at the USTR, Lula reminded Zoellick that, in politics, frankness counts for a lot, and that a *no* delivered with sincerity is more valuable than a dissimulated *yes*. On that note, he repeated that just as President Bush defended the interests of the American people, businessmen and farmers in trade negotiations with Brazil and others, they could expect the Brazilian government to do the same on the FTAA. He added that if the negotiations proceeded in that spirit, there was every chance they would reach a deal.

Lula then went on to tell Zoellick that he had committed a "gaff" earlier that day during the White House interview by announcing, in an apparently inadvertent way, two of his future ministers, and that the Brazilian press had already pounced on the names. He said that he had two very experienced names in mind to handle trade negotiations, one as minister for Development, Industry and Foreign Trade, and the other as minister for Agriculture. The first of these would be someone from the food industry that exports to over seventy countries and the second a businessman with ties to agribusiness and the cooperatives sector in Brazil. He was referring to Luiz Fernando Furlan and Roberto Rodrigues, who assumed their respective positions in 2003. Zoellick asked who his main interlocutor on foreign trade would be, adding that he and his counterpart during the FHC government, Celso Lafer, had made good progress on the Doha Round with regard to development and the FTAA. Lula responded that the Ministries of Industry and Foreign Trade and Agriculture would work in tandem with the Foreign Ministry on these issues. He also said that the new government's aim would be to impose more pragmatism on trade negotiations, which, as he saw it, had been handled in a very theoretical way.

Zoellick added that he would be prepared to visit Brazil as soon as the new trade negotiations team was up and running to exchange opinions and perceptions on where matters stood. Zoellick also talked about certain discussions underway on the FTAA and at the WTO.

As for the FTAA, he said he wanted to better understand—through ample, frank, and transparent dialogue—what Brazil's real expectations were, and those of other countries in the bloc. To get things moving in this direction, he said that the negotiations could avail themselves of the ministerial mini-meetings that were being organized at the WTO. Zoellick also stated that the United States was open to discussing other forms of integration with Brazil and that it wanted to get a clearer idea of what the country had in mind when it mentioned a model already in place with the European Union. He observed that negotiations would become more active as of 2003, which was why he wanted to talk and achieve a better understanding so as to avoid and overcome possible divergences. Lastly, he stressed the need to organize the working schedule for the two countries' co-chairmanship, which would begin in February.

On the subject of the WTO, Zoellick said that the United States and Brazil could continue to make a positive contribution to the advancement of the Doha Round on development and could establish important partnerships, seen as they shared many positions within the forum, such as on the elimination of agricultural subsidies.

President-elect Lula accepted the USTR's offer to come to Brazil once the negotiating team was in place and agreed on the need to thrash out the issue once and for all. He also underscored the importance of not adopting a stance for or against the FTAA a priori, or on principle. Convincing and being convinced, he said, depend on the reality of the facts, but also on negotiations. He agreed that there is no politics without divergences and that it was essential, not only in foreign trade, but in various walks of life, to learn to handle diversity democratically.

When Zoellick asked how things were progressing with the rest of the cabinet, Lula said that the process was almost complete, but that it had been a difficult one, especially given the need to accommodate names put forward by the various parties in order to build a congressional majority and ensure governability. In relation to the Central Bank, Lula informed Zoellick that the team had opted for a gradual transition over the first months of government, but did not specify the line of action to be adopted. This doubt was left to linger until the announcement of Henrique Meirelles as president. In other words, there would be no transition after all, but continuity of the previous government's economic policy.

At the end of the meeting, Zoellick recognized that Brazil's main problem lay in the financial area, saying that he had been a staffer at the Treasury Department and that he knew all its inner workings. He offered to help the new team, if and when appropriate, in its dealings with Treasury Secretary John Snow, recently appointed to the post. Zoellick said that what really mattered was that Brazil and the United States continued to make progress and succeed in their work together.

OTHER VISITS AND MEETINGS

One of the highlights of Lula's first trip to Washington was his visit to the headquarters of the AFL-CIO (American Federation of Labor–Congress of Industrial Organizations), arranged by the embassy and by Stanley Gacek, a representative of the powerful union and a longtime friend of PT. In an unprecedented move, Lula was received with rapturous applause by the unionists. John Sweeney, then-president of AFL-CIO, made an inflamed and emotional speech in which he said that Brazil had succeeded where the United States had always failed, in electing a working-class president of the Republic. And all the while PT's famous campaign jingle "Lula Lá," from the 1989 elections, blared over the loudspeakers.

At the same time that Lula was receiving a hero's welcome at the AFL-CIO, we saw in the American press a number of critical articles orchestrated by the conservative right. *The Washington Times* bemoaned Lula's election and the fact that the new government would certainly drag Brazil to the left. I wrote letters and articles in response, criticizing the level of disinformation in relation to what was actually going on in Brazil.

In this debate I took the opportunity to mention the "Letter to the Brazilian People" and to underscore the former union leader's pragmatism and relatively ideologically unbiased position on major issues. I also stressed that he was a leader elected by direct vote who had always respected the political system, even after losing three elections in a row.

The fears expressed by the government, the political right in Congress, and the media that President Lula would join the "new wave" of leftist governments in Latin America, led by President Hugo Chávez, had, I argued, lost much of its force after this visit. Gacek went so far as to contact Secretary Otto Reich in a bid to debunk some of the myths surrounding Lula and PT.

Even before Lula took office, the prevailing perception of him in Washington had begun to change, though the financial system continued to harbor reservations.

Lula also met with the heads of the World Bank and the Inter-American Development Bank, emphasizing his plans to maintain economic stability and honor all contracts and commitments assumed by the previous government.

There were also talks with democratic and republican congressmen from the Congressional Brazil Caucus, who, seduced by Lula's charisma, began to take a positive view of the government's future plans.

While the president-elect was still in Washington, Henrique Meirelles was invited to become governor of the Central Bank. Through the mediation of the businessman Ivo Rosset, who had ties to PT, Meirelles, who was visiting the United States at the time, arranged with Palocci to meet at a dinner in Lula's honor held on the night of December 10th at the embassy in Washington. During the aperitifs, Palocci and Meirelles talked for over an hour in my study in the private wing of the residence. What took so long was that Meirelles wanted to be sure he would have the autonomy and independence he needed to exercise his function before accepting the invitation. Palocci, the future Finance Minister, said, "So, let's go ask the president."

Lula, who was becoming impatient, was asking why we were taking so long to serve dinner when Palocci and Meirelles came up to him to put their question and have it answered in the affirmative. It was a commitment that would be respected throughout Lula's eight years in power.

With the matter resolved, we moved into the dining hall, where an eclectic assortment of guests was seated at eight round tables. Among those in attendance were the Brazilian photographer Sebastião Salgado, on a visit to the city; the democratic senator Christopher Dodd, who would later run in the primaries (on being introduced to the photographer, Dodd showed him a picture of his new-born daughter); the African American leader and former presidential candidate Jesse Jackson, who insisted on having his son seated at the table even though he was not invited; and Lally Weymouth, a journalist and heir to Katherine Graham of the *Washington Post*, who had come down from New York curious to meet this much-vaunted leftist president.

Upon Lula's return to Brazil, I accompanied Palocci to New York, where he made his first contacts with the financial sector on Wall Street, with the help of Tim Geithner, then-president of the FED in the city, and future treasurer under Barack Obama. On this occasion, Palocci stuck to the "Letter to the Brazilian People" and made all the necessary assurances on the economic policy Wall Street could expect from the Lula government, saying that it would be based on security, balance, consistency, and sustainability. He told his interlocutors that the government would work resolutely and unwaveringly to achieve long-term economic stability for the Brazilian citizenry and institutions.

For the visit to New York, I also arranged an informal meeting on social policy between Palocci and Joseph Stiglitz, Jeffrey Sachs, and Albert Fishlow, scholars and economists with a keen knowledge of Brazil's problems.

From Lula's perspective, the visit was a major success. The new president returned to Brazil having opened a direct channel of communication with Bush and having clearly stated his intentions to maintain economic stability and honor the contracts sealed by the outgoing government. By so doing, he dispelled much of the concern his election had caused. All of this was accompanied *pari passu* by unequivocal declarations of the priority the new government would place on social issues and the fight against hunger.

Lula in Washington during the Iraq Crisis

President Lula's second visit to Washington took place in June 2003, some three months after the United States invaded Iraq. During the few months between his first and second visits, the world context had greatly changed. The Bush government's obsession with the invasion and the pressure it was putting on every country in the hemisphere to support the war were responsible for some considerable revisions to our relationship with the United States.

The argument that there were connections between the Al-Qaeda terrorists and Saddam Hussein and that Iraq was hiding an arsenal of weapons of mass destruction had not been enough to convince countries like France and Germany to support the invasion. Britain and Spain, however, did not hesitate to throw their weight behind the American position. The focus of US foreign policy was thoroughly on Iraq. Internally, the population had rallied behind the war effort, which had the express aims of capturing Saddam Hussein alive and installing democracy in Iraq and of discovering the whereabouts of Bin Laden.

For the United States, Brazil was a friendly nation with a firmly established democratic order and economy at an advanced stage of recovery. The signs of stability were clear for all to see and renewed economic growth was brushing aside whatever uncertainties had lingered since the election.

In relation to foreign policy, however, suspicions persisted that Brazil might join the Latin American axis of evil, captained by Cuba and Venezuela. This distrust was piqued by a visit the president's international advisor, Marco Aurélio Garcia, made to Hugo Chávez during the ten first days of Lula's government, and by an interview that Minister for Science and Technology Roberto Amaral gave to BBC Brazil, during which he said that Brazil ought to acquire the capacity to build nuclear weapons. "We are against nuclear proliferation; we are signatories to the non-proliferation treaty. We renounce the production of warheads, but we should not renounce any body of scientific knowledge," said Amaral. When asked if this "knowledge" included that required to build a nuclear bomb, the minister replied: "It includes all knowledge. Knowledge of the genome, knowledge of DNA, knowledge of nuclear fission." Our government's criticism of the US attack against Iraq and its promise to vote against military action at the United Nations, in consonance with Havana and Caracas, added to the climate of doubt as to Brazil's intentions.

In the economic area, the Treasury Department and the FED were beginning to question the president's commitment to pursue orthodox economic policies and honor agreements made with the IMF. In short, the FED was worried about the economy under the new government, and displayed as much in its actions.

This bad impression only began to dissipate midway through the year, given the positive performance of the financial market in Brazil and the higher consumer and corporate confidence that came with the strengthened economy.

"To speak of Brazilian debt as a high-quality asset really is a big change," said Alan Greenspan, a tad ironically. A "populist with a large following"—that was how the FED president described Lula, making no attempt to conceal his major reservations concerning the new president.

The international community and that mysterious entity known as the market began to believe that Lula would give a wide berth to the radicalism PT had adopted in its campaign and that he would pursue an economic policy based upon that of the previous government.

The Washington press, both the *Post* and the *Times*, which had been publishing articles and editorials critical of the Lula government, was soon contradicted by events in Brazil.

The change of perception toward the country's economy in the second half of 2003 can be credited to the Finance Minister Antonio Palocci and his team, and to the many contacts maintained in Washington and New York, an effort in which I was able to participate personally. On the strength of this initial effort, Palocci came to be seen as the guarantor of economic policy continuity and as the man behind the stability of the Brazilian economy. It was a perception passed on to me not only by qualified personnel at the US Treasury, but especially by representatives of financial companies and institutions in Washington and New York.

The gradual improvement of Brazil's image in the areas of foreign policy and the economy was, in part, the reason for the excellent welcome President Lula received in Washington on his state visit in June 2003.

I learned from the Portuguese ambassador that his prime minister had made an official visit to the United States some days before Lula's. At a meeting with Bush at the White House, the American—in yet another demonstration of his lack of knowledge of world politics—asked whether Portugal had a special relationship with Brazil. The prime minister said that it did, and praised Brazil's economic policy and stability, but demurred that President Lula was, after all, a leftist politician. Bush apparently replied that he didn't have any problem with that, as Lula had shown himself to be serious and competent. He said that Lula defended the interests of his country, seemed to be handling the economy well, was taking measures to tackle hunger and poverty, and, most importantly of all, had not demonstrated any anti-American feeling.

Lula's second visit was carefully planned. It took three inter-ministerial meetings with members of the Bush administration and countless others with US officials to go over the documents and draft the joint statement to be released afterwards. This statement would cover points of convergence between the two countries and would highlight the positive elements of the agenda. This time, the focus would be social and political rather than economic. The embassy in Washington made suggestions as to how to institutionalize the bilateral relations, as discussed by the two presidents back in December.

Preparations for the visit on the Brazilian side, much of which fell to the embassy, were greatly facilitated by the goodwill shown by the US authorities, demonstrating the importance Washington attributed to the new Brazilian leader.

In my contact with Itamaraty, I began to detect the first signs of Brazilian resistance to the formalization of some of the thematic working groups to be created during the visit and an unwillingness to approve the wording of the joint statement. Various passages that had struck me as very positive, such as those recognizing Brazil's regional importance, were attenuated or dropped altogether, and the part that described the existing mechanisms of coordination between the two countries was reduced.

During our preparations, Allan Larson, economic secretary at the State Department, expressed his concern about this Brazilian intransigence on certain aspects of the joint statement. As he saw it, certain relevant points were still open, such as the financial issue, terrorism and, particularly, trade, seen as the Brazilian government did not want any reference made to the FTAA negotiations. I passed Larson's concerns on to Brasília and submitted a request to the State Department for a meeting between Bush and Lula at the Conference in Monterrey, Mexico, which would take place before the visit to Washington.

Richard Haas, political planning director at the Department of State, less interested in the present conjuncture than with the medium to long-term vision, used an interview prior to Lula's visit to stress how important the Brazilian president's visit would be to the United States. An economically strong and stable Brazil would have a global impact, its active presence in the hemisphere would be important to the resolution of regional problems, and, in the sphere of trade negotiations, the country's position would be relevant to the Doha Round and to a potential agreement on the FTAA.

The initial caution the Bush government exercised in relation to the Lula administration was also based on the Department of State's concerns (limited though they were) about the political and economic direction being taken by certain South American countries. The new Brazilian government continued to be seen as a moderating influence in the region and, for that reason, deserved to be treated with prestige, exactly as it had under Fernando Henrique Cardoso.

President Lula came to be seen as a democratic left-wing leader who served as a counterweight to the radical Bolivarians. Nevertheless, the more conservative sectors of the Bush administration continued to criticize the Brazilian government's support for Hugo Chávez and its opposition to the threatened attack on Iraq. Itamaraty had repeated Brazil's traditional position that all peaceful means should be exhausted before military action was taken.

The government's official declarations against the US military buildup were the subject of many a talk I had with Itamaraty, José

Dirceu, Antonio Palocci, and President Lula himself, as discussed in the chapter on the invasion of Iraq.

US Trade Representative Robert Zoellick came to Brazil to go over the economic agenda to be discussed during the visit. Priority topics such as the FTAA and trade disputes were debated with Itamaraty and the Ministry for Development, Industry, and Foreign Trade. I was able to accompany Zoellick on his meetings with the ministers Luiz Fernando Furlan, Celso Amorim, Roberto Rodrigues and Vice-President José Alencar.

On our visit to Brasília, the secretary-general of the Brazilian Foreign Office, Ambassador Samuel Pinheiro Guimarães, asked me to make a presentation to Itamaraty's leading diplomats. The recently appointed secretary-general had introduced the new and positive practice of having visiting ambassadors speak on the work underway at their posts overseas.

On this occasion, it became evident to me that a change of direction had occurred in the broader strokes of Brazilian foreign policy, with a new and accentuated party-political bias in the decisions taken and growing restrictions on closer ties with the United States. In my presentation to the diplomats, I went against the official line and argued for a continued policy of cooperation with the US, our largest trade partner—a country that had, only months earlier, given us the financial support we needed to ride out the 2001 economic crisis.

As always happens in bureaucratic circles, some will always rush to defend the official line. That was the case with Ambassador Adhemar Bahadian, who was quick to question and criticize the positions I had just expounded. But at the end of the lecture, much to my surprise, I received a standing ovation from the hundred or so colleagues who had packed the auditorium—something I interpreted as a demonstration by a silent majority uncomfortable with the party-politicization of foreign policy the new administration was imposing upon Itamaraty.

STATE VISIT
President Lula traveled to Washington with a cortege of ten ministers: Celso Amorim, Foreign Relations; José Dirceu, chief of staff; Dilma Rousseff, Mines and Energy; Antonio Palocci, Finance; Roberto Rodrigues, Agriculture; Luiz Fernando Furlan, Development, Industry and Foreign Trade; Jacques Wagner, Labor; Humberto Costa, Health; Roberto Amaral, Science and Technology; and Marina Silva, Environment.

On the American side, there were eight ministers present: Richard Armitage, vice-secretary of state (Colin Powell was away from Washington); Donald Evans, Trade secretary; Ann Venneman, Agriculture; Spencer Abraham, Energy; Tommy Thompson, Health; Elaine Chao, Labor; Andrew Card, chief of staff; and Condoleezza Rice, from the National Security Council.

On the day of his arrival, after a dinner at the embassy residence, President Lula assembled his ministers so that I could give them a general outline of the political and economic situation in the United States and a briefing on the Brazil–US relationship, on which I spoke at greater length.

Defending a continued policy of closer ties with the United States before a group aligned with the more radical left and therefore, in general, against such rapprochement, was for me a curious experience, to say the least. My position met with objections from some of the ministers, such as Roberto Amaral, who criticized the US position on nuclear non-proliferation.

It was obvious that certain sectors of the government harbored anti-American feelings and that their inexperience with international issues was bound to cause the Brazilian government some embarrassment.

On the American side, there was clear willingness to strengthen ties. The Bush government decided to innovate on the format of this visit as a way of expressing its public support for Brazil. On Bush's suggestion, there would be a private meeting between the presidents, followed by a meeting between the cabinets and a working lunch. For the first time, Brazil was given special treatment in Washington, something previously the preserve of the United States's North American Free Trade Agreement partners, Canada and Mexico, and a handful of European allies.

The reception laid on for Lula was even more prestigious, if we take into consideration that we were two months into the invasion of Iraq, at a time when Washington was facing major problems with the security of its troops on the ground and also facing mounting political instability due to a succession of Iraqi suicide bombings.

The three presidential meetings were held in a positive atmosphere, with genuine interest on the American side in finding formulas to raise US-Brazil relations to a new level.

At the private meeting, the two presidents, with such different agendas and styles, picked up where they had left off in December. Participating in the meeting were the Brazilian ministers Celso Amorim and José Dirceu and the Americans Condoleezza Rice, Richard Armitage, and Tom Shannon, then-special advisor to the White House and director of the National Security Council, as well as the ambassadors of the two countries.

In a frank and objective conversation, Bush said that sections of their internal publics had distorted images of both he and Lula, according to which Bush was "a madman who liked bombing and killing people in other parts of the world," while Lula was "a lefty who didn't understand economics." He added that the Brazilian had already supplied ample proof to the contrary.

The conversation flowed on politics and the economy in Brazil. Lula spoke of the main decisions that had been taken in the first days of his term of office toward stabilizing the economy and curbing inflation; the priority his government placed on social issues—the eradication of poverty, hunger and illiteracy—; and his recalibration of foreign policy, previously focused on the United States and the European Union, with little emphasis on South America, where Brazil intended to fully assume its responsibilities.

Bush praised the social programs and measures taken to preserve the main lines of the country's economic policy. He said that Brazil stood out among its South American counterparts for its political, economic, diplomatic, and military importance. He expressed interest in cementing the bond between the two countries and in expanding their bilateral relations, observing that while he did not expect them to agree on everything, they had a lot in common, and that, in itself, justified a solid relationship in the future. He also added that he hoped to be able to draw upon Brazil's good counsel on matters affecting the national security of both countries.

In the exchange of pleasantries that followed, President Lula said that he planned to fortify Brazil–US relations and consolidate mutual trust, adding that "no topic should be taboo between us." Once again, the official rhetoric bore little relation to the facts as they would unfold over the coming years.

In relation to South America, Lula spoke positively of Argentina and Brazil's Mercosur partners, and said that he was closely following developments in Venezuela and Colombia, and that Brazil was ready and willing to do what it could to help them. He also said that he wanted to cut through the rhetoric surrounding the process of regional integration, a key issue in Brazilian foreign policy, and that he would concentrate a lot of effort on physical integration.

For his part, President Bush was emphatic about the invasion of Iraq and spoke at length about his reasons for opting for war and about his concerns for the territorial integrity of the United States. Lula was subjected to an enflamed defense of US policy and assurances of a swift end to hostilities. Bush said he believed the war would be "brief and the mission quickly accomplished." Even at such an early stage in the war, the case Bush made for the attack was far from convincing, but we abstained from openly stating as much so as not to spoil this friendly encounter. Lula's non-response to Bush's impassioned defense of the operations in Iraq was to say that, for Brazil, the only combat that mattered was the fight against poverty and hunger.

Bilateral trade and the Doha Round negotiations were also on the agenda. Lula emphasized the difficulties caused by US trade barriers against Brazilian products and his reservations about how the FTAA talks would develop.

The two presidents exchanged opinions on the need to reform the United Nations, especially the Security Council, but Bush was not very receptive to this. He recalled the frustrating experiences they had had with the UNSC and the agency's ineffectiveness. "The UN is a shopping center of good ideas," said Bush, making no attempt to conceal his disdain for the organization.

The Brazilian president set forth some of his own priorities on the world stage, particularly his interest in a peaceful, UN-sponsored solution to the Israel/Palestine conflict, and announced that he would be visiting the region and also Africa. President Bush expressed his contentment with the appointment of Mahmoud Abbas as Palestinian prime minister, which he saw as a step forward. He added that he had been working to convince Israel to strengthen Abbas' position, all too aware of the fragility of the Palestinian Authority. On that note, Bush told Lula to avoid undermining Abbas on his visit to the Middle East, since the Palestinian leader Yasser Arafat "continued to pursue his terrorist strategy" and would not be in a position to honor any agreement that might be made. Bush said that he saw no chance of building a Palestinian nation so long as Arafat was involved: "If he comes back, I'm out."

During the wider meeting, with the full ministerial delegations, the emphasis was on the bilateral relationship and how to expand it. Among the main topics were the two nations' possible collaboration in the agricultural, commercial, and energy sectors, not only because of the contributions Brazil could make in terms of renewable energy sources such as ethanol, but also because of the store the Bush administration placed in the theme of energy, particularly in the light of the new energy bill the government was discussing with Congress with a view to reducing oil dependency.

Minister Palocci spoke of a long telephone conversation he'd had with Treasury Secretary John Snow, in which they had agreed to create a consultation mechanism, the Group for Growth, to study macroeconomic issues of interest to both countries. During this conversation, Brazil had also agreed to support the names the United States had put forward for the new executive directors of the IMF and World Bank.

At the end of the meeting, President Lula underscored the symbolic aspect of the inter-cabinet meeting and gave assurances that Brazil would press forward with the institutionalization of the bilateral relations.

The proposal to institutionalize relations between the two countries as a means of consolidating Brazil's special position within the hemisphere was already under examination by the State Department and National Security Council. As I mentioned earlier, the first initiative in this direction had been taken on President FHC's last visit to Washington.

In the document drafted by the Department of State, we restated the reasons for institutionalizing relations between Brazil and the US, the proposal for regular meetings between the two presidents and their ministers, and the creation of joint working groups for the development of a new positive agenda. The idea was to establish these groups in areas of mutual interest, such as energy, agriculture, and science and technology, in the manner of the ministerial group on education set up during the FHC government.

During the build up to Lula's visit, I presented a draft of the institutionalization proposal to Richard Haass, director of the Political Planning Department; to Otto Reich, secretary for Western Hemisphere Affairs; and to John Maisto and Tom Shannon, at the National Security Council.

To an extent, Haass should be credited with the success of this visit, as it had been he who drew attention to Brazil's increasing relevance and undertook to pursue the initiative presented by the embassy, which was a help when it came to putting Brazil into the order of the day. Later, Haass left the government to assume the presidency of the Council on

Foreign Relations, the most important think tank on international relations in the United States. In 2009, during a visit to the US, Haass told me that the diplomatic action to institutionalize relations between the US and Brazil had been one of his most successful interactions with the Department of State, and one of which he was most proud.

Finally, at the working lunch between Lula and Bush, the participants gave some general treatment to the situation in Latin America and the US government's mounting concern over the growing animosity it was encountering in certain South American countries. The main global themes were also broached, such as terrorism and the environment, on which the US held dogmatic perceptions which Brazil did not share.

Most of the discussion, however, concerned Argentina, Venezuela, Bolivia, and Peru. The US government was clearly worried about the region's stability, business climate, and security, in the light of guerrilla activities in Colombia.

Deteriorating relations with Caracas was another key subject, given the coup d'état recently launched against Chávez, with ostensible US support. Lula and Minister Celso Amorim reaffirmed Brazil's policy of seeking an understanding with Venezuela and Bolivia, and of avoiding isolating presidents Hugo Chávez and Evo Morales by working to integrate them with the rest of the region.

In addressing the crisis in the Middle East, Lula praised the US for its engagement in the peace process and brought up the creation of a Palestinian state. President Bush renewed his attacks on Yasser Arafat and said that he thought Prime Minister Mahmoud Abbas had assumed good positions, but was politically weak.

When the talk turned to relations between Brazil and the United States, the participants examined formulas for deepening cooperation in the areas of energy, agriculture, trade, and the environment. The theme of the FTAA was also raised, with Brazil emphasizing that the issue of subsidies was one of the nerve centers of negotiations. Referring to Lula's comments on Brazil's interest in free trade, Bush vigorously defended it, but admitted that there was still some resistance toward free trade within his political party. Minister Roberto Rodrigues noted the importance of agriculture to Brazil and the obstacles Brazilian products faced in the US market, especially the impact US subsidies had on our exports. President Bush said he had discussed the theme of agricultural subsidies at length at the last G8 meeting. He said he was in favor of adopting a "zero subsidy" policy, but that it depended on agreement with Europe.

Lula said that he would be visiting London the following month and that he also planned to discuss the matter with President Jacques Chirac of France and the German Chancellor, Gerhard Schröder, to which Bush retorted: "Schröder will agree with you, but Chirac won't."

During the visit to Washington, Lula also attended four parallel meetings with the president of the World Bank, James Wolfensohn; of the Inter-American Development Bank, Enrique Iglesias; of the AFL-CIO, John Sweeney; and with the managing director of the IMF, Horst Köhler. The last two of these warrant special mention. Köhler used the entire meeting with Lula to discuss Argentina and ask for Brazil's support in convincing President Nestor Kirchner to give assurances that he would not renege on the existing financial understandings. With Sweeney, Lula discussed how American workers' pension funds could invest in his government. Sweeney also offered to provide training to Brazilian pension fund directors. Later, with the support of Stanley Gacek and the AFL-CIO, representatives of these multi-billion-dollar pension funds visited Brazil to negotiate with the government.

Months after these meetings between Lula and Bush, I learned from an American diplomat that Bush, Colin Powell, and Condoleezza Rice had mentioned Brazil's particularities, characteristics, and interests at a White House meeting and had recognized that our country was no longer just another South American nation and that it deserved differentiated treatment within the regional context. According to this diplomat, personal comments were also made about Lula, especially the good chemistry between he and Bush, and how this facilitated their relationship. The US president had taken to Lula and learned to appreciate him. "What you see is what you get" was how he summed up the impression the Brazilian president had left in Washington.

Lula's charisma, his simple and direct way of talking to people, from the lowliest housemaid at the embassy to the president of the United States, perhaps explains why these two political leaders had developed such mutual respect and communicated so fluidly despite their opposing ideologies. There was a clear contrast between the lukewarm treatment that marked the relationship between Bush and FHC and that shown to Lula. It was often said in Washington that FHC's intellectual capacity and brilliance, which Clinton had praised so highly to Bush, had caused the Texan some discomfort.

At the end of the visit, US acceptance of the proposal to institutionalize relations and its approval of the high-level consultation program and creation of joint working groups in the areas of science and technology, agriculture, and energy were perhaps the most significant decisions over the medium and long term.

The presidents announced the creation of a Brazil–US Group on Energy, which would include research and development on hydrogen, carbon sequestration, modernization in the generation of electricity, renewable energy, and new technologies geared toward energy efficiency and security in offshore energy infrastructure. Though the group was assembled during my time in Washington, it never got off the ground.

One thing that did materialize was the commitment to facilitate and broaden direct contact between the two countries' business communities, in order to expand trade and investment. A special CEO forum was created for Brazilian and American company presidents and ministers from both governments. The group remains active today.

In another important decision, the two presidents announced their willingness to work together on AIDS prevention throughout Portuguese-speaking Africa, which would be a significant boost to our presence there.

The deliberations and decisions reached during the state visit were recorded in a joint statement issued at the end of the presidential talks, which spoke of a more mature relationship between the countries. Lula and Bush agreed to establish regular, high-level consultations and work together toward prosperity, democratic governability, and peace in the Americas, and, above all, to defend democracy, tolerance, religious liberty, freedom of the press, the expansion of economic opportunities, and the rule of law.

However, as often happens in these situations, most of the intentions expressed in the statement were forgotten in the years that followed.

At that very moment, the US government was approving secret decisions and new regulations that clearly violated the Geneva Convention on the treatment of prisoners of war, constituting a serious threat to the physical integrity of those it considered terrorists. Against such a backdrop, it was impossible to move ahead on the commitments that had been made on human rights.

On the commercial side, the renewal and expansion of subsidies and introduction of sophisticated new regulations imposed further barriers against Brazilian access to the US market and thus also to the conclusion of the Doha Round and the hemisphere-wide negotiations on the FTAA.

If, on one hand, there was no reason for naïve optimism concerning any future understandings between Bush and Lula, neither was there any call for minimizing the relevance of the bilateral summit held at the White House in 2003.

It is important to emphasize that the meeting between Presidents Lula and Bush served to show that there was a real possibility of the two governments being able to work together, even if, as we would see over the eight years of Lula's administration, the opportunity was ultimately wasted.

One positive outcome was that the meeting helped delineate areas of convergence on which the relationship could be strengthened, with a new institutional framework and inclusion of wider-ranging and more positive themes on the agenda, all of which was reiterated in the documents signed and the information bulletins circulated by the White House and State Department. This new level in discussions on US–Brazil relations was only possible because of an apparently sincere recognition, based on mutual respect, that we would continue to disagree on matters of our national interests and to express our divergences in the area of trade, but that none of this was to be construed as anti-Americanism, but rather as a natural defense of our own real interests.

There were no illusions that whatever future yields might come of the presidential meetings would depend on the governments' ability to lend momentum to this initial impetus. The US government seemed willing to dialogue and cooperate with Brazil on those areas flagged as priority to both countries—to wit: science and technology, energy, education, health, economic growth, and agriculture—and to extend this into other areas to be identified in conjunction.

Below is an outline of the diversification and amplitude of the areas examined during the summit meeting:

- Energy, the most promising area for convergence and a positive agenda, given the prospects for cooperation that arose for both the government and the private sector;
- Reform of the United Nations, including the Security Council. The US President was forthright on this issue, including the possibility of Brazil's candidacy for a permanent seat on the UNSC. Bush agreed that there was a need to rethink the UN system,

but, as the US had no official position on the matter, he did not want to commit himself on either point;

- Investment funds for infrastructure. President Lula asked the US government to urge financial institutions based in Washington to create investment funds for infrastructure projects in South America, which would involve US construction companies in undertakings in Brazil and across the southern continent;
- The FTAA. The theme was only touched upon, without going into any aspect of the negotiations in depth. Referring to the two nations' responsibilities as co-chairs of the negotiating process, the joint communiqué stipulated January 2005 as the deadline on talks, in accordance with the original 1994 provisions. To make this deadline viable and to safeguard the Brazilian position, an important item was included to the effect that only a win-win agreement could be considered a successful and balanced outcome to the negotiations.

The action plan was approved. There was no time to waste if we wanted to take full advantage of the impetus provided by the presidential meeting.

In my notes, I jotted down some telling comments made by the State Department diplomats who attended the presidential meetings, and which testified to the United States's gradual change of perceptions toward Brazil.

For different reasons, however, neither government was able to focus on the agreements and little progress was made.

Energy is a good example of a partnership that did not come to fruition, despite Brazil's eagerness to promote ethanol and Bush's interest in having Brazil as a partner in the area. In short, Brazil lost an excellent opportunity. Had we played our cards right, we might have embarked on a highly beneficial partnership with the United States on renewable sources of energy, ethanol, biodiesel, and other more advanced forms, such as hydrogen and cellulosic fuel.

On the American side, obviously we cannot ignore the effects of the government's more blatant unilateralism post-9/11, the transformations that occurred on the international scene and the Bush administration's new policy directions, and the events that followed the attacks on Afghanistan and Iraq. The so-called "War on Terror" was foremost in US priorities.

The resistance of certain sectors of our government to following through on the decisions made in Washington by the two presidents largely stemmed from the ideological penchants of PT politicians. Up until the end of my ambassadorship in April 2004, I detected various difficulties of this order in certain departments of Itamaraty and among advisers to the Presidency and Ministry of Science and Technology.

We must also bear in mind that, at that time, the United States was receiving widespread criticism for its military offensive on Iraq, so one could have expected the Brazilian government to be a bit shy about cozying up to the superpower.

The promised bilateral relationship seen through a whole new prism has yet to materialize. Brazil could have drawn major benefit in a number of fields—from the economic–financial to the technological, the military and strategic to the academic and cultural—had the Lula government not insisted that openly good relations with the US would be bad for grassroots support. A solid relationship could have borne a lot of fruit, including robust backing for Brazil's application for a permanent seat on the United Nations Security Council.

CHAPTER 4

Diplomatic Negotiations in Washington

EMBASSIES PLAY A KEY ROLE in supporting diplomatic negotiations in the countries in which they are accredited. While the Foreign Ministry is in charge of these discussions, the work of the embassy and ambassador can be decisive when it comes to obtaining privileged information from a range of sources and skillfully conveying the positions of its own government. In many cases, the embassy fulfills a central function in the conversations, hence the crucial role of the ambassador and the absolute importance of having a reliable team.

The FTAA Negotiations

Since the beginning of my time in Washington, the FTAA was the theme that most occupied the embassy's time and demanded my direct and active participation. The negotiations, conducted from 1994 up to 2003, were without doubt the most complex and difficult I experienced during my term in the US capital. For the duration of my mission, I maintained close contact with the USTR and Department of Trade, preparing technical and political meetings between Brazilian and US authorities. The economic sector of the embassy, initially coordinated by Minister Regis Arslanian, and later by Minister Evandro Didonet, was also responsible for the detailed analysis of specific points and for developing parallel studies on themes of everyday interest.

Before going into the embassy's role in the negotiations in greater detail, it would be useful to present an overview of the issue.

The hemispheric integration project was launched by President Bill Clinton at the December 1994 Summit of the Americas in Miami. The main objective of the FTAA was to negotiate the reduction or elimination of trade barriers and, as the name itself suggests, to promote free trade throughout the Americas. Once in place, it would create one of the biggest economic blocs in the world.

At the meeting in Miami, the thirty-four governments approved the agenda for negotiations. Cuba was still suspended from the American community and was the only nation not to participate. The agenda included the opening of markets to manufactured goods and agricultural produce; governmental services and purchases; and rules governing intellectual property, investment, competition, dumping, safeguards and the resolution of disputes and commercial compensations in proven cases of subsidization. Nine negotiating groups were formed, one for each theme. Also formed were a consulting group for smaller economies and committees on electronic trade and civil society participation.

On the Brazilian side, President Itamar Franco, in the last month of his presidency, and his then-Foreign Relations Minister, Ambassador Celso Amorim, accepted the proposals presented by Washington in Miami, which envisioned the creation of an integrated zone from Alaska to Patagonia. Fernando Henrique Cardoso, then president-elect, was reluctant about participating in the summit.

As I was about to take over as ambassador to London, just a few months earlier I had stepped down as undersecretary for the Economy, Regional Integration, and Foreign Trade, a post in which I was able to follow the US preparations for the launch of the FTAA project. I was one of those who advised the president-elect not to go to the summit meeting, so as to avoid committing to future negotiations and be in a better position to justify later decisions that defended our interests. However, on Itamar Franco's insistence, FHC agreed to attend.

From the beginning of the FTAA negotiations, Brazil played an active and constructive role, as it saw the agreement as a means of eliminating tariff and non-tariff barriers, an opportunity for greater debate on food assistance programs and agricultural subsidies, and for more transparency in the rules for commercial compensation and additional obligations. The aim was to prevent these rules from being used as protectionist measures against Brazilian products, especially by the United States.

The US government said it was ready to set up a free trade agenda. At the meetings I had with my counterparts, from mid-1999 on, time and time again I heard the same line: "Everything is on the table, everything is negotiable."

At the time the negotiations began, the American hemisphere—North, Central and South—was the destination for 55 percent of Brazil's exports, with manufactured goods accounting for roughly 80 percent of those. For the Brazilian government, the FTAA represented broader access to the US market and the prospects of increasing the exportation of goods and services to other countries throughout Central America and the Caribbean with which the country did not have any trade preference agreements in place. The FTAA could also be seen as an opportunity for Brazil to deepen its tariff preferences with other South American nations, already negotiated under the auspices of the Latin American Integration Association (LAIA).

At Itamaraty, there was a clear perception that FTAA negotiations would only make sense if they yielded balanced results. One of the basic principles defended by Brazil, and accepted by all the other nations at the ministerial meeting held in Belo Horizonte in 1997, was the single undertaking, i.e., the idea that the negotiations could not be partial and could only be declared complete when a definitive agreement was reached on all the aspects up for discussion. To that end, it was important for each party to bring its full range of primary and industrial products to the table, so long as the hemispheric rules complied with those at the WTO. Another condition was that the existing sub-regional agreements—Mercosur, for example—would be maintained. Only sensitive agricultural and industrial products, such as automobiles, toys, and chemical compounds, would be bracketed out.

Drawing up a free-trade agreement between thirty-four vastly different countries, from the richest and most developed nation in the world to some of the poorest, from some of the physically largest to some of the smallest, was no easy matter. From the very beginning, the negotiations ran into a series of obstacles. From 1995 to 2000, financial and political crises in many countries throughout the hemisphere made talks almost impossible. New security imperatives post-9/11, followed by economic slowdown in the United States, also weighed heavily on trade agreements.

By mid-2002, the backdrop to the negotiations had changed considerably in the US and throughout South America. There was growing opposition to the FTAA in Brazil. The creation of the Bolivarian Alternative for the Americas (Alba), through the initiative of Hugo Chávez, also signaled greater resistance to the bloc. For its part, the United States withdrew important aspects from discussion and began to argue that systemic themes, such as subsidies and dumping, should be handled in Geneva, under the Doha Round of WTO talks, and not as part of a regional framework. However, they also tried to add other themes, no less systemic, related to trade and intellectual property, which were also on the Doha agenda.

The United States's new negotiating position caused immediate problems because of the refusal to discuss subsidies and anti-dumping laws within the hemispheric context, which was a breach of the principles originally established in Miami. From that point on, Brazil moved to develop a new agreement that could guarantee its own interests. In late 2003, the United States approved the Brazilian proposal, only to reverse its decision soon after, effectively bringing negotiations to a halt.

THE EMBASSY'S PARTICIPATION IN THE NEGOTIATIONS

My view, formed during my time as economic undersecretary at Itamaraty and reinforced later during my ambassadorship in Washington, was that it was highly unlikely that Brazil would stand to gain enough in terms of access to US markets to justify its signing an agreement on the FTAA.

The power of the United States's protectionist lobbies, especially in the area of agriculture, transformed the US Congress into a frank opponent of opening the market to products it considered to be "sensitive." Taking the issues of subsidies and anti-dumping off the negotiating table was a clear example of this. Even so, it seemed to me that we could not go back on our commitment to negotiate down to the wire in defense of our interests.

In procedural terms, concerning FTAA negotiations, I made two suggestions to strengthen Brazil's negotiating hand: minimize the political, ideological, and emotional factors involved in the debate on the costs and benefits of the FTAA, approaching the discussions objectively and calmly, as had occurred during the negotiations on the European Union, and upgrading the role that could be played by the embassy in Washington by giving it more clout in its interactions with the US government.

The embassy was in constant contact with the American government on the FTAA, especially with the White House National Security Council and the USTR, and with the embassies of other countries involved in the negotiations, such as Chile, which was always in close agreement with Brasília. Our conversations with the Chilean embassy were useful and informative, as the country was conducting parallel negotiations with the United States on a free trade agreement.

Given the North American tradition of favoring close contact between the public and private sectors on themes of a commercial ilk, I was often invited to outline Brazil's position at meetings with captains of industry and the members of producer and export associations.

The perception nurtured by the private sector in the US, ignorant as it was of the Brazilian reality, was that Brazil continued to be extremely protectionist, with high tariffs and strong trade barriers. In fact, during the FTAA negotiations, it was the US that increased restrictions in order to favor local industries that had lost competitive ground internationally. The Trade Department and USTR decided to introduce a series of safeguards to keep Brazilian products out of the US market, especially our steel.

The embassy was directly involved in discussing how to overcome the difficulties these protectionist measures created. Despite the FTAA negotiations, the aim of which was to establish a common market, the American government never showed any willingness to suspend the restrictive measures on steel, for example, or the surcharge on ethanol and orange juice, much less abolish the cotton subsidies.

On two distinct occasions over the course of the ministerial talks on the FTAA negotiations and trade relations between the two countries, Foreign Minister Celso Lafer received complaints about my insistence on defending Brazilian positions. Although presented in a respectful and blithe manner, these complaints showed the discomfort my stance was causing. Zoellick even asked the Brazilian minister to tell his ambassador in Washington to tone down his criticisms of the restrictive measures imposed by the US government.

For me, there could have been no better praise for my work than to be criticized by a high-ranking US official for "defending the Brazilian national interest."

THE FHC ADMINISTRATION AND THE FTAA

With my personal involvement in the discussions, both in Washington and as economic undersecretary at Itamaraty, I was able to maintain frequent contact with private foreign trade organizations in the US that were interested in the FTAA negotiations.

Following the discussions at close quarters, on numerous occasions I drew Washington's attention to the fact the US government's change of position was proving a real obstacle to our making any headway in the negotiations. I pointed out the problems that a harder American line would cause in Brazil. I reminded the US authorities that we were approaching a presidential election in which the PT candidate would voice his party's forceful anti-FTAA stance, adding that the Worker's Party had even helped to organize a referendum on the FTAA.

During the first years of FHC's administration, the opposition, led by PT, campaigned strenuously against the FTAA on the grounds that it was tantamount to the commercial annexation of Brazil to the United States.

Throughout the FHC government, dialogue on FTAA-related themes with US authorities was difficult and sometimes even tetchy. In March 2001, in the company of Minister-Counselor Marcos Galvão, I recall having harsh words with Ambassador John Maisto, then-secretary of the White House National Security Council, when, faced with the new bases presented by the United States, we tried to explain the difficulties we would have in proceeding with the negotiations. In addition to the transference of systemic themes, such as subsidies and antidumping, to Geneva, the US also wanted to bring the talks deadline forward from January 2005 to before the end of Bush's first term, so as to give Congress time to approve the agreement. They also wanted to anticipate the Brazil–US co-chairmanship by a few months, starting in February, despite the fact that Ecuador's term would only expire in October 2002.

On these two themes the discussions with John Maisto were particularly tough. The secretary dispensed with the rhetoric and went straight to the point: President George Bush wanted to wrap the process up before running for re-election. Furthermore, it was essential that the Summit of the Americas in Quebec, scheduled for April 2001, not only produce, but be seen to produce, results in the trade area.

On bringing forward the co-chairmanship, I told Maisto that we had difficulties on two fronts. First, we were worried about the effects a change of date would have on internal politics, and, second, we were worried about how Ecuador would react, considering that we were already detecting signs of discontent from the Ecuadorian government and did not want to be seen to be responsible for cutting short their term as co-chair of the group. Peter Allgeier, an alternate trade representative participating in the meeting, informed us that Secretary Peter Romero had spoken with Ecuadorian Chancellor Heinz Moeller, and that he had reacted positively to bringing forward the meeting and the change of co-chairmanship. On the possibility of a US–Brazil–Ecuador troika running through to the end of Ecuador's mandate, Moeller had not given any clear position, but neither had he lodged any complaints. He did, however, insist on the importance of Ecuador's role as a representative of the hemisphere's "smaller economies." I tried to respond candidly: "Maybe they've been saying one thing to you, and something else to us." My interlocutors laughed, and insisted no further on that line of argument.

Maisto asked whether it might not be better in terms of public opinion in Brazil, given the country's "anxiety" about the FTAA, to be in command of the negotiations sooner. I answered that it was not as simple as that, as the earlier co-presidency was being offered to us as part of a larger package that also meant an earlier deadline for negotiations, around late 2003, considering that it would take a year to have the agreement ratified and approved by the signatory nations.

Despite the divergences, the atmosphere remained friendly and cordial, and I told our American interlocutors that we understood the political necessities of the Bush administration in relation to the Quebec summit, but that the United States had to recognize that we, for reasons of our own national interests—which had been clearly enumerated—were not prepared to alter the position we had defended since the very start. I went still further: I said that if they insisted on taking this calendar change proposal to Quebec, the press would focus all its attention on that point and we would risk having the summit labeled a failure if consensus was not reached on it. I said that we ought to accentuate the progress the thirty-four nations had made in the relatively short period of three years and stick to the original schedule, which had set the start of negotiations on a free market, the plan for the final agreement, and the beginning of the Brazil–US co-chairmanship for October 2002 and the final deadline for 2005.

In talks with FHC and his diplomatic advisor, Ambassador Eduardo Santos, I insisted on the convenience and, indeed, the need for Brazil to draw clear limits for the FTAA negotiations at the Quebec summit.

After attending a meeting at the Chamber of Foreign Trade (Camex) in March 2001, I suggested a draft of a text designed to stiffen the Brazilian line. On that occasion, we discussed the importance of the government defining a bottom line that could, at the end of the negotiations in December 2004, justify signing a hemisphere-wide free trade agreement.

Domestically, the debate on the FTAA was becoming increasingly politicized and short on information concerning the scope of the talks, which meant we had to be more transparent and resolute in the defense of our interests.

The Brazilian position had to incorporate concrete gains, without which it would have been difficult to obtain support for the negotiations. The process would entail trade-offs in areas in which we had interests to defend, especially in such sensitive sectors as electronic trade, services, investments, and government procurement.

I agreed with the position Ambassador Celso Amorim assumed at the WTO regarding a technical aspect that, though apparently minor, was crucial to the negotiations. As the mandate for discussions on industrial tariffs was sufficiently loose to allow us to maintain a degree of flexibility, I thought it was important, in the final stage of definitions, to ensure that the consolidated tariff—that negotiated at the WTO—served as a basis for the negotiations. The consolidated tariff would give Brazil more room in which to maneuver, so it was imperative that we held firm against pressure for the applied tariff—that currently in force—to be taken as the base. I was outvoted on this, and Brazil ended up agreeing to the use of the applied tariff.

I registered my concerns over the possibility of bilateral pressure from the US putting us at a disadvantage in future trade negotiations. With the preferential tariffs the United States had granted, or was going to grant, to the Andean, Caribbean, and Central American nations, and to Chile in their free trade agreements, I reckoned it would be difficult to avoid isolation in negotiations on rules for market access, especially considering the need to extend to Brazil the tariff concessions the US had granted to other Latin American countries.

Knowing the US position on the FTAA negotiations, I informed Itamaraty of the points I believed had to be preserved:

1. Balanced progress in the negotiations and equitable results;
2. Effective access to the US market for Brazilian products hitherto subject to protectionist restrictions through the gradual and continual elimination of tariff and non-tariff barriers over an agreed time frame;
3. All areas should be negotiated at the same time, with nothing left out (agriculture, for example);
4. No unilateral application of US defensive trade measures on antidumping, countervailing duties, and safeguards;
5. The negotiations should obey the general principles of consensus and single undertaking; in other words, "nothing is agreed upon until everything is agreed upon";

6. No linkage between labor and environmental protection standards and sanctions/other trade obligations;
7. Presidential Trade Authority must be granted to the US President by the US Congress;
8. The negotiations had to be consistent with WTO rules;
9. Mercosur would continue to exist as a sub-regional trade agreement.

A short time later, at the summit in Quebec, FHC limned Brazil's position on FTAA negotiations.

As support material for the draft of the presidential announcement, I sent some comments designed to transmit a firm message according to which only an FTAA based on balanced benefits would receive the support of Brazil and the Mercosur and have any real chance of success. The President's speech had to be upbeat on the FTAA, but only on an FTAA that met the minimum requirements set by Brazil and the Mercosur bloc.

Brazil vigorously reaffirmed the concept of balanced negotiations at the summit meeting in Canada.

On that occasion, FHC recognized the need to put the Brazilian position across in a clear way and very decisively determined the need for balance and reciprocity when he stated that:

The FTAA will be welcome if its creation is a step toward providing access to more dynamic markets; if it is effectively the path toward shared anti-dumping regulations and reduced non-tariff barriers; if it avoids the protectionist misuse of good sanitation regulations; if, in protecting intellectual property, it simultaneously promotes the technological capabilities of our peoples. And further, if it goes beyond the Uruguay Round and corrects the imbalances crystallized there, above all in agriculture. Unless it is all this, it will be irrelevant, or, in the worst case, undesirable.

As part of the strategy, Itamaraty, under Minister Celso Lafer, defended the position that we ought to proceed with negotiations, stating our positions firmly but without stalling the talks. The Brazilian government believed that, in the end, with a package finally closed, it would be possible to make a real assessment of whether or not the agreement was consistent with Brazil's interests. If it was, then it would be signed, but if it wasn't, Brazil would not simply follow the majority.

For my part, given the number of interests involved, I told Itamaraty that it would be difficult not to sign the agreement and have it ratified by Congress once the negotiations were complete.

When it was first launched, the FTAA was, for internal and external political reasons, a project of immense interest to the United States. However, the project lost its priority as the negotiations progressed, in view of the mounting resistance in Congress and the impossibility of accommodating the demands of the Brazilian agriculture sector in the face of the US lobby.

In 2002, the US Congress granted Trade Promotion Authority to the Executive so it could engage in trade negotiations, including the FTAA. However, the TPA imposed limits on the USTR's scope of action and, in practice, removed from the negotiating table many areas of interest to Brazil, such as anti-dumping legislation and subsidies.

With FTAA talks at an advanced stage, at the Americas Summit in Quebec in 2002, the thirty-four nations in the hemisphere appointed Brazil and the United States as co-chairs of the final phase of negotiations. This choice was certainly inspired by the fact that the two countries were, respectively, the largest economies in South and North America and because their markets were attractive enough to urge the other thirty-two countries to give serious discussion to the creation of a free trade area. It was also a way of engaging Brazil in the talks, precisely at a time when the Brazilian government was beginning to have doubts as to whether it really was in the country's interests to continue negotiating. From that point on, the talks were tense, especially after the new government was sworn into office in January 2003.

THE LULA ADMINISTRATION AND THE FTAA

When Lula took office, he reaffirmed the importance of the trade negotiations to Brazil and the country's commitment to continued active participation in the talks, although along the same lines as set down by FHC in Quebec in April 2001.

However, in a clear message to the United States, he stressed that Brazil would always defend its sovereign right to make the decisions it judged to be consistent with its model of development. This stance was reinforced by our concerns with keeping employment figures up, improving social conditions and preserving our freedom to set the course of our own industrial policies, something Lula emphasized time and again.

Despite the initial declarations, the technical difficulties that arose made it hard to maintain the same level of ambition as originally envisioned for the FTAA and to complete the negotiations on schedule, in January 2005. In 2003, the internal economic and political contexts in the main American markets were much changed. In the US, the economy was slowing down and Congress was staunchly against opening American markets, as was clear from the TPA it granted to the Executive. In Brazil, opposition was growing among sectors of the government strongly influenced by PT.

If the United States felt entitled not to discuss certain sensitive themes with its hemispheric partners, naturally Brazil could do the same. So from 2003 on, following the orientations given by Minister Celso Amorim, Itamaraty became more trenchant in its position and began discussing the remaining points directly with the United States, which, in itself, was a clear signal that if there was no agreement on the themes of interest to Brazil, there would be no agreement at all.

Influenced by sectors within the Foreign Ministry that were militantly against the FTAA negotiations, such as the general secretariat, under Ambassador Samuel Pinheiro Guimarães, the initiatives taken by the Brazilian government became more declaredly geared toward preventing rather than fostering a satisfactory conclusion to the talks.

The Brazilian government's perception was that the United States was not going to negotiate market access to Brazilian agricultural produce, much less anti-dumping legislation. In the spirit of our chronic disposition toward conspiracy theories about the US, it was even believed that the US government, by starting to negotiate bilateral agreements with Central America, Colombia, and Peru, was trying to isolate Brazil in the region. However, similar free trade agreements were already in place with Mexico and Chile.

For most of that year, there were successive consultations with our partners in Mercosur, with the United States, and with other nations in the western hemisphere to find some way to balance the negotiations. After the visit to Brazil made by the US Trade Representative Roberto Zoellick in the final days of May 2003, the debate on the FTAA intensified, both within the government and in public. There were various options, including the postponement and restructuring of the negotiations.

Despite his declarations against the Free Trade Area, which he said meant the region's "annexation" to the United States, President Lula repeated that Brazil would continue to negotiate in good faith.

In August 2003, Brazil and the other Mercosur nations proposed an alternative ("three trails") suggestion that accepted the US demands on anti-dumping and subsidies, but lowered the FTAA's ambitions by establishing the following premises: 4+1 bilateral negotiation—that is, between the Mercosur as a bloc and the United States—on market access for goods (agricultural and industrial), services, investments, and government procurement; reduction of mechanisms related to market access, as a means of better solving disputes and rules of origin, with the rest referred to the multilateral forum; norms related to services, investments, intellectual property, and competition would be transferred to the multilateral negotiations in Geneva (Doha Round), just as had occurred with subsidies and anti-dumping.

OUTCOME

The final stretch of the negotiations saw an exchange of gibes between Brazilian and American authorities. In one of these, the US Trade Representative Robert Zoellick, faced with growing Brazilian reluctance to negotiate, quipped that Brazil would end up isolated and trying to boost its exports to the penguins in the Antarctic. President Lula returned that he wasn't interested in what "the sub of the sub of the sub" had to say.

In the months building up to the meeting in Miami, scheduled for November 2003, I was in frequent contact with the USTR in a bid to clarify the Brazilian position and learn what we might expect on the US side concerning the bilateral agreement with Mercosur.

In August, I met with Peter Allgeier, the deputy USTR. Allgeier spoke of the Brazilian proposal, which he said had sparked concerns among many countries who feared that its implementation could Balkanize the FTAA negotiations. He said he believed that, instead of a single integration agreement, it would lead to a handful of bilateral accords with only one common denominator, the chapter on the resolution of disputes.

According to Allgeier, many countries had sent analyses of the Brazilian proposal to the USTR saying that, if adopted, it would radically alter the philosophy of the FTAA negotiations and that they wanted to stick to the original negotiating mandate. He mentioned the Chilean and Mexican delegations in particular and reaffirmed January 2005 as the deadline. Picking up on the question of timeframes and mentioning the rocky state the WTO was in, Allgeier also stressed the importance of pressing ahead with the process of trade liberalization in the hemisphere.

For my part, I said that 2005 was looking increasingly unlikely given the existing difficulties, evidenced by the seven thousand points pending in the texts under discussion and the non-revision of the negotiating targets and mandate. I also emphasized that our proposal was a response to the United States's change of position and that I could not see its adoption leading to Balkanization, as the USTR thought it would, but that if any such breakup did occur, it would be due to the bilateralization of the negotiation initiated by the United States. I also added that US insistence on sending such themes as "domestic support" and "trade defense" to the multilateral talks on the WTO Doha Round could make it impossible to close the negotiations in 2005, given the principle of single undertaking.

Not long after this conversation I had a meeting at the USTR with Ambassador Ross Wilson, recently appointed as chief negotiator on the FTAA. I wanted to learn what the United States had planned for the ministerial meeting in Miami and get a sense of their reaction to the Brazilian document and to the proposal by the Mercosur ministers on a maiden 4+1 meeting.

I told him that after the three meetings Minister Celso Amorim had held with the USTR, Brazil's understanding was that Zoellick was in agreement with our proposal as a way of getting the negotiations completed on time—pending bilateral talks to iron out the details.

I repeated my position that the US attempt to tie in the fate of FTAA negotiations with the results of the Doha Round posed an added impediment, not only in relation to the deadline, but in terms of the overall balance of the final FTAA package. I stressed that the idea behind the proposal was to arrive at the kind of FTAA that would be possible to achieve by January 2005, and asked his opinion on some specific points in the document, such as the referral to the WTO of rules in the areas of investments, government procurement, services and intellectual property, even if other countries opted to negotiate rules that were more ambitious than those existing within the WTO-plus.

Ross replied that, as he saw it, most of the thirty-four countries wanted an agreement on the FTAA so long as it was wide-ranging, but that he recognized that the real objective of the FTAA had not yet been clearly set. He said that the US Congress would not approve an agreement that did not contain disciplines in the areas of investment, services, government procurement, and intellectual property. He went on to say that the United States was still interested in negotiating an FTAA that was broad in scope and had a minimum of rules to satisfy not only Congress, but the business community too. For Ross, the main aims at the ministerial meeting in Miami would be to define how the models of a future FTAA agreement would relate to each negotiating discipline and to draw up a plan of action to meet that goal. Lastly, he said that at no time had the USTR formally signaled its acceptance of the Brazilian proposal, but merely a willingness to understand it.

In mid-October 2003, the international advisor to the Presidency, Marco Aurélio Garcia, made a visit to Washington. Among the subjects we discussed with the USTR and Security Council were the WTO/FTAA trade negotiations and the Brazil–US bilateral relationship.

Marco Aurélio Garcia took the initiative to say that it would be important to find a formula so that a negotiated solution could be reached in Miami. He added that we had to change the mood of the talks and avoid ideologizing matters, and that the Lula government wanted to preserve the excellent relations the countries had developed together. He also said that we ought to make an effort to bring the negotiations to a satisfactory conclusion without confrontation, and that the Lula administration did not have an ideological bias against the FTAA. At a PT meeting before the elections, Marco Aurélio and Minister José Dirceu had tried to avoid the possibility of the party pushing for a referendum on the FTAA.

I completely agreed with Marco Aurélio Garcia. I had already spoken to the Department of State on the matter of pursuing more harmonious negotiations, saying that we should not risk spoiling what we had achieved in recent years, especially since the June 2003 meeting between Lula and Bush, when new and important areas had been introduced to the agenda and were now in development. I said that "both sides had to use the appropriate channels to help iron out the differences on trade so as to avoid friction that might contaminate other aspects of our relations, as I had already begun to detect." It was essential that we reached a satisfactory agreement in Miami so that the outcome there would not negatively affect the Doha Round Summit in Mexico, scheduled for September 2003.

Ambassador Tom Shannon, then in charge of Latin America at the

White House National Security Council, also present at the meeting, said that the US authorities continued to see the relationship with Brazil as "strategic" and that it had to be as ample as possible, as the two presidents had agreed in June. He acknowledged that we ought not ideologize the trade negotiations, but rather "encapsulate" them within the context of Brazil-US relations. He also said that the US government did not see it as a strictly trade-related problem. At this time, Shannon made a broader political point, mentioning that Brazil had previously teamed up with China and India, among others, on the Doha Round negotiations in Cancun and within the financial G20 (created to replace the G7 on many aspects). He said that at these fora, Brazil and these countries had defended joint positions on the multilateral talks that were contrary to the American position. The United States had understood this as a sign that Brazil was less willing to negotiate.

However, Shannon affirmed that he would continue working to ensure that the bilateral relationship was not damaged by all this. On that matter, I observed that if the US had misread our positions within the sphere of the G20, for many in Brazil the intransigence of the USTR had sent out similar signals, that the US did not want to proceed with negotiations.

Marco Aurélio Garcia's opinions on the FTAA and our policy toward the United States as expressed at this meeting still bore the afterglow of Lula's discussions with Bush in December 2002 and June 2003. However, moderate and constructive positions toward our relationship with the United States were gradually undermined or forgotten.

In Brazil, controversy was building internally on the FTAA. The ministers for Development, Industry, and Foreign Trade, Luiz Fernando Furlan, and of Agriculture, Roberto Rodrigues, both in favor of the negotiations, publicly criticized the Foreign Ministry's growing reservations on a potential agreement. President Lula had to intervene and ask his ministers to keep their disagreement under wraps and Chief of Staff José Dirceu, announced that the president would be keeping a close eye on the negotiations.

In the midst of this tense climate, José Dirceu had lunch with the US ambassador to Brazil, Donna Hrinak, at which he told her that President Lula wanted to seal an agreement on the FTAA and had instructed Minister Celso Amorim to work with Zoellick, at the USTR, toward that end when they met late in October.

In November 2003, after countless comings and goings, the eighth ministerial meeting on the FTAA took place in Miami, and there the governments of Brazil and the United States, as co-chairs, agreed that the thirty-four countries should follow one of two paths: those who wanted deeper negotiations with the United States—such as Chile, Costa Rica and Mexico—should continue to negotiate and close a more ambitious deal on the FTAA; and those who did not so wish could close a more limited agreement, with few economic clauses and a list of products to be given free market access.

The new FTAA vision, outlined by ministers commanded by Celso Amorim and Robert Zoellick, confirmed what many observers called "FTAA *à la carte*," that is, a minimal set of rights and obligations applicable to all countries and additional obligations and benefits to be arrived at through further pluri- or bilateral negotiations.

The negotiating framework was set forth in a ministerial declaration at the close of the Miami meeting. The commitment reached between Brazil and the United States paved the way to the formation of the only FTAA that was possible at the time and that could meet our interests.

It was decided that those ministers still interested in proceeding with broader negotiations within the FTAA should complete them by January 2005. With a dose of realism, given the near insurmountable difficulties that divided the different nations, it was clear that some flexibility would be required from all concerned in terms of taking into account the susceptibilities of the different economies.

Against all expectations, in the media and among many of the countries present at the meeting, Brazil and the United States had reached an agreement that might at least keep the possibility of a viable FTAA alive. A compromise had been found for two-track negotiations, with different degrees of integration.

A few days later, however, under pressure from various countries—especially Mexico, Chile, and Costa Rica—the United States, which had agreed to the dual-track approach, went back on the deal with Brazil and decided to pursue only the more ambitious project.

As was to be expected, Brazil, Venezuela, Argentina, Bolivia, and Ecuador refused to return to the table and the negotiations were brought to an abrupt end. They have not been resumed since.

It was the end of the project to form a free trade area from Alaska to Patagonia, which, since its launch in 1994, had caused so many expectations and so much noise. It was also a victory for those within the Brazilian government who had been against the process all along.

AN ALTERNATIVE STRATEGY PROPOSED:
A BILATERAL AGREEMENT

I always believed it would be extremely difficult to reach a balanced agreement on the FTAA, given the natural complexity of the trade issues involved and the political difficulties that became clear from the outset, both on the Brazilian side and in the US.

I saw a 4+1 format as a possible alternative. The idea had already been presented to the United States in March 2001, on FHC's visit to Bush, but it was not followed up on, as I recounted earlier.

There was a series of arguments to justify a 4+1 bilateral agreement.

First of all, the Brazilian understanding was that the FTAA project would lose momentum after the agreement with Chile, and that other bilateral arrangements in the pipeline between the United States and Central America, Colombia, and Peru would cause interest in the region-wide plan to drop further. As had happened with Mexico after NAFTA, many of these countries would no longer need to pursue tariff concessions from the United States.

Another important question was that there had been no indication in the proposals examined in the working groups that the United States was likely to change its position in the negotiations and agree to significant concessions in the areas of most interest to Brazil (market access for agricultural produce, reduction or elimination of dumping practices, subsidies, and tariff hikes). Brazil also reckoned that these interests would be diluted by demands from the other negotiating nations, also interested in gaining access to the US market for priorities that were much less ambitious and more concrete than ours.

The very negotiating structure for the FTAA was stacked against Brazil. The trade-off on the final agreement would end up involving unequal concessions, given the economic differences in size between Brazil and its Latin American and Caribbean partners.

As the most important American market for the US, Brazil would always be left to pay a higher price for the concessions it received than did the other Latin American nations. As for market openness in the US, Brazil would be forced to accept a supposedly balanced package that considered demands made by other countries, but which did little to service Brazil's priority interests.

The Brazilian assessment was that a bilateral project for the United States and Mercosur would not invalidate the FTAA commitment. They were processes that could easily run parallel, as had NAFTA and other agreements with Chile and Central America. The FTAA would continue to be the undertaking upon which all other free trade agreements would converge. Mercosur, for its part, would preserve its institutional personality, as a customs union. Brazil also calculated that Argentina, always seduced by the idea of a special trade relationship with the United States, would not refuse a bilateral negotiation under the auspices of Mercosur in tandem with the regional discussions on the FTAA.

For all of these reasons, a bilateral negotiation with the United States could have given Brazil more bargaining power on the FTAA than it would have had as just one of thirty-four nations in the hemisphere.

The negotiating process with the United States would certainly be more predictable if we could present concrete proposals for a free trade agreement. And it would also safeguard our aim of entering into a preferential schema only if the US proved genuinely willing to discuss the items of priority interest to Brazil.

Furthermore, in the event that the United States came to accept a free trade agreement with the Mercosur, the Brazilian government had strong indications that the protracted discussions with the European Union would accelerate dramatically.

Of course, the United States–Mercosur strategy implied its own set of risks. The most evident of these was that the bilateral negotiations would run up against similar difficulties to those with which the FTAA talks were fraught, seen as the United States showed no interest in revising the protectionist measures that so badly affected Brazilian exports.

There was also the possibility that the Brazilian proposal would be accused of going against Brazil's traditional policy of prioritizing South America and our traditional strategy of regional integration. Then again, doubts might be raised to the effect that Brazil's gains in a bilateral US–Mercosur negotiation would come to the detriment of a multilateral regional option.

Be that as it may, the risks were worth taking. It was possible, perhaps even probable, that the US government would reject a 4+1 agreement with Mercosur, but the fact is, were that to indeed occur, it would be clear that the US Congress and agricultural lobby were not willing to make concessions, whether within a bilateral framework or within the wider sphere of the FTAA. The blame would lie squarely with the United States, while Brazil would have shown a will toward negotiation and liberalization. We would also be very clear on the United States's narrow margin for maneuver in negotiations, something that had not been totally evinced within the context of the FTAA.

Alcântara and the Technological Safeguards Agreement

The privileged location of the Alcântara rocket-launching base in Maranhão opened major commercial prospects for Brazil. Situated two degrees south of the equator, it can launch rockets with 13 percent lower fuel costs than at Cape Canaveral in the United States and 31 percent lower than at Baikonur in Kazakhstan, where Russia launches its satellites.

The commercial viability of the Alcântara Launch Center and its technological upkeep depended on revenues from the leasing of parts of the site for satellite launches.

However, there was one important detail: over 85 percent of the commercial satellites built worldwide belonged to American companies and not one of these would be launched from Alcântara unless a technological safeguards agreement was first sealed with Washington.

On June 11, 1999, when I arrived in Washington as ambassador, Minister for Science and Technology Ronaldo Sardemberg was in town to discuss the possibilities of a Technological Safeguards Agreement (TSA) with the US authorities. Brazil's aim was to develop a competitive launch center so that it could break into the niche market for the launch of telecommunications and meteorological satellites. With a safeguards agreement in place, the Brazilian teams working on launches would reap the benefits of the knowledge acquired through contact with foreign technicians.

There would be no international difficulties in establishing the base, as Brazil was a member of the Missile Technology Control Regime (MTCR). The treatment would be exactly the same as that dispensed to other countries, such as Russia and China, which had signed similar safeguards agreements with the United States.

The discussions with the United States were not easy, as Brazil had been developing a manufacturing program for a satellite launch vehicle (SLV), which could be used for either civilian or military ends.

Despite the US government's suspicions as to the nature of the Brazilian program, the safeguards agreement was signed in April 2000, with one condition: Brazil was not allowed to channel the revenues from the agreement into its launch vehicle program, though it could invest those funds in its space program, at the Alcântara Launch Center, and on improving infrastructure systems. The income generated could also be spent on assistance programs for the population that was displaced during expropriations for the construction of the base.

Once signed, the agreement was to be submitted for ratification by the Brazilian Congress. However, from the outset, the opposition to the FHC government, led by the Workers' Party, had fought hard against negotiations with the United States, alleging that Brazil was making concessions that went against its own interests.

The main and most systematic criticism made by the opposition was that the agreement did not include any transfer of technology from the US companies to Brazil, and that it posed a threat to national sovereignty, as components for the satellites to be launched from the base could only be opened and handled by staff from the American companies, with no interference from the Brazilian customs. PT also objected to the fact that revenues from the agreement could not be used on Brazil's own launcher program.

In light of this opposition, the agreement signed with the US and sent to Congress was not ratified.

At the end of the FHC government and the beginning of the Lula government, when Brazil's position became more trenchant, I participated in conversations at Congress and the Department of State on how to overcome the technical and political difficulties standing in the way.

I also met with deputy Waldir Pires (PT for Bahia), who was the rapporteur at Congress, and the president of the foreign affairs commission, then-deputy Hélio Costa (PMDB for Minas Gerais), who wanted to block the TSA. I tried to show them the advantages for Brazil and the need to accept certain conditions in order to make the base a viable concern. I always strove to emphasize that it was not a matter of technology transfer, as the opposition liked to pitch it. I drafted some comments on Deputy Waldir Pires' report, analyzing and responding to the questions he raised.

In an interview with Marcio Aith of the *Folha de S. Paulo* newspaper in November 2002, I showed that the Brazilian Congress, by virtue of a discussion that was out of focus, was about to exclude Brazil from a market worth US$12 billion per year. I highlighted the fact that Brazil had approached the US to offer the Alcântara base as a possible launch site for American satellites precisely because it was in our interests to do so. I also observed that neither the American government nor private sector had ever suggested an agreement of this type for fear that a missile launch vehicle would be put to military use and because of the absence of a safeguards agreement.

Despite resistance and skepticism from Itamaraty, already under the influence of PT, in the second semester of 2003 I reopened negotiations with the State Department to temper some of the points on which the now-ruling party was most vocally in disaccord. To the surprise of many, progress was made and certain bones of contention were eliminated. When I left the embassy in April 2004, the biggest political objections to ratification had been overcome. The Brazilian government would officially request certain minor adjustments and these would be accepted by the US authorities. Once the amendments were approved, the agreement would be passed by the Brazilian Congress.

However, PT's opposition continued for the duration of the Lula government and to this day it has not been possible to resume talks with the United States.

As a practical example of the politicization of decisions in the area of foreign affairs, it is worth recalling that a very similar safeguards agreement was signed with the Ukraine during Lula's first term. The Ukraine agreement met with no opposition from PT; quite the contrary, it was submitted to Congress and swiftly approved. However, though the agreement is in effect, it has never brought any commercial benefit to Brazil. Ideology won out, and Brazil lost a major opportunity to become a competitive player in the communications satellite launch market.

It is also important to remember that a serious accident occurred at the Alcântara base in August 2003. The launch vehicle SLV-1 exploded while preparing to launch a rocket, killing twenty-one scientists. It was a major setback to the Satellite Launch Vehicle program and signaled the end of Brazil's aspirations to a dominant position in the commercial satellite market.

The Bustani Affair

Ambassador José Maurício Bustani was re-elected director-general of the Organization for the Prohibition of Chemical Weapons (OPCW) at The Hague, Netherlands, for the period 2001–2005. One of the first actions he took in his second term was to invite Syria, Iran, Iraq, and

Sudan to join the organization. The US soon realized that Iraq's signing up to the OPCW would be a major blow to its justification for a unilateral attack on Saddam Hussein, and embarked on a campaign to have Bustani unseated.

In January 2002, the under-secretary for Political Issues at Itamaraty, Luiz Augusto Araújo Castro, was in Washington for periodic talks with the Department of State, a meeting prescribed under a Brazil–US consultation mechanism.

During his stay in the capital, we were called to a meeting with John Bolton, Secretary for Disarmament and International Security, responsible for the area of nuclear non-proliferation at the Department of State. I had met John Bolton in 1999, soon after my arrival in Washington. He was a far-right, ultra-conservative politician and fierce critic of Clinton-era foreign policy, and there was little surprise that he had been incorporated into the Bush Administration.

When we entered Bolton's office I noticed that there was not a single document or file on his desk, just a hand grenade, a decoration that was certainly apt.

Without mincing words, and with the arrogance so typical of many in Bush's team, the secretary cut straight to the point, and began to outline the administrative problems the United States was having with Ambassador Bustani.

Bolton said that Bustani was "threatening to fire an American administrative director who was trying to fine-tune the organization's work." He said that if the situation remained uncomfortable for this American staffer "there would be serious consequences" for the director-general. Bolton also insinuated that there were financial mismanagement issues within Bustani's administration and the fact that this American official knew about them was the reason behind Bustani's threats.

Both Ambassador Araújo Castro and I reacted immediately and vigorously. First, I contested the need for the subject to be discussed with the Brazilian Embassy or with representatives of the Brazilian government because Ambassador Bustani held an international post, to which he had been elected by signatory nations including the United States. As such, it was not the Brazilian government's place or obligation to take a position on the matter, whether for or against. Second, I stressed that we would not accept aspersions being cast upon Ambassador Bustani, who we had known for forty years, saying: "You might criticize him on other aspects which we would not be in a position to assess, but on a question of ethics we summarily reject any insinuation."

Araújo Castro and I left the meeting in dismay at the manner and tone in which Bolton had approached the subject. It was the first time the matter was being officially addressed with the Brazilian government. I immediately informed Itamaraty of the content and nature of the conversation. I also rang Ambassador Bustani at The Hague and told him that we had just learned of a serious problem involving his position at the head of the OPCW and that the Americans were on a crusade to oust him.

From a distance, even without full possession of the facts, it was clear that Bustani's attempts to engage Iraq, followed by Syria, Sudan, and Iran, and persuade them to sign up for the chemical weapons convention went against the US government's strategy for confrontation with these nations—a strategy that would soon lead to the invasion of Iraq and the arrest of Saddam Hussein.

If Iraq had been incorporated into the OPCW, it would then have been subject to the same regular controls as the other member states and there would have been international inspections at its facilities to verify the existence of weapons of mass destruction. This would have resolved the impasse between Baghdad and the United Nations, considering that the Security Council Committee's weapons inspectors had been expelled from the country, accused of spying for the United States.

However, it was not in the interests of the US to have Iraq join the OPCW Convention, as it would have opened up Iraqi installations to inspection and therefore would have eliminated the US contention that the country possessed an arsenal of weapons of mass destruction and therefore also its grounds for war. In one more demonstration of unilateralism, the United States began to press aggressively for Bustani's removal from the post and to hound him to resign as director-general.

The issue dragged on for some months and became a full-blown international incident involving the OPCW, Brazil, and the United States. From the American capital, the embassy followed the developments at close quarters. Late in January 2002, I received instructions from Itamaraty to inform the State Department that the Brazilian government would support Bustani's permanence in the post, a message I conveyed immediately.

Soon thereafter, during one of the working visits by Minister Celso

Lafer to Secretary of State Colin Powell, the issue assumed new propor-
tions, given its direct handling at that level of government and the fact
that the Americans were beginning to question certain attitudes adopted
by the Brazilian authorities.

Having gone over the themes on the agenda in the presence of their
respective aides, Powell asked everyone to leave the room so that he and
Lafer could converse alone. On his return to the chancery, I asked the
minister if the subject of their private discussion had been the Bustani
case, and he replied that, yes, it had, but said no more and I asked no
further questions.

After this meeting with Bolton, I was called in on two further occasions to hear complaints from American authorities, who claimed the
Brazilian government was maneuvering to keep Bustani in the post,
when the reality of the situation was that the Brazilian diplomat had
himself rallied the support of various member states in The Hague.

On April 8, before the ninety-eight signatory nations were to take
a no-confidence vote moved by the United States against Bustani, I received an *aide-mémoire* from Brasília addressed to the Department of
State. In this document, the Brazilian government gave the United States
advance notice that it would vote in favor of the ambassador.

The United States failed to secure enough votes to pass its motion of
no confidence in the OPCW director-general, but they did take the matter to an extraordinary assembly in April 2002, when the preparations
for the invasion of Iraq were at full-steam. The US campaign against the
director-general culminated in his removal from the post by forty-eight
votes to seven, with forty-three abstentions. An end was brought to a
regrettable episode, a clear expression of the Bush government's foreign
policy and arrogant unilateralism.

From the US perspective, it was not a bilateral issue with Brazil. In
fact, we were given the opportunity to appoint another Brazilian diplomat to the post.

Be that as it may, the episode nonetheless left a bitter taste in the
mouths of all those who had followed the events as they unfolded. When
I learned of Ambassador Bustani's departure speech, I sent a message
of support, emphasizing that his career and professional conduct spoke
far louder than the often unjust machinations of international hardball.
What mattered was that Bustani's work at the helm of the OPCW was
duly recognized, as could be sensed from the standing ovation he received at the close of his speech.

Coup d'État in Venezuela

The coup d'état that ousted Hugo Chávez in April 2002 was openly backed by the United States, which, at that time, further compromised its relationship with the rest of the western hemisphere. From the very beginning, Brazil opposed the unseating of a democratically elected leader and supported every initiative to restore the Venezuelan president to power.

President Chávez was deposed by sectors of the army acting in collusion with the business elite, and they held power for two days. Pedro Carmona, president of the Venezuelan Federation of Chambers of Commerce (Fedecámaras), was declared president. The situation rapidly deteriorated, with tumult in the streets and clashes between Chávez loyalists and supporters of the coup.

The western hemisphere secretary Otto Reich, in charge of Latin American Affairs at the State Department, invited the region's ambassadors to declare their support for the new government, which had captured and imprisoned Hugo Chávez.

I don't know to what extent the State Department heads were aware of the pressure applied by Otto Reich, as they were too busy focusing on the war against terror and on preparations for the invasion of Iraq, but the fact is the secretary's behavior immediately allied the government with the coup, severely damaging the US image region-wide in the process. This was perhaps the US government's single biggest foreign policy blunder in Latin America so far in the twenty-first century.

Brazil was one of the few South American countries to condemn the coup. On orders from Brasília, the embassy in Washington, represented by Minister Roberto Jaguaribe, emphatically expressed Brazil's repudiation of the overthrow and its hopes for the immediate restoration of order. Any recognition of the new government would be roundly condemned by Brazil. After all, Chávez had been democratically elected and his government supported by a likewise democratically elected Congress.

Less than twenty-four hours after the coup, Chávez was re-installed to the presidency amid civil unrest and a standoff between segments of a divided military.

There was no doubt that US oil interests spoke louder than the contradictions and incoherence of supporting a coup against a democratic government. At the time, Venezuela supplied over 15 percent of US oil imports. Yet despite patent US opposition to Chávez, Caracas had never threatened to cut off its oil supply to the United States.

With Chávez back in power, government and opposition positions escalated, causing widespread uncertainty and concern for the political situation in the country. At the behest of the Organization of American States (OAS), the secretary-general created a Group of Friends to keep abreast of developments in Venezuela. The tense and uncertain atmosphere intensified when a referendum, provided for under the constitution, was called on whether or not to revoke the president's mandate.

The Group of Friends—made up of the foreign ministers of the United States, Mexico, Brazil, and Chile—was coordinated by Celso Amorim. At various meetings attended by American Secretary of State Colin Powell, Brazil took an active role in suggesting formulas for conciliation that would help resolve the issue while respecting Venezuelan sovereignty and the will of its people.

The political situation in Venezuela and Chávez's decision to embrace the role of socialist doyen for the twenty-first century began to feature on the agenda with US authorities, who continued to view Brazil as a moderating influence in the region. This perception, which had existed since FHC, had gained strength in the light of the ideological affinities between the Lula Government and that of Hugo Chávez.

Air Transport Problems

In 2001, air transport and travel risked being seriously disrupted when the US filed a complaint with the International Civil Aviation Organization (ICAO) against the Brazilian Civil Aviation Department (DAC), replaced in 2005 by the National Civil Aviation Agency (ANAC).

Since my arrival in Washington, the Federal Aviation Agency (FAA), the agency in charge of civil aviation in the United States, had been stepping up its restrictions on certain aspects of Brazilian air transport.

The situation, which was entirely new in Brazil, came to a head in March 2001, when the ICAO—the executive agency behind the Chicago Convention, which regulates civil aviation worldwide—threatened to downgrade Brazil's air-safety rating.

Concerned with flight safety, the FAA contacted the Brazilian government to push for internal measures to strengthen the DAC and improve its performance as a certifying and inspection agency. In particular, the FAA was worried about the shortage of technical staff at the

DAC, which it felt compromised its oversight of security procedures and inspection of maintenance hangers, especially those of Varig Airlines.

If Brazil failed to meet the ICAO's demands and did not move to comply with the baseline requirements, American airplanes would cease to land at Brazilian airports and Brazilian air traffic would be prohibited from entering US airspace, which would have had massive political and economic consequences. I became directly involved in the discussions in the hope of broadening the scope of the negotiations and, by the end of March, gave the subject a political spin by contacting the Department of State. In my talks there, I broached the matter of Embraer plane certifications and the homologation of our airports, stressing the safety of our air transport and committing to reinforcing the DAC's human resources.

In April 2001, the crisis worsened when the FAA brought up an accident that had occurred in 1997 involving a Comair-owned EMB-120 Brasília built by Embraer. The National Transportation Safety Board (NTSB) joined the FAA in alleging that the accident with the Brazil-built plane was the result of "lessons not learned" from a similar crash in 1994, involving an American Eagle ATR-72. The questions raised, however, were of an operational rather than technical nature. The investigation had been completed satisfactorily thanks to "outstanding cooperation and responsiveness" from Embraer, as the FAA formally recognized.

Be that as it may, the FAA began to demand painstaking inspections and certification of all Embraer aircraft flying over US territory and continued to insist that the DAC was understaffed to carry out that supervision.

Both Embraer and the Brazilian aviation bureau asked for the Washington embassy's help to solve the problem. I accompanied the Brazilian delegation, led by Brigadier Reginaldo Santos, on numerous meetings with the US authorities to try to clarify the functioning, limitations, and planned expansion of the DAC.

As sometimes occurred, Itamaraty overzealously sought to limit the embassy's involvement. The secretary-general, Ambassador Luiz Felipe Seixas Corrêa, rang me to say that he had been against the inclusion of my name on the Brazilian delegation, but that Brigadier Venâncio Grossi, director of the DAC, and Chief of Staff Pedro Parente had insisted that I participate in the meetings. When President FHC was in Washington in November 2001, we spoke about the subject and I asked for his direct intervention, given the potential consequences to the country if the FAA decided to carry through with its threat to penalize Brazil.

When Finance Minister Pedro Malan learned of the chance that Brazil would be downgraded, and understanding the repercussions this would have on the economy and on air transport, he contacted me to find out how matters were unfolding.

Months went by with this tension hanging in the air, because if the FAA had made good on its threat—the first in forty-four years—it would have created strong friction in Brazil–US relations and would have had a considerable economic impact on Brazil.

After tough negotiations between the DAC and FAA, we reached an agreement that was satisfactory to both parties and the Americans lifted their threat to downgrade Brazil on air safety.

After the meetings with the FAA, Brigadier Reginaldo Santos, accompanied by Brigadier Venâncio Grossi, made much of the role the embassy had played in the negotiations and the support I always gave to businesspeople on official delegations. I replied that, since my time in charge of the Eastern European Trade Commission (Coleste) in the late 1970s and early 1980s, I had always tried to include businesspeople in Brazilian delegations so that they could participate in coordinating issues related to foreign trade.

In this particular episode I was able to make a substantial contribution to defusing a bomb that could have derailed Brazil's bilateral relations with the United States, with untold consequences for the Brazilian economy.

The Triple Border

After September 11, 2001, the obsession with the war on terror led the US government to identify the existence of cells of Palestinian militants with ties to Hezbollah and involvement in acts of terrorism at the tri-border region between Brazil, Argentina, and Paraguay, the so-called Triple Frontier.

In Foz do Iguaçu, Brazil; Puerto Iguazú, Argentina; and Cuidad de Leste, Paraguay, there is a significant Palestinian presence, mostly people who have taken refuge there from the conflict in the Middle East. Ever since this aggregation made the US Defense Department's watch list there have been intermittent denunciations of the existence of terrorist cells infiltrated within the region's Arab community.

This perception of a potential threat to US security was ratcheted up by the United States Southern Command in Miami, responsible for assessing security issues in South America. In an attempt to gain visibility and a bigger budget from the US Congress, sources at Southcom peddled these denunciations in the press.

In news items fed to American newspapers via Miami, the Triple Frontier started to feature prominently as a point of concern for the US government.

In November 2002, CNN broadcast a program in which it claimed that Al-Qaeda had agents in São Paulo. The report caused a public backlash and immediate response from the Brazilian government. In contact with the network's management, I pointed out that official intelligence from Brazil and the US had found no proof of any terrorist activity at the Triple Frontier, much less any trace of Al-Qaeda in São Paulo. I added that the Brazilian government had asked the US authorities to send all the information it had on alleged terrorist-group activities in the region, despite there being no evidence to suggest that there was any. In April 2011, the issue came to light once again in a report by the weekly magazine *Veja*, which claimed to have identified figures with ties to terrorist organizations living in São Paulo.

Given the recurrence of these stories, on various occasions I made contact with the State Department and CIA to verify the existence of the terrorist activities mentioned in the press and to reiterate Brazil's interest in examining any evidence on these alleged terrorist hotspots in the region. Nothing concrete was ever presented to the embassy. The chief of the presidency's Institutional Relations Cabinet, General Alberto Mendes Cardoso, visited the CIA in Washington and "underscored the importance of not demonizing the Triple Frontier without any evidence of terrorist activity."

Even so, the theme acquired a certain relevance in the context of relations between the two countries and was the subject of an exchange of opinions between the Defense Minister José Viegas, and US Defense Secretary Donald Rumsfeld in July 2003, when Brazil reiterated its position that there was no evidence to suggest that terrorist cells were operating at the Triple Frontier.

All the Brazilian government's investigations were able to prove was that money was being sent from the area to the Hezbollah in Lebanon. Though Brazil could trace the origin of the transfers, it could not follow the money trail to its final destination, as a political party can legally receive donations and it is often difficult to determine where the money goes from there.

In order to better follow this sensitive issue, the Brazilian and US governments created a coordination group called 3+1, made up of Brazil, Paraguay, Argentina, and the United States, so the countries could exchange information and monitor these financial transfers to the Middle East.

Between 2002 and 2004, when I left the embassy, the United States never did find concrete evidence of terrorist activity or cells operating in the region.

The embassy's proactive engagement was important in clarifying information that had cast the shadow of terrorism upon Brazilian territory, had brought disquiet to the border region, and had caused concern within the intelligence community in both countries.

Cooperation on Defense

The creation of the Brazilian Ministry of Defense in 1999 made it possible to establish more extensive contact with the higher echelons of the Pentagon and to deepen collaboration between Brazil and the United States on military issues. Rapprochement between the two countries gradually increased during the FHC and Lula governments after their respective defense ministers Geraldo Quintão and José Viegas Filho made visits to Washington.

The two countries' relationship in the area of defense had not always been smooth. Through the Military Assistance Agreement of 1953, the United States committed to materials transfers and to facilitating the sale of services to the Brazilian Navy, Army, and Air Force. The agreement was part of a US Security Assistance policy pursued with allied nations in the wake of the Second World War.

In 1977, in one of the single most significant acts in bilateral relations between the two countries, the government of Ernesto Geisel withdrew from the Military Assistance Agreement as a reprisal against Washington's repeated criticisms against the dictatorship's human rights abuses. As a result, all negotiations on the purchase and supply of armaments and services were cancelled and the Joint Brazil–United States Military Commission dissolved.

In March 1984, the Brazilian Liaison Office was opened at the Wright-Patterson base in Dayton, Ohio, the headquarters of the Air Force Material Command. The aim of the office was to set up the technical management of a program to foster better interaction with the logistics command of the US Army, Navy, and Air Force.

During my time in Washington, the training of officers for the three armies at US academies remained unchanged and was limited to their different professional and strategic aspects. I maintained close contact with the attachés to the three armed forces, general officials, and military materials procurement committees, especially on replacement parts.

Cooperation in the military area was further expanded in 2000, when Agreement 505 permitted the transfer to Brazil, on a concessionary basis, of decommissioned military material belonging to the US Armed Forces.

Contact and cooperation grew until 2003, when the United States decided to suspend its military assistance to some fifty countries, Brazil included, in retaliation for their refusal to sign a bilateral agreement proposed by the Bush government that would have exempted US nationals, including military personnel, from the Rome Statute of the International Criminal Court. As Brazil understood the proposal, the agreement would have exonerated US military personnel of responsibility for crimes committed in the theater of war in other countries, and so refused to sign. It was not hard to explain the position adopted by the Brazilian government, which was not particularly worried about the suspension of military assistance anyway, as it was negligible and would have had no effect on the Brazilian armed forces.

During my ambassadorship in Washington, given the creation of a Brazilian Defense Ministry, high-level contact with the US Defense Department was resumed. The integration of the Navy, Army, and Air Force under a single civilian minister was proof of the consolidation of our democracy.

The visits to Washington made by Ministers of Defense Geraldo Quintão and José Viegas Filho were largely arranged by the embassy, a task that was greatly facilitated by the frank and direct dialogue maintained with American Assistant Secretary for Defense Rogelio Pardo-Maurer, who was in charge of Latin American policy.

It was during the FHC government, in June 2002, that the first meeting was held between a civilian Brazilian defense minister and his US counterpart, in this case, William Cohen, Clinton's defense secretary. This was a watershed in the politico-strategic relationship between the two countries.

Among the main issues discussed by Minister Geraldo Quintão and Secretary Cohen were the preparations for the first bilateral Brazil–US defense meeting and the creation of three subgroups: cooperation in the area of defense; science, technology, and logistics; and relations between civil and military personnel. Also discussed was the agenda for the fourth Defense Ministerial Conference of the Americas, to be held in Manaus in October 2002, and, briefly, other themes such as hemispheric security in the twenty-first century, measures for boosting mutual trust across the region, and defense and development.

Minister Quintão highlighted the striking differences between North, Central, and South America in the strategic field and how these make it hard to define a single security policy for the three regions.

Though a peaceful continent—far removed from the international flashpoints—in which countries were working to consolidate democracy and development through a process of regional integration, the absence of obvious conventional enemies did not mean that South American countries could afford to be lax about their defense structure, as the international environment, fluid and unstable as ever, could at any moment present the most unexpected threats. The message was that no nation had ever renounced the right to legitimate self-defense, so in order to ensure sovereignty the Armed Forces had to be adequately sized and appropriately structured, well-trained, and properly equipped.

Quintão reaffirmed that his ministry strove to keep foreign policy and defense strategy in sync, in order to determine not only the most adequate form of strategic insertion for Brazil on the South American, hemispheric, and global levels, but also the military structure the country would need to meet its defense needs.

The Brazilian minister also met with General Henry Shelton, Chair of the Joint Chiefs of Staff, and with representatives of the Brazil–US Congressional Caucus. No mention was made on either side of the preparations then underway for the war in Iraq.

In July 2003, José Viegas Filho became the second minister of defense to visit Washington. On this occasion, he met with Bush's defense secretary, Donald Rumsfeld.

It was a delicate moment, as the visit took place not long after the invasion of Iraq, and the US government was facing increasing difficulties in the theater of war.

In addition to the meeting with the defense secretary, Minister José Viegas also had a working meeting with Assistant Secretary of State for

Political-Military Affairs Lincoln Bloomfield. At the Pentagon, he received a wide-ranging briefing on US defense strategy, the war against terrorism, and Plan Colombia, and met with members of the House of Representatives Foreign Affairs Committee.

These meetings dealt with a number of regional themes of interest to both nations and with matters of bilateral defense.

Minister Viegas welcomed the intensity and density of Brazil–US relations, including the field of defense, and said that President Lula's government wanted to take the relationship between the countries to a higher level. He also emphasized the stability of South America and noted that the subcontinent possessed certain features that set it apart from the rest of Latin America. He spoke at length on the concepts of democracy, peace, and development, and recalled that there were no military conflicts underway in or among South American states.

The Brazilian minister also remarked that Brazil was seen, and saw itself, as an international moderator. He spoke about Brazil's contribution to South American stability, underlining the fact that Brazil shared borders with ten neighbors with whom it had enjoyed over one hundred thirty years of peace. Viegas showed Rumsfeld that if the United States was genuinely interested in a stable and prosperous South America, dialogue with Brazil would be indispensable.

Rumsfeld recognized Brazil's role and relevance not only in South America but worldwide.

Viegas said that Brazil was serious about taking its place as a regional power and that the country was engaged in increasing its presence in South America, albeit in a smooth manner, true to the national style.

In response to the secretary's question about the threats Brazil could see South America having to face, the Brazilian minister mentioned narcotrafficking, contraband, money laundering, and even the possibility of terrorist attacks. On the latter topic the minister said that, while there was no Brazilian terrorism or anti-Brazilian terrorism, the country had to remain on constant alert so as not to be caught unawares. On the issue of money laundering, he said there was no reason to believe that this activity in Brazil was linked to terrorist initiatives.

On the subject of Colombia, Rumsfeld said that the United States was fully behind Plan Colombia and that he believed it could help the country to iron out its difficulties. In his view, Colombia had a clear strategy and it was carrying it out. About whether the US was interested in deepening its engagement with Bogota, Rumsfeld said that he was satisfied with the level of involvement between the two countries. He explained, however, that the US Congress had some problems on the issue, insofar as the plan had originally been viewed as an exclusively counter-narcotics measure, when it was clearly much more than that.

Donald Rumsfeld took the opportunity to ask Brazil whether or not it considered the FARC to be a terrorist organization. Viegas explained that the country did not work with lists of terrorist organizations, but that, as made clear in the OAS resolution, which we had supported, the Brazilian government did recognize that the FARC had committed acts of terrorism. In a broader sense, the minister made it clear that the country did not have any sympathies for the methods the Colombian organization employed.

Donald Rumsfeld also mentioned the political situation in Venezuela and recognized the country's successful cooperation with Brazil on the OAS secretary-general's Group of Friends, a model that he said should be replicated with other countries. The Special Security Conference in Mexico, held the following year, was the last to be hemispheric in scope.

As for themes of a bilateral interest, the shoot down policy warranted special attention.

Minister Viegas explained what Brazil saw to be a need to regulate the existing law on the issue so as to make the control of Brazilian airspace more effective in the clampdown on illicit drug trafficking. Viegas expressed his concern that the Brazilian rules on the shoot down option needed to be coherent with those in place in Colombia, Peru, and the US, and clarified that Sivam (Amazonian surveillance system) efficiency in fighting the drug trade would be weakened without the shoot down option.

In response to the minister's reflections, Secretary Rumsfeld was direct in saying that the United States did not have a unified position on the shoot down policy. He said that the Defense Department would not cause any problems in that regard, but that it would be necessary to "work on" the Departments of State and Justice.

Rumsfeld said that the main problem lay in determining with absolute certainty whether or not a plane was involved in drug trafficking. Viegas spoke of the procedures Brazil would adopt prior to taking the final decision to down any aircraft and suggested that US reticence on the issue could be interpreted as a lack of trust.

In order to deal with the matter more thoroughly, Rumsfeld proposed creating a panel of American experts that would go to Brazil to "map out obstacles." The Minister replied that the difficulties were already known and that all that was needed from the US at this point was a change of attitude.

The theme had been dragging on for years, since Minister Luiz Felipe Lampreia first discussed it with Secretary of State Madeleine Albright in 1999. It was finally settled shortly after Minister Viegas' visit, when Brazil passed the legislation and put its counternarcotics policy into practice on the border.

The minister for defense said that as he saw US interests in South America, Brazil and the United States were aligned on the aim of working to foster an environment predicated on democracy, prosperity, peace, and stability throughout the subcontinent. For the minister, the problems Brazil did have with the United States in the area of defense were minor and isolated, but nonetheless underscored the need for the two countries to maintain constant and fluid dialogue. To illustrate his point, Viegas mentioned three specific issues.

The first of these concerned the unsubstantiated declarations by US authorities as to the existence of terrorist activities at the Triple Frontier. The Minister said that the Brazilian authorities had stepped up their surveillance in the tri-border area and that our intelligence agencies had found no evidence to suggest a terrorist presence there. The minister stressed that in the absence of proof, there was nothing that could be done, and he asked the American side to send the Brazilian government any information that may arise.

The second issue concerned a letter written by General Hill, of the Southern Command, to the commander of the armed forces in Colombia pressuring the country, which was in the process of substituting obsolete fighter planes, not to opt for Embraer's Super Tucano—the most suitable option, according to preliminary technical studies—but to go for planes manufactured by an American company. Rumsfeld said that the Brazilian government's reaction to the letter was comprehensible, but that Brazil had to understand the American official's position, which was simply to defend US interests in a transaction of considerable value. Donald Rumsfeld added that the US Congress would find it hard to accept that a country that received as much financial aid as that currently dispensed to Colombia should choose against American suppliers when it came to buying aircraft.

Viegas' third and final point concerned the "theoretical exercises" used by the Southern Command in the training it administered to the Paraguayan military. These exercises envisaged scenarios in which "Braziguayans" (Brazilian nationals living on or across the border with Paraguay) were threatening the integrity of Paraguayan territory. Rumsfeld, who had already received an informal document on the subject (a 'non paper,' in diplomatic parlance) admitted the absurdity of the situation and said that he had instructed one of his aides to look into it. With theatrical flair, Rumsfeld held up the paper and asked: "What the heck is this? Tell them to stop with this nonsense."

The Amazon

Amazonian deforestation, the demarcation of indigenous homelands, drug trafficking, the threat posed by the Colombian guerrillas, and Brazil's concerns about external meddling in the region kept the Amazon high on the embassy's agenda during my time in Washington. Two examples illustrate the attention this topic required.

In February 2003, at a meeting at Inter-American Dialogue, a center for Latin American studies, General James T. Hill, chief of the US Southern Command, made an ample presentation on narcotrafficking in the Amazon and the US-sponsored measures being taken by the Colombian government to stamp it out.

General Hill stressed the idea that the Colombian conflict was a hemispheric problem and that the new challenges of the twenty-first century (such as organized crime, drugs and terrorism) demanded a "reassessment of the role of the Armed Forces in the region." For Hill, only military institutions had the capacity to deal with violations of national sovereignty, represented, for example, by the use of Brazilian rivers in the Amazon to transport the chemical products needed to refine drugs or the use of ports in Chile by drugs and arms traffickers.

The chief of the Southern Command related the drug trade with terrorism. In addition to mentioning narcoterrorists in Colombia and the issue of the Triple Frontier, he also cited northern Chile and Margarita Island in Venezuela as areas that might be sheltering terrorist organizations or the money laundering operations that bankrolled them. Hill classified drugs as "weapons of mass destruction" and cited the consumption statistics in the United States and Brazil, which he identified, respectively, as the first and second largest cocaine-consuming countries in the world.

What was most worrying about Hill's speech was the number of generalizations and simplifications about the region and about Brazil and the extent to which these might tarnish our image or, worse still, end up on the US policy agenda by compounding certain distorted concepts already inhabiting the "collective mindset" of US decision makers. For our part, we understood that Hill was trying to sweep certain "hot" US Security themes under his jurisdiction in order to command a bigger budget from the Pentagon.

Ambassador Valter Pecly, Brazil's representative at the OAS, had informed me that at a speech a few days earlier in Miami Hill had been even more emphatic in his proposal to engage the military in the war on drugs, suggesting that the legal impediments to this should be "simply removed."

After his presentation, I took the floor to say that General Hill had spoken more as a politician and diplomat than as a soldier, since he had chosen to omit the suggestion he had made in Miami that the legal impediments to broader military action in combating drug trafficking in countries like Brazil should be summarily removed. In this context, I asked the chief of the Southern Command how he expected such changes to be made by democratic governments, and why the US was insisting on the policy when its own Constitution prohibited the involvement of the Armed Forces in such activities. I also asked why the United States did not involve its military directly in the war on drugs on home soil—the world's largest drugs market—at a time when the FBI was transferring over five hundred agents from the drug division to the war on terrorism.

The Southcom chief denied having said in Miami that Latin American countries should remove the legal impediments to military engagement in tackling drugs and said that he had never suggested that local law be disrespected, but that it was important for the military to "take the debate on the reformulation of its role to political leaders." Hill also said that, with the democratization of the region, the possible dangers to Brazil would not come from its neighbors, but from narcotraffickers, gunrunners, gangsters and other elements of organized crime that could erode the social fabric. The general explained that he did not defend the use of the Armed Forces to police cities, but to patrol vast swathes of forest in places like the Amazon.

Then-Secretary Julio Bitelli, an efficient diplomat and collaborator of mine, asked Hill to clarify more thoroughly what was meant by "effective sovereignty," something Defense Secretary Donald Rumsfeld had mentioned in passing during the ministerial meeting on Defense in Chile some time before. On that occasion, Rumsfeld had declared that "elected governments have the responsibility to exercise sovereign authority, conferred at the ballot box, throughout their national territory. We are all benefited by helping democratic nations across this hemisphere exercise effective sovereignty over their territories." A document that circulated at that same meeting proposed effective sovereignty as a response to those "ungoverned spaces" that are "a threat to peace and consider themselves to lie beyond the authorities' reach." Hill did little to elucidate our doubts on what looked to be the embryo of a new operational concept for US security policy in Latin America. As an example of what effective sovereignty was not, he mentioned Colombia, where "there are parts of the national territory to which the government simply cannot send its representatives, be they soldiers, police, mayors, teachers."

The non-definition of this innovative concept, put forward by the US government's highest-ranking officials on the subject, was grounds for serious doubt in a country like Brazil.

Was the Pentagon simply proposing the regimentation of regional military aid as a means toward resolving the crisis in Colombia and eliminating the threat posed by these "lawless territories"? Could the "ungoverned space" tag also apply to large demographically empty areas in which the state has a weaker presence, such as the Amazon? Or might sovereignty be considered "ineffective" in urban areas where organized crime and drug gangs exercise a de facto parallel power? What, then, could be said of areas like the Triple Frontier, a point of convergence for criminal organizations (drugs and arms smugglers and money-launderers) through clandestine networks?

Answers to these questions would go a long way toward clarifying the real position the United States was adopting on the involvement of the Armed Forces in the fight against organized crime.

If the Triple Frontier, or even the urban shantytowns, fit the definition of areas lacking "effective sovereignty," we might infer that what the United States expected was that the Brazilian Armed Forces be deployed to engage the narcotraffickers in combat. After all, the state has the responsibility to control these areas (Rumsfeld) and the Armed Forces are the only institutions equipped to ensure that control (Hill).

Another issue involving the Amazon was the news that schools in the United States were using a book entitled *Introduction to Geography*, by one David Norman, which illustrated the Amazon as lying outside Brazilian territory.

According to the news, which popped up periodically online, this book depicted the Amazon as being an independent reserve under US/UN protection. The reason for the creation of this zone was that "the Amazon is located in South America, one of the poorest regions on earth" and because it was "part of eight different and strange countries, which are in the majority of cases kingdoms of violence, drug trade, illiteracy and a [sic] unintelligent and primitive people."

According to the same news report, this explained "Plan Colombia" the American troops in Suriname, the appropriation of the rocket-launch base in Alcântara, Brazil, the United States's intention to set up a CIA office in Foz de Iguaçu so it could keep the Tripe Frontier under surveillance, and the creation of military bases in Ecuador. In other words, the Amazon was surrounded on all sides by the US military, which could seize control of the region at a minute's notice.

News of the book's content hit the headlines and many people and organizations contacted the embassy for clarification. We conducted a thorough search and discovered, hardly surprisingly, that it was all a hoax. Neither the book nor its author existed. The map in question was a montage and the texts, distorted and full of lies. It was not possible to identify the creators of the map or ascertain their political intentions.

The Immigration Issue

With nearly thirty-eight million Latino immigrants living in the United States at the turn of the twenty-first century, the issue of illegal immigration became one of the most delicate problems in internal US policy.

In the mid-1990s, given the problems with the economy and the prolonged period of slow growth, Brazil became an emigrant nation, with the US the destination of choice for those searching for better job opportunities and living conditions.

According to estimates made by the embassy in Washington, by the beginning of the 2000s, there were about two million Brazilians living in the United States, with particularly strong concentrations in California, Florida, and the Massachusetts–New York corridor.

After the September 11 terrorist attacks, particularly from 2002 on, the Americans adopted more stringent measures to control the influx of illegal immigrants. Where before it was Mexico and Central America that had been on the receiving end of harsher US action, the terrorist attacks widened the net, with deportations affecting a growing diversity of foreign nationals.

In the case of Brazilians living illegally in the United States, the number of detentions and deportations rose in accordance with the general trend. The Brazilian community, known to be peace-loving, hardworking, and well integrated with the rest of American society, was now exposed to a new, harder line of policy and growing insecurity.

The forced return of Brazilian nationals living illegally in the United States became a source of rising tension between the two countries. Brazil had always respected a nation's right to apply its immigration legislation, but felt it could not accept the growing number of detentions and deportations due to visa irregularities. US practices were becoming a source of embarrassment to Brazilian travelers and were having a negative impact on public and government opinion.

In May 2003, roughly eight hundred Brazilians were detained and had removal proceedings brought against them by the US government. According to the authorities in Washington, each individual was given full legal protection, including the right to appeal the deportation decision issued by the US Citizenship and Immigration Service. According to the immigration service, far from being treated unfairly, the rights of these people were actually being protected throughout the process.

According to USCIS, deportation was being done aboard specially chartered flights so as to ensure a "safe, humane and dignified return for the Brazilian nationals involved." The charter system to El Salvador, the Dominican Republic, Nigeria, and Pakistan, among other countries, had been in use for years. The US government had decided to release the detainees as the chartered flights were filled, but if, for whatever reason, those flights could not depart, the detainees would remain in detention for indeterminate lengths of time.

The embassy endeavored to give all possible support to the Brazilian deportees. Our staff and diplomats were invited to visit detention centers holding Brazilian nationals and to accompany them on their return on the chartered aircraft.

For internal political reasons, pressured by Congress and public opinion, the Bush government had undertaken to remove as many illegal immigrants as it could in the shortest possible time.

However, Itamaraty and some Brazilian states considered the deportations to be an outrageous abuse of human rights.

I was instructed to inform the Department of State that the Brazilian government would not collaborate with the US authorities on any mass deportation of Brazilian citizens, nor issue visas to the American officials designated to accompany the flights, and that these would not be given clearance to fly over or land at Brazilian airports.

The repercussion in the Brazilian media was immense, and for some time we had an impasse in our talks with the US immigration service.

In the end, good sense prevailed and the Brazilian government decided to accept the deportees back home.

It was the solution I had argued for, as it would have made no sense for the Brazilian government to leave its citizens stranded in US detention centers, unable to start afresh in Brazil, having been prevented from continuing their lives in America.

Cooperation in Third Countries

In 2003, I started discussions with the US Department of State about our possible cooperation in other countries, particularly Africa and its Portuguese-speaking nations, such as Angola and Mozambique.

Brazil had cooperation and technical assistance programs in place in Africa through the Brazilian Cooperation Agency, but these were running on limited resources. The United States, on the other hand, had plenty of funds, but the disadvantage of a language barrier, not to mention the political resistance it encountered in certain places.

A joint US–Brazil endeavor could have helped overcome the problems of funding, language, and relations and perhaps could have broadened prospects of getting assistance into Africa through an agenda that strengthened its institutions and such pivotal sectors as education and health.

At meetings with US Secretary for Africa Susan Rice, now the Obama administration's ambassador to the United Nations, I proposed the creation of joint action between the Brazilian Cooperation Agency and similar institutions in the US. The idea was to offer assistance projects to African nations in the areas of health and education that would be staffed by Brazilian doctors and teachers and include Portuguese-language teaching materials.

The Department of State considered the suggestion both positive and opportune, but said that the viability of the project would depend on deeper analysis.

The idea only got off the ground in 2009, when concrete examples of joint Brazil–US cooperation—in the area of health, for example—began to take shape and be handled directly by presidents Bush and Lula.

Brazil and the G8

Brazil first sat in on a G8 meeting as a non-core member in May 2003—at the summit held in Evian, France—alongside the United States, United Kingdom, France, Germany, Italy, Japan, Canada, and Russia. Brazil's first presence at the meeting of the world's eight biggest industrialized nations triggered widespread interest among the international community and so warranted special attention from the Brazilian government in its preparations for the meeting.

Brazil's debut—and that of President Lula—at a summit meeting was a unique opportunity for Brazil to air its ideas about the reorganization of the international economic order.

Given the importance of the issue, and the fact that the embassy in Washington was closely monitoring the American position on proposals for the reduction of hunger and poverty, I was able to make some concrete suggestions to Brasília in its preparatory discussions for the meeting.

Inspired by positions PT had championed during its election campaign for the presidency, and on the Fome Zero (Zero Hunger) program, Brazil drafted a proposal for a global anti-hunger program funded by a tax on financial transactions, specifically those that were speculative in nature or that involved certain types of merchandise (such as weapons).

Straight off, I said there would certainly be opposition from G8 members on any compulsory receipt mechanism based on a transaction tax (following the example of the Tobin Tax, a charge proposed by the American economist, Nobel laureate and Yale scholar James Tobin in 1981).

I also warned of the low receptiveness of developed countries to proposals to create or expand traditional anti-hunger or poverty instruments within the United Nations. Developed countries tended to show little enthusiasm for UN-administered "funds," which they considered to be inefficient.

I suggested that a more effective approach would be to work on ideas that already had the approval of the developed nations, such as the International Financing Facility, suggested by British Chancellor of the Exchequer Gordon Brown, and the Millennium Challenge Account (MCA), announced by President George Bush at the Monterrey meeting in 2002.

The MCA, for example, was an assistance program for poorer nations, those with annual per capita earnings of less than US$1,435. Another criterion for eligibility could be having received aid from the International Development Association. Brazil would automatically not qualify for a program of this kind, but the northeastern region of the country might be eligible, as would other regions and social groups elsewhere. I suggested that the government use its US and UK embassies to gauge the level of receptiveness that there would be to such a proposal and to start preparing for dialogue with the respective heads of state.

However, the Brazilian government decided to run with its proposal to tax financial transactions and arms deals to raise funds for a global anti-hunger and anti-poverty program. As was only to be expected, no such program came to fruition, given the difficulties of its application and a lack of political support from the developed nations.

The US idea, on the other hand, was approved by the financial institutions, and the Washington government pressed ahead with the MCA, albeit under the slightly changed title of Millennium Challenge Corporation (MCC). Ambassador John Danilovich, the US representative in Brazil, accepted the invitation to be the first leader of the entity.

It is perhaps worth remembering an episode that occurred at the beginning of the G8 meeting and which was telling with regard to the future attitudes Lula would take in order to assert Brazil's self-esteem. At the first meeting with the leaders of the developed nations, Bush came into the room and all the heads of state stood up, except Lula, who remained seated. "If no one stands up when I enter the room, why should I stand up for the US president?" asked the Brazilian president. It's a question perhaps best answered by a psychologist.

CHAPTER 5

Being Ambassador in Washington

I BELONG TO A GENERATION of diplomats that reached posts of the highest level in Brazil and abroad after first acquiring the experience and maturity indispensable to the successful fulfillment of the missions with which we were entrusted. My appointment as ambassador to the United States was the culmination of a whole career of hard work, and it was, without doubt, my biggest challenge yet.

From Ambassador in London to Ambassador in Washington

For over thirty years, I held leadership positions in the government and economic sectors at the Ministry for Foreign Affairs. As executive-secretary of the Trade Commission for Eastern European Countries (Coleste) between 1976 and 1983, I was responsible for Brazilian economic and trade relations with the communist bloc. I also held the post of liaison officer to the Congress in 1984. Outside the Itamaraty, I had two professional experiences which I consider particularly enriching: the first was on the Debureaucratization Program to the Presidency, in 1985, and the second was as international secretary to the Finance Minister, in 1986. During the government of José Sarney, having served as chief of staff to Olavo Setúbal, the foreign affairs minister, and as general under-secretary for Multilateral Affairs, I was appointed permanent representative to the Latin American Integration Association (LAIA) in Montevideo.

    During the three years I remained in the post, I participated actively in the integration process then underway in South America. Upon my return to Brazil in 1990, I suggested to Francisco Rezek, then-minister for Foreign Affairs, the creation of the Regional Integration Department, of which I became the first head. Later, I was appointed the first under-secretary-general for Integration, Foreign Trade, and Economic Affairs at the Foreign Ministry and coordinator of the Brazilian Section of Mercosur. When Senator Fernando Henrique Cardoso became foreign minister in 1992, the whole economic area of Itamaraty was unified under my command. Among my most important missions in that capacity was the coordination of the Uruguay Round of talks on the General Agreement on Tariffs and Trade (GATT), which gave rise to the WTO.

In 1994, at the suggestion of Fernando Henrique Cardoso, then finance minister, President Itamar Franco appointed me ambassador to London. In the British capital, I also served as Brazil's representative to the International Organizations for Coffee (ICO), Sugar (ISO) and Cocoa (ICCO), and held a five-year term as president of the Association of Coffee-Producing Countries (ACPC).

I remained in the ambassadorship when Fernando Henrique Cardoso assumed the presidency in 1995 and throughout his first term.

THE INVITATION

Before the elections in 1998, I spoke to President FHC and Minister Luiz Felipe Lampreia and mentioned my interest in serving as ambassador in Washington, should the president assume a second term. On one of his trips to London, FHC commented, with a dose of humor and irony, that "sending Rubens to Washington is easy; the problem is getting Paulo Tarso to leave." He was referring to Paulo Tarso Flecha de Lima, then Brazilian ambassador to the United States.

On January 2, 1999, President FHC rang me at the embassy in London. It was a Saturday, and the day after his inauguration to his second term of office.

Accompanied by my friend, journalist Rosental Calmon Alves—director of the Knight Center for Journalism in the Americas at the University of Austin, Texas, who was visiting us at the time—I was in the Audley, a pub a block away from the residence on Mount Street. Maria Ignez, my wife, rang to inform me of the call. I returned immediately to the residence and phoned the president, who made the anticipated and prestigious invitation for me to assume the post of Brazilian ambassador to the United States.

The appointment proceeded through the necessary channels and was submitted for approval by the Foreign Affairs Commission. At the Senate hearing that approved my nomination, there was, as is usual practice, ample debate on my experience in London, my ideas, and my program for the future post.

Before assuming the ambassadorship in Washington, I met with President FHC in Brasília and received clear instructions to broaden

Brazil's relationship with the United States and to do everything in my power, and in line with Brazil's interests, to diversify and strengthen our bilateral understanding.

With my program to enhance the Brazil–US relationship in the political and commercial fields approved by the President and by Itamaraty, I began my tenure in Washington.

I could not have imagined the magnitude of the challenges that awaited me, nor of the changes and crises that would fill up the 1,782 days I spent as Brazil's representative to the most economically, politically, and militarily powerful and influential country in the world.

Without doubt, being appointed Ambassador to the United States was an extraordinary privilege and the greatest challenge of my career, a mission I had earned in recognition of my work at Itamaraty and at the Brazilian Embassy in London.

To be an ambassador in Washington, the most prestigious foreign post to which a diplomat from any country outside the US can aspire, is the career dream of most competent and well-prepared diplomats, but it is not always a realizable one. The appointment depends not only on qualifications, but also on a series of professional and personal circumstances, including, of course, a window of opportunity.

I believe my performance in London, in both the financial area and in the promotion of Brazil abroad, had done much to put the British capital on the agenda of the Brazilian government. During the 1999–2000 crisis, our economic authorities were invited to attend a series of official meetings and other conversations and debates with the British financial sector. Throughout the FHC government's privatization program, the Brazilian embassy in London gave total support to the Ministers Sérgio Motta and Pedro Malan, and to the president of the Central Bank, Gustavo Franco, in organizing meetings with the European financial community. Our most constant endeavor during those years was to help dispel doubts as to the viability of the Brazilian economy at that time.

During my ambassadorship in Britain, I made contact with the leader of the Labor Party, Tony Blair, who expressed interest in meeting the sociologist and presidential candidate Fernando Henrique Cardoso. On one of the president's visits to London, a meeting was arranged between the two at the Embassy residence.

The Labour Party's historic victory over the Conservatives in 1997, which I witnessed in England, enabled Tony Blair to introduce his "Third Way," a political movement that sought some middle ground between Marxism and capitalism.

Soon after Blair came to power, FHC was invited to join this group, whose members also included the then-president of the United States, Bill Clinton. *In loco*, I was able to see the extent to which Fernando Henrique, who was only beginning his "presidential diplomacy," was already widely known and respected as a sociologist by the European academic milieu. His government had gained a reputation abroad for having stabilized the economy and vanquished inflation. Furthermore, the attunement among the three leaders generated substantial good will toward Brazil, which made my job easier in London and, later, in Washington.

ARRIVAL

My wife and I arrived in Washington in June 1999, nearly six months after the official end of my term in London. Ambassador Paulo Tarso Flecha de Lima, whom I was to succeed in the US, had stayed on longer in the post while waiting for the previous occupant to vacate the embassy in Rome, his new mission.

Leaving London was not easy, emotionally speaking, as it was a city in which I had lived at different times throughout my life. First, for six years back in the 1960s, as embassy secretary and deputy consul; then, after my marriage, when I had two children there and defended my master's degree thesis at the London School of Economics; and, finally, two decades later, when I was able to return, for another five and half years, as Brazilian ambassador.

After a brief stay in Paris, on one hot summer's afternoon we arrived at the embassy residence on Massachusetts Avenue, where we were received by the diplomatic and administrative staffs.

Washington is a bureaucratic city with very special characteristics. Because Maria Ignez had lived in Brasília for a total of seventeen years, and I had lived there for twenty-three (although not consecutively), moving back to a federal district after major cosmopolitan hubs like London and São Paulo was not as strange as it might otherwise have been.

It was quite emotional for Maria Ignez to find herself in a house that had once been occupied by her father, the diplomat Sérgio Corrêa da Costa, between 1983 and 1986, and by her grandfather, the politician Oswaldo Aranha, who served as ambassador to Washington from 1933 to

1938, both in the company of her mother and grandmother. She was, therefore, the third generation of women in her family to assume the role of ambassadress and live in that house. After I assumed the post, it did not take long for that curious coincidence to make it into the social pages of the Washington newspapers. When asked about how such a coincidence had come to pass, I replied, jokingly, that the women in Maria Ignez's family knew how to choose a husband.

PRESENTING CREDENTIALS

The presentation of credentials is the inaugural act of an ambassador's work and involves delivering into the hands of the president of the receiving nation a letter from the head of state of the sending nation granting diplomatic accreditation to the bearer. American pragmatism and objectivity was already apparent to me from the ceremony.

Unlike in England, where protocol tends to follow far older rituals, complete with horse-drawn carriage and a meeting with the Queen, in the US, everything is streamlined. The Department of State sends a limousine to pick up the ambassadors and the car is carefully checked for security upon arrival at the White House. Once inside, and after taking various corridors and crossing numerous rooms, the ambassadors are received by the President in the Oval Office, normally in small groups.

On the eve of the presentation of my credentials, in a telephone call with FHC, the president asked me to invite Clinton, on his behalf, to visit Brazil. During the ceremony, I ended up spending ten minutes alone with the US leader, seven more than the protocol allows. After receiving my credentials, a very pleasant Clinton lavished praise on FHC and Ruth Cardoso and revealed that he already knew me by name, as a friend we have in common had spoken highly of me and of my personal connection with Fernando Henrique. The friend in question was Mack McLarty, chief of staff during Clinton's first term. I extended the president's invitation to visit Brazil and Clinton not only expressed his thanks, but spoke positively of the possibility to his National Security advisor, Sandy Berger.

Having Clinton's sympathy was a positive factor in my relationship with staff at the president's office. After leaving the government, McLarty became Clinton's envoy to the Americas and resumed his successful career as a businessman.

On the first meeting with the American president, it is customary for ambassadors to prepare a speech and the president, a response, although, in practice, these texts are normally exchanged, but not read. The speech I presented at the White House, entitled *Mission Statement*, summarized my plan of action, outlined my projects for the embassy and transmitted Brazil's interest in broadening and diversifying its bilateral relations with the United States, while also referring to Brazil's growing standing worldwide.

In the United States, a newly-arrived ambassador is advised not to meet officially with ministers or members of Congress before the presentation of his credentials. However, necessities of work and sometimes the delay in scheduling the date for the presentation of credentials mean that, more often than not, this tradition is ignored—as was the case with me.

Four days after my arrival in Washington, in a gesture of deference to Brazil, the representative of protocol at the State Department scheduled a visit so that I could present a copy of my credentials. As Secretary of State Madeleine Albright was absent, I was received by her interim, Strobe Talbott, a journalist and academic who had a distinguished career as a diplomat and presently presides over the Brookings Institution.

Talbott and I had an agreeable conversation in which we discussed some initiatives to boost the bilateral relationship. I mentioned my plans, the work I had done in London, the programs in place for the embassy, and President FHC's express desire to strengthen Brazil's ties with the United States.

Among other themes, such as the real conditions in certain South American countries, we spoke at length about the situation in Central America and the US position on various episodes in that region. Off the cuff, but in a way that is perhaps indicative of the routine fashion in which superpowers deal with serious issues, Talbott turned to a diplomatic advisor and asked: "Remind me, when was our intervention in the Dominican Republic?" The secretary could not recall that it was in 1965, an episode in which the Brazilian military government not only supported the US, but even sent troops.

The Agenda

When I arrived in Washington in June 1999, my first concern was to decide the mission I would set for the embassy, a choice that would also determine our priorities and the instruments of work.

At the time, Brazil was in the process of normalizing its relations with the international financial community after three major crises

(Mexico, Asia, and Russia), so economic-financial-commercial dialogue with the United States seemed to me the natural priority.

Later, in view of the economic and political uncertainty in Brazil on the eve of the 2002 elections, set against the backdrop of an economic policy predicated on fiscal adjustments, the curbing of inflation, and the resumption of growth, it became increasingly important to keep information flowing about what was going on in Brazil. The recovery of foreign trust and credibility was something that had to be imparted.

In this context, my immediate goal was to broaden the contact and deepen the relationship the embassy maintained with the US government and Congress, as well as with the universities, think tanks, international and private financial institutions, and the media. The aim was to make the embassy a proactive interlocutor in what we considered to be priority sectors: Congress, the financial sector (private banks, international financial institutions), foreign trade (promotion of exports and the defense of concrete interests), defense, universities and schools, the media and NGOs (human rights and the environment).

All of this was based on a set of factors that justified the effort:

- asymmetry in Brazil's relationship with the world's sole super-power and syntony between our interests and perceptions;
- priority of bilateral relations with the United States within the context of Brazilian foreign policy;
- importance of the United States as Brazil's main trade and investment partner;
- excellence in the phase in our bilateral relations, facilitated by a special relationship between FHC and Bill Clinton, and between Minister Luiz F. Lampreia and Secretary of State Madeleine Albright;
- Brazil's relevance to the US in terms of private investment and foreign trade (at the time, Brazil was among Washington's top-ten strategic partners);
- low priority of South America and relative ignorance about Brazil on the part of economic policymakers in the US.

When I arrived in Washington, there were 194 embassies there. Over the first few months, I noticed the clear disparities that existed in the treatment dispensed to foreign embassies. Those representing the major industrial powers—such as Britain, which enjoys a historically privileged position—had ready access to the US authorities. A second tier, the so-called rogue states, also received special treatment in contact with the government as their ambassadors tended to be called in to discuss specific or "problematic" issues. The representatives of the remaining 180 or so embassies had to wrangle for visibility and recognition. Brazil, without major political problems with the United States and not being a threat to its national security, belonged to this last group.

In light of that, I endeavored to expand the embassy's network of contacts as much as possible, so that Washington would begin to identify Brazil as an important interlocutor for the United States, and thus set it apart from the rest.

In the globalized world, in which communication is instantaneous and presidential and ministerial visits are multiplied, there is enormous competition for space in the media, in the cultural milieu, and in access to the academic community.

The ambassador in Washington has to be up-to-the-minute not only on events in the home and host countries, but on developments worldwide, hence the importance of cultivating local sources and of maintaining intensive dialogue with the authorities and the media.

In the face of all these challenges, I assumed the post fully aware that the dispute for space and influence would be one of the embassy's main lines of action, and its raison d'être. I began my ambassadorship assured that the primary motivation of our endeavors had to be the defense and promotion of the Brazilian national interest.

My arrival in Washington coincided with the end of the Clinton government and the city was already in full campaign mode. The US was experiencing a period of major affluence, with society brimming with wealth, the economy growing at 3 percent per annum, the balance of payments in a healthy state, and the nation running a budgetary surplus.

The first week in the capital was spent in meetings with the embassy staff and the military attaches. I wanted to get up to speed not only on matters in progress, but also set the coordinates for my management, and start dispensing instructions to my team. From the very beginning, it was clear that the team of accredited diplomats was apprehensive that the arrival of the new ambassador would come with a heavier workload and an accelerated pace. At those first meetings with the embassy staff, we went over the strategy for the future, which aimed to invigorate certain sectors at the chancery and to create others to handle public diplomacy and Congressional relations.

The activities the embassy was to pursue, and report on periodically, were defined in detail and registered in new directives.

Among the initial priorities were increased contact with the American authorities, an emphasis on economy and trade, and development of a public diplomacy program involving seminars and meetings on Brazil. I also worked to strengthen our presence in Congress and establish a solid relationship with the academic community.

I always made a point of surrounding myself with competent diplomats so as to ensure that I received quality counsel. My team responded to the challenge with dynamism and efficiency and it is to them that I owe the concrete results obtained for Brazil during my term. I cannot fail to mention the minister-counselors who helped me lead the embassy over the nearly five years I spent in Washington: Regis Arslanian, Roberto Jaguaribe, Paulo Roberto de Almeida, Marcos Galvão, Evandro Didonet, and Carlos Alfredo Lazary Teixeira, excellent diplomatic staff who continue to serve Itamaraty and Brazil with the same brilliance they showed during my ambassadorship.

Unlike most posts, Washington deals almost entirely with highly sensitive and politically delicate issues that demand the direct involvement of the president of the republic or ministers of state. As such, it is imperative that the ambassador have the full trust of the president and foreign minister and direct, unimpeded access to them, as matters of urgency and public impact can arise without a moment's notice.

That is how things were with President FHC, the Ministers Luiz Felipe Lampreia and Celso Lafer, and, later, with President Lula and Minister Celso Amorim.

Beginning with my arrival in Washington, taking into account Itamaraty's interests, I determined that the embassy would systematically cover the main themes in US–Latin American relations, particularly Colombia, Venezuela, Mexico, Cuba, and the Southern Cone. Much of this was done through contact with the Department of State, the Treasury, the Pentagon, Congress, the Latin American diplomatic community and the various think tanks, which are important shapers of opinion on foreign policy in Washington and fulfill a very singular role.

The attraction Washington holds over authorities of all sorts is one of the facets of life in the US capital. With each passing day, presidents, prime ministers, and high-ranking officials sweep in and out of town, meeting with their counterparts in the US government. The think tanks avail themselves of these visits to organize seminars, meetings, and lectures that are a precious source of information in diplomatic activities. The presence of diplomats from the Brazilian embassy at meetings arranged to debate the situation in the western hemisphere, US foreign policy, and the foremost global themes was a major help to us in collecting information and analyzing developments throughout the continent and worldwide.

On many occasions, the embassy supported our authorities at meetings with their US counterparts. Our ministers of finance and planning and the president of the Brazilian Central Bank visit Washington periodically for meetings with the World Bank, the IDB, and IMF. The finance minister and president of the Central Bank, in particular, meet regularly with the secretaries of the Treasury and the FED.

When looking for loans from the IDB or World Bank, the state governors and their finance secretaries would ask for our support, and we received delegations from almost every state in the Federation.

The embassy always accompanied these Brazilian authorities on their meetings with the US government and with the capital's multilateral institutions.

The constant presence of some government member or other national figure in Washington made the post a particularly privileged vantage point from which to observe regional and global themes as they unfolded and to gauge the political and economic temperature in Brazil.

From this perspective, and mindful that there is more to the United States than just Washington, my diplomatic endeavors included travel and personal contacts outside the capital.

I had heard much talk of an ultra-exclusive gentlemen's club called Bohemian Grove, located amongst the best vineyards of the Napa Valley, California, where a yearly meeting was held among the key figures of the US establishment. Bohemian Grove is the wealthiest private club in America, with 2,500 members including Republican politicians like Henry Kissinger and George Schultz, the CEOs and top executives of companies and the press, and members of powerful traditional families, such as the Bush clan and the Rockefellers. Members and their guests gather there, informally, at campgrounds nestled among some 2,700 acres of century-old sequoias.

I was invited to one of these camps by Howard Leach, then US ambassador in Paris, to whom I had been introduced by my friend John Danilovich, former US ambassador to Costa Rica and, later, to Brazil. Howard Leach and his wife, Gretchen, visited us at the residence in

Washington prior to assuming the post in France, where, on more than one occasion, they received us at the beautiful US embassy on Faubourg Saint-Honoré.

Howard Leach has a seven- or eight-room chalet at the Bohemian Grove campsite. Like all the other chalets, this simple wooden construction has rather precarious installations, a shared bathroom, and beds that resemble military bunks.

Meals are served in a dining hall, and the gathering lasts for four or five days, with a weekend in the middle. The program includes concerts in the gardens, discussions of current political themes, and many informal encounters that allow those in attendance to rub shoulders with major figures from the government and business community. I attended lectures by Schultz and Kissinger in an open-air conference space; had dinner with numerous politicians, Congressmen, government staffers, then-Secretary for Trade Don Evans, and Karl Rove, a close friend of George W. Bush, the architect of his rise to power and one of the most influential figures in his administration—and all this without the slightest luxury or formality. It is part of the club's philosophy that the country life be lived to the letter, so it is not unusual to see people urinating in public, irrigating the park's great sequoias. As far as I know, no other Brazilian ambassador has participated in this adventure, and I was told that foreigners are rarely received at the club.

First Contacts

One of my first visits upon my arrival in Washington was to the Western Hemisphere Secretary, Ambassador Peter Romero, a man with close ties to the Cuban lobby in the United States and therefore largely ignored by the Democratic Party. He exercised his functions on a precarious and interim basis, having never succeeded in being approved by the Senate. His radical and party-political opinions were always controversial.

Before we discussed certain themes of common interest and my desire to broaden and improve dialogue with the US, I was taken aback by Romero's criticism of my predecessor, Ambassador Paulo Tarso Flecha de Lima. The secretary, visibly irritated, seemed convinced that the former ambassador had breached his trust by not adequately reporting conversations with the State Department to Brasília. As a new arrival in the city and not yet in a position to assess the observations and the visible irritation of the secretary, which struck me as exaggerated, I was vehement in defending the ambassador's professionalism. I gave no credence to Romero's comments, but, given the delicate nature of the situation, I thought it best not to register them in the Embassy's annals, though I did convey the content of the conversation verbally to Minister Luiz Felipe Lampreia.

To be succeeding Ambassador Paulo Tarso Flecha de Lima—former secretary-general of Itamaraty and one of the most highly-regarded diplomats of his generation—for the second time in my career was a major professional challenge in itself.

Peter Romero's comments reinforced my conviction that the foremost concern of an ambassador should be to expand the scope of dialogue, earn the trust of one's interlocutors, and instill credibility. In order to achieve that, I would have to keep contacts and information sources open and unobstructed.

Part of the work of any embassy today, especially those in strategic countries, is to accrue value to the information that the home nation's foreign office can obtain by its own means. To that end, I had the embassy staff draw up reports that went beyond the news that could be found pretty much anywhere and in near-real time.

Unlike the British, who are reserved and formal, Americans do not hesitate to pick up the phone at any hour of the day for a quick consultation or exchange of ideas. I soon realized that life would be much easier if I started to do the same.

On my second day in Washington, I received a phone call from Christopher Meyer, the British ambassador, inviting me for coffee at his embassy, located near our own, on Massachusetts Avenue. Upon receiving me in his office, Meyer said: "Ambassador, it is a pleasure to meet you. You must have been very popular in London, given the sheer number of e-mails, phone calls, and letters I've received introducing you. It made me curious to meet you." Some years later, Meyer wrote a highly controversial memoir in which he gave details of his time in Washington and his divergences and disputes with and within the Foreign Office and with influential members of Tony Blair's ministerial cabinet.

As at many other posts, in Washington diplomatic missions tend to huddle together in regional groups, such as the Asian, the European, and the Latin American. The latter group, nicknamed Grula, met monthly over lunch to discuss subjects of mutual interest and to exchange information. In my second week in Washington, I had my first meeting with the group. The ambassadors habitually discussed how to strengthen the Latin American lobby and the Hispanic presence in the United States.

Mexico and the Central American countries have very solid institutions in this respect, the strongest amongst them being La Raza, an association set up to defend the interests of the Mexican community, which the Grula people referred to as Hispanic rather than Latin American. I decided to stay quiet, and not interfere, until one of the ambassadors asked me what the problem was; why hadn't I given my thoughts on how to fortify the Hispanic lobby? I replied that, as Brazil is not an Hispanic country, I didn't feel it was really my place. The other ambassadors hurried to correct themselves, saying that the discussion was on the *Latin American* lobby. Be that as it may, it was clear to me that Brazil did not have much to contribute in that forum.

Another curious meeting I had during my first weeks in Washington was at a lunch I was invited to by Lincoln Gordon, US ambassador to Brazil between 1961 and 1966. The lunch was at the Cosmos, a private club in downtown Washington, obviously modeled on the old gentlemen's clubs in England. Gordon told me that he was preparing a book on Brazil, in which he intended to clarify what had really happened during the military coup of 1964. In Brazil, the abiding impression was that the ambassador had participated in the coup as an intermediary between the Washington government and the Brazilian military, and that he had even offered the support of US troops, if needed.

At that lunch, Gordon wanted to explain that he had had no prior knowledge of the coup and could not be accused of having conspired about, much less influenced, the course of events. He gave me his version of what happened on that dramatic day of March 31, 1964.

Gordon told me that, on that day, he was following a speech by João Goulart at the Clube Naval on TV and the radio, when Secretary of State Dean Rusk called him on the phone for the "first and only time in four years," worried about the political situation in Brazil. Later, Gordon learned of the coup from General Vernon Walters, the US military attaché to Brazil since 1962. Walters knew Portuguese and had ties to the Brazilian military, especially General Mascarenhas de Morais. He was also a good friend of Colonel (and future president) Humberto Castelo Branco, whom he had met while working as an interpreter and official liaison between the Brazilian Expeditionary Force and US army in Italy during the Second World War.

Gordon went on to tell me about his telephone conversation with President Lyndon Johnson, who called him the following day looking for information on what had transpired.

On this, our first meeting, Ambassador Gordon said that it was important to him that Brazil and the Brazilian people knew, through my intermediation, that "the American embassy played no part whatsoever in the revolutionary movement of 1964." In his book *Brazil's Second Chance: En Route Toward the First World*, Gordon is categorical in saying that the first he knew about the coup was after it had occurred, on March 31.

It is hard not to harbor doubts about the veracity of what I was told that day. Official US Government documents from the time, released by the Department of State and the Lyndon Johnson Library in March 2011, contradict Lyndon Gordon's version of events and reveal his active participation in arranging the supply of arms, fuel, ammunition, and even money so that the CIA could assist forces opposing João Goulart.

Later, with his book completed, Gorden asked if he could hold the launch at the embassy, to which I agreed as a gesture of courtesy.

On the occasion, the Washington correspondent with *Gazeta Mercantil*, Paulo Moreira Leite, called me to say how incensed he was that the embassy had agreed to host the event and that he planned to write critically of the decision in the newspaper. However, democratically, and without further problems, other than the journalist's reaction, I held the event, of which the secretary-general of the Presidency, Minister Aloysio Nunes Ferreira, had been informed. I must also remember the fraternal welcome I received from the President of the IDB, Enrique Iglesias. We had been in frequent contact since back in the days when I was chief of staff to Minister Setúbal and Iglesias was foreign minister for Uruguay, and, later, during my time as permanent representative to the regional trade organization (LAIA), in Montevideo. Soon after my arrival, Iglesias organized a highly representative meeting with some forty influential figures in Washington at the Inter-American Dialogue, directed by Peter Hakim, so that I could get an overall view right from the beginning. Given this opportunity, I spoke publicly for the first time about the agenda the embassy would pursue and received some very creative suggestions on how to do that.

The Wife's Role

In all diplomatic functions, but particularly in the embassy to the White House, the role of the ambassador's wife is extremely important. As Washington is an administrative city, the social scene is basically composed of members of Congress, the government, the courts, the media, and the thousands of card-carrying lobbyists.

The fact that the Department of State is encouraged to create women's clubs in Washington so that the ambassadors' wives can gather socially is an illustration of the Americans' practical spirit. Once a month, the women meet for lunch with the wives of local personalities and authorities, which can open doors for the ambassador to people of relevance to his mission.

If the wife of a high-ranking official makes friends with an ambassador's wife, she will certainly want her husband to choose a dinner or event at the embassy over the myriad other invitations that rain in by the day.

The Brazilian ambassador's wife is a member of the Number One Club, alongside the wives of the ambassadors from Britain, France, Italy, Russia, Egypt, Jordan, Argentina and Senegal. It is one of the most hotly disputed clubs and its members traditionally include the wives of the vice-president, some secretaries of state, such as defense and trade, the presidents of the Library of Congress, top-notch White House staff, well-known journalists and newspaper chiefs, and the directors of prestigious museums, such as the National Gallery.

It is an unwritten rule that if a women belonged to one of these clubs under a previous administration, she should return to that same club if or when her husband was appointed to another important position in Washington D.C. Another rule was that a wife should leave the club as soon as her husband vacates his post.

A concrete example of these rules in action concerned Joyce Rumsfeld, the wife of Donald Rumsfeld, the secretary of defense under George W Bush. She had been a member of another club in Washington, but after her husband's appointment as secretary of defense, she accepted an invitation to lunch at the Number One Club, of which her predecessor, Janet Cohen, had been a member. However, news reached her of the disapproval this caused among the women at her former club and she ended up deciding not to participate in either.

Maria Ignez witnessed Joyce Rumsfeld's disappointment at being unable to join the Number One Club and decided to arrange a lunch for the club's cast-offs, which included certain widows, such as the wife of the recently deceased journalist Don Evans. It was a kind gesture and it enchanted the defense secretary's wife. Although Brazil had not supported the war in Iraq and had therefore not been added to Donald Rumsfeld's good book, Joyce always treated Maria Ignez kindly, with some nice personal gestures, such as occurred after the death of Sérgio Vieira de Mello. Later, on the eve of our departure, in addition to a personal memento, Joyce presented my wife with a copy of the book *The Substance of Style*, on which she wrote "To Maria Ignez, whose friendship I cherish. You are the substance of style. Affectionately yours, Joyce Rumsfeld."

Maria Ignez made some good friends at the Number One Club, including Karyn Frist, wife of Senate Majority Leader Bill Frist. Some years after our return to Brazil, Karyn invited Maria Ignez to participate in a book in which some prominent women—including Hillary Clinton, Condoleezza Rice, and Barbara Bush—wrote about their relationships with their fathers. In 2006, Maria Ignez returned to Washington for the launch of *Love You, Daddy Boy* at a gathering of the authors and other members of society, held at the Frist residence.

On the occasion of the presidential visit in March 2001, it was my wife's suggestion to hold a meeting between Ruth Cardoso and Laura Bush. Ruth was a little reticent at first, because she was close to the Clintons, but she ended up appreciating the visit to the White House. Accompanied by Mary Lafer and Maria Ignez, she was received in the Yellow Room, on the second floor of the private wing. Ruth introduced Mary Lafer to Laura Bush as a Professor of Ancient Greek at the University of São Paulo. Laura Bush did not seem much impressed, but her brother-in-law Neil, also present, mentioned that he had been to Greece. Mary asked which parts he had visited and what he had liked the most. For those who know the American style, his answer will come as no surprise; the president's brother said that he had seen practically nothing of the country, because, for reasons of security, he had spent the whole time aboard ship with his father, George Bush. For her part, Laura Bush chatted about her first weeks as First Lady and took the three Brazilians on a tour of the residential wing, and spoke of the changes she planned to make to the décor.

At Lunches and Dinners

The residence, a few dozen yards away from the chancery, functioned as a sort of support wing for diplomatic actions. Very often, the day would begin with a working breakfast. Sometimes together, but occasionally separately, Maria Ignez and I would receive our American guests, members of the diplomatic corps, Brazilian authorities, and friends over lunches and dinners.

More so than in other posts, in Washington, what counts the most for an ambassador is to have access and influence. The building process that translates into prestige before the local government and society is largely done through contacts made and deepened on occasions at which the interests of the represented nation are expounded and defended, and, in my case, this often occurred at the residence.

According to the chancery records, between June 1999 and April 2004, Maria Ignez and I received, on average, some three thousand people a year for breakfasts, lunches, dinners, and receptions at the residence on Massachusetts Avenue, not to mention the dozens of official Brazilian guests who stayed there on visits to the US capital.

Within days of our arrival, as we had been recommended by friends in London, we were invited to dinner at the house of the millionaire Elizabeth Smith-Bagley, US ambassador to Portugal during President Clinton's first term. This small and relaxed dinner party was a welcome opportunity for us to meet a group of US Congressmen, high-ranking White House officials, including Hillary Clinton's private secretary, and influential journalists with whom we soon became friends.

Obviously, for ambassadors, the more quality contacts they have, the better they can perform their function. In Washington, the foreign ambassadors compete for this privilege, and the competition is stiff. Our circle of friends gradually expanded, and the turn out en masse of authorities from the White House, the government, and Congress at our farewell reception was, for us, proof of a mission accomplished.

Late in 2002, at a reception to celebrate the decoration of General Norman Schwarzkopf, commander-in-chief of the US troops during the Gulf War in 1991, I spoke with Staff General of the United States Army, General Henry Hugh Shelton, about the preparations for the invasion in Iraq and the likely results of the apparently imminent offensive. He told me that part of the cost of the war would be covered by revenues from the sale of Iraqi oil and that oil prices in general would come down after the ouster of Saddam Hussein and the end of his regime.

In contrast to London, where protocol is rigid and based on precise rules, the sometimes unexpected behavior of the Americans was one curious aspect of life in Washington. Our staff even caught guests swapping placement cards on the dinner tables so they could sit beside some more interesting friend. Again, unlike the British, who appreciate culture and good conversation, most Americans seem to view receptions and dinners primarily as an opportunity to network. It was fun to see how, in London, royalty and foreign authorities are treated with special deference, but in the United States this VIP treatment is dispensed more liberally and ostensibly to the power set of the moment, the millionaires and possible donors to charity organizations, cultural institutions, and political campaigns, which is not the case with ambassadors.

On a certain occasion, after dinner at the residence, I noticed Vernon Jordan, a well-known lawyer, close friend to the Clintons and one of the most influential members of the black community, gazing at length into my cigar box, as if unsure which to go for. Noting his hesitation, I went over and offered him a pure Cuban cigar from my pocket, which he took immediately. The box on the table contained only cigars from the Dominican Republic and Costa Rica (good ones), as, in light of the US embargo against all things Cuban, I figured it might not be politically correct to just lay them out.

In addition to the routine official events, the residence also hosted decoration ceremonies for Brazilian and foreign personalities. It was in the magnificent French salon on the first floor, where mirrors line some of the wainscoting, creating an infinite effect (or *mis en abyme*, in French), that I bestowed the Orders of the Southern Cross, Rio Branco, and Merit upon the likes of maestro Lorin Maazel, Under Secretary of State Tom Pickering, Governor Kenneth MacKay, Ambassador Mickey Kantor, the former USTR Arturo Valenzuela, then responsible for the Brazilian program at Georgetown University, and, posthumously, the banker Edmond Safra, represented on the occasion by his widow, Lili, and dozens of other guests.

During our time at the residence, on numerous occasions we hosted Ruth and Fernando Henrique Cardoso, both during and after FHC's presidency. Other frequent guests were Pedro Malan and his wife, Catarina, and Armínio Fraga, given the various meetings he had to attend at the World Bank, IDB, and IMF. FHC's Vice-President Marco Maciel stayed with us once, and José Serra two or three times as Minister for Health when he came to Washington to defend his positions on intellectual property rights over medications and to have Brazil taken off the US watch list for the imposition of possible trade sanctions, and again after running in the 2002 elections, when he spent some months at Cornell. Others who stayed at the embassy were Aécio Neves, as president of the Senate, and Geraldo Alckmin, governor of São Paulo, who, on the occasion, decorated me with the Order of Ipiranga, the highest honor bestowed by my home state. President Lula's minister of Mines and Energy, Dilma Rousseff, and the mayor of São Paulo, Marta Suplicy, also stayed at the residence.

One of the stories that has stuck in my mind involved Senator Eduardo Suplicy, a long-time friend of mine who stayed with us when he was invited to participate in meetings on the minimum wage, his favorite subject, at the American union AFL-CIO and the American Institute. On the Saturday before he was to return to Brazil, we went to see the documentary film *The Fog of War*, about the life of Robert McNamara, US defense secretary during the Vietnam War. Impressed by what he saw in the film—especially the secretary's willingness to participate in over a dozen public audiences at Congress, at a time when, back in Brazil, some of the figures involved in the *Mensalão* (big monthly pay-out) scandal were refusing to do just that—Suplicy decided to seek out McNamara. I told him that I did not have his telephone number at home, but that I could get it from the chancery on Monday. But Suplicy, unwilling to wait, and on the spur of one of his surprising whims, asked me for the telephone directory. After trying various McNamaras, he finally found a Robert that his intuition told him was the one he was looking for. He left a message on the answering machine identifying himself as a senator of the Republic of Brazil and requesting a meeting. I watched the whole maneuver, a little incredulous as to its final result. However, on Monday, the day he was scheduled to leave, a euphoric Suplicy called me at the office to say that McNamara had returned his call and invited him to a meeting at his house. However, as he could not reschedule his return to Brazil, and to his immense frustration, he'd had to decline.

To mark the release of the film *Oriundi*, we held a dinner at the residence to honor the director, Ricardo Bravo, Anthony Quinn, the star, and his wife, the widow of the author Jorge Luis Borges. The event was held at the behest of Milena Gaviria, the wife of the secretary general of the OAS, César Gaviria, who was responsible for the Festival of Latin American Cinema.

We were also visited by various friends from London, such as Micheline and Sean Connery; Princess Esra Jah; Ira Furstenberg; the Prince and Princess Michael and Marie Christine of Kent; Luce and Winston Churchill, grandson of the English statesman and regular guest speaker; and James and Shirley Sherwood, who had come to Washington to exhibit his botanical drawings at the Smithsonian.

In relation to the Brazilian government, especially from 2003 on, various people on official business to Washington wanted to save on hotels and asked to stay at the embassy, which was not always possible.

Yet not even the life of a Washington ambassador is all official commitments and routine. In addition to being a privileged observer of the way of life in another country, an ambassador in the US capital has his fair share of unexpected and memorable experiences.

One curious if not surreal adventure was a weekend trip to Florida with some ambassador colleagues to attend the traditional and glitzy Red Cross Ball in Palm Beach. At the behest of the organization, the tycoon Donald Trump kindly agreed to give the group of diplomats a round-trip ride on his private plane. However, to general surprise, and bordering on discourtesy, the billionaire spent almost the entire journey locked in a private cabin with his new girlfriend.

As was customary, we were accommodated in the houses of local businesspeople who vied to have the ambassadors from the most important countries as their guests. There was a whole ritual to follow on this gala evening at the famous Breakers Hotel. The attire, as in the English Court of Saint James, was tailcoat and decorations. On arrival at the main hall, each ambassador and his wife was escorted by impeccably uniformed guards and had their names read out, under the spotlight, as they took their places for the official photo.

After a weekend of lunches, dinners, and sporting events, we boarded Trump's plane to return to Washington. The weather forecast was for rain followed by snowstorms. It was the middle of winter and we were informed that it was snowing in Washington and New York. Shortly after take-off, we were shocked to learn that, for reasons of security, we would not be able to land in the capital, but would have to fly on to John F. Kennedy airport in New York. The reality, however, was quite another. The bad weather was but a ruse so that Donald Trump could see to some business or other in the city. The result was an exhausted and grumpy bunch of ambassadors abandoned in the airport; we had to ride the bus back to Washington, where we would only arrive four hours later. The most disgruntled amongst us was the Israeli ambassador, who found himself stripped of his customary security guards. The only thing for it was to take it all in good spirits and mark it down as one more story for the memoirs. Some days later, however, the Washington newspapers managed to transform the boorishness of the famous billionaire into joke-of-the-week.

Lula's Ambassador

Toward the end of 2002, the smooth transition from the FHC adminis-tration to the Lula government was a genuine demonstration of political maturity in Brazil. The coordination of this civilized handover fell to Chief of Staff Pedro Parente, in charge of fulfilling the outgoing Presi-dent's express request that the Brazilian Workers' Party be given open and harmonious access to the halls of power. The personal and frank conversations between FHC and Lula contributed to this atmosphere of understanding between those on their way in and those on their way out.

Indirectly, I ended up involved in this transition. My job was to ease the minds of the authorities in Washington, who were afraid that Lula was going to steer the economy off the course that the FHC government had set for it.

Even before the 2002 Brazilian elections, faced with the significant prospects of the opposition winning, I had decided to retire from the diplomatic corps of Itamaraty, a request I filed in December 2002.

Given my connections with the FHC government, it would be only natural for the new president to recall me from Brazil's most important foreign post. Furthermore, my time abroad was approaching the ten-year limit, which would have obliged me to return to secretary of state in Brasília anyway, for a period of two years, in order to qualify for an-other international post.

Having led the embassies in London and Washington, I felt that my career goals had been achieved in full. My mind was made up; it was time to leave Washington and pursue some experience in the private sector.

I had first met President Lula, in passing, in São Paulo some years before. The next time we met was on a visit he made to London, when I was ambassador there. On that occasion, he dined with us at the em-bassy, in the company of Marco Aurélio Garcia, PT's international sec-retary, and Jorge Mattoso, a party advisor. That was the first time we conversed informally. During the electoral campaign in 1998, the em-bassy in London helped some PT envoys to make contact with the Brit-ish government, as we did with other candidates too.

During his initial conversations with Lula in Brasília, President FHC suggested that he keep me on as ambassador in Washington, something I would only learn some time later, from FHC himself. In December 2002, when Lula visited Washington and stayed at the embassy residence, the future finance minister, Antonio Palocci, and the mayor of São Paulo, Marta Suplicy, made the same suggestion.

It was on that same visit, shortly before assembling his cabinet, that the president-elect asked me to stay on as ambassador. I accepted the invitation as a professional challenge, but fully aware that my work would be limited.

The fact that I was remaining in the post under an opposition government was read by the US authorities as a sign that there would be no dramatic rupture or change of course in Brazil–US relations.

My retirement request was already being processed, so when President Lula made my continuation in the post official in January, it was as political ambassador, in other words outside of Itamaraty.

I spent the holidays and New Year in Brazil and, on January 3, 2003, two days after the President's inauguration, I was the first ambassador to meet with Lula at the Government Palace.

I prepared myself to receive the new president's instructions, and our conversation was frank, direct, and lasted for nearly half an hour. In response to my question about how he saw relations with the United States, Lula rolled out some of the metaphors that would become a staple of his public speeches, saying: "I want to play the game. So if I can play with them, I will."

I mentioned the importance of lending continuity to the initiatives introduced by the previous government and of deepening our relationship with the United States in all areas. The new president gave me precise instructions to continue to pursue the course FHC had set.

He asked me what sort of routine contact I had maintained with President FHC and I told him how important it was that an ambassador to a place like Washington have the full trust of the president and foreign minister and the freedom to contact them directly if and when the need arose, day or night. Lula said that I was to continue with that practice and feel free to call him whenever I felt it was convenient or necessary to do so.

President Lula spoke of his justified concern over the situations in Iraq and in Venezuela and told me that he had decided to attend both the Social Forum in Porto Alegre and the Economic Forum in Davos, and that he would deliver the same speech at both. It was an early indication of the pragmatism that would become a defining characteristic of his government.

From his first stay in Washington, still as president-elect, my contact with Lula was always frank and friendly, and throughout the time I served his government in Washington, and even after my return to Brazil, and despite my articles in the *O Estado de S. Paulo* and *O Globo* newspapers, and my critical perceptions on various aspects of his foreign policy and strategy in trade negotiations, I never received anything other than appreciation and cordiality from President Lula.

On that visit to the Planalto, I also spoke with Minister Celso Amorim and Secretary General of Itamaraty Samuel Pinheiro Guimarães about the priorities of the post.

Leaving Washington

It is understandable and indeed to be expected that Minister Celso Amorim would have wanted to appoint someone from his inner circle to the embassy in Washington, and as he gained the trust of the president, he set about gradually replacing the ambassadors that had remained in their posts after the transition, especially those of greater visibility.

In August 2003, when rumors began to appear in the Rio press that Ambassador Roberto Abdenur had been chosen as my replacement, I saw that the time had come to take some action.

That same day I called Minister José Dirceu, Lula's chief of staff, and told him that after forty-two years of service to Itamaraty, the time had come for me to stand aside. I mentioned the story in the newspaper and reiterated my satisfaction at having had the fascinating experience of serving under two different governments in Washington. I then asked him to inform the president of my decision to leave my post. Dirceu said that he had not read the note in the press and that he was unaware of any change planned for Washington. He said that I retained the total trust of the government and that my position was not in jeopardy. However, my decision was made and I asked him to arrange a meeting with the president in New York, during the United Nations General Assembly that September, so that I could tell him in person.

In early September, Ambassador Mauro Vieira, Celso Amorim's cabinet chief, called me to say that the minister wanted to talk to me about his plans for the post.

As requested, I met Lula for a breakfast meeting at the Waldorf Astoria in New York, where the Brazilian delegation was staying during the UN General Assembly.

During a long conversation, I told him that I perfectly understood Minister Celso Amorim's interest in entrusting the most important post in Washington to someone from his inner circle, such as Roberto Abde-nur, who had been Amorim's secretary-general at Itamaraty during the government of Itamar Franco.

I said it was a pity, however, that some had seen fit to plant in-trigues in the press to try to cause friction between myself and Lula's government.

I also told him of my plans to set up a private consultancy firm in São Paulo.

Affable and frank as always, the president reaffirmed his apprecia-tion for me personally and for my work at the embassy, both before the elections and during the first year of his government. He said that Celso Amorim had spoken to him on the matter and of the Minister's plans to overhaul the senior staff at Itamaraty.

During our cordial conversation, President Lula was full of praise for Itamaraty. In a clear attempt to pander to my ego, a trademark of Lula's, he said that, from what he had been able to observe, there were "three important figures" in the Foreign Office: Celso Amorim, Ronaldo Sar-demberg, and me.

In another demonstration of appreciation, Lula invited me to remain with the government as a director at the national development bank (BNDES). I thanked him for the offer, but said that I had really decided to have a go in the private sector.

I said, however, that I did have one request. As I was leaving the post amicably, and the government, from what Lula had said, had been sat-isfied with my work, I asked to be allowed to leave the embassy in the manner that is customary in the United States, in other words, with a fixed date of departure. In Brazil, things tend to be handled differently, with the egress of ministers and high-ranking officials being effective as of notice and the substitute announced forthwith.

The President did not hesitate to agree: my exit would be announced immediately and my congé scheduled for six months' time, or March 31, 2004. The agreement was communicated to Minister Amorim that same day.

I said goodbye to the President and thanked him for his trust and for a year and eight months of his administration. Soon afterwards I met Celso Amorim, who was already apprised of my arrangement with the President. Though my departure had been scheduled for March 2004, he asked me to request an *agrément* for the new ambassador for the end of 2003.

On the same afternoon, still in New York, I informed accredited Brazilian journalists that I would be standing down and expressed my desire for a smooth transition, without speculation concerning political divergences at the helm of the country's most important foreign post.

Back in Washington, I met with my closest collaborators, the minister-counselors Marcos Galvão, Evandro Didonet, Paulo Roberto de Almeida, and Carlos Alfredo Lazary Teixeira, who had recently been appointed to Washington, and informed them that I would be leaving the post.

 From that moment on, I set about planning my definitive return to Brazil and building a new life in São Paulo, a city I had left in the 1960s when I went to study at the Rio Branco Institute in Rio de Janeiro.

In early November, Antonio Palocci, in a gesture of trust and friendship, offered me the top job at the Finance Ministry's Secretariat for International Affairs (SAIN) in the event that I decided to return to Brasília. I would be replacing Otaviano Canuto, designated to the World Bank in Washington. Palocci knew that I had previously held this position and made a point of emphasizing how important the function was. I thanked him for the offer, but repeated what I had told Lula in New York, that the time had come to leave governmental bureaucracy.

On Friday, December 9, I received the request for *agrément* for Roberto Abdenur and, on the following Monday, took the document to the State Department to request its approval of the new appointee.

On February 29, in my last phone conversation in Washington with President Lula, I suggested that he speak to Bush to discuss the political situations in Venezuela, Haiti, and Argentina, as these were areas of concern we shared with the Americans. I also informed him of a visit to Brazil by the Saudi Arabian ambassador, the all-powerful Prince Bandar, who, married to one of the main heiresses to the Saudi royal family, had held the post in Washington for twenty years. I told him that the Ambassador was going to Brazil for talks with Brazilian businesspeople and that he would like to meet the President to discuss investment opportunities of interest to the government in Riad, to which Lula responded positively.

During what was a long phone call, Lula was receptive to my suggestions and said that he would call Bush. He also mentioned that he intended to propose to the American president that he spearhead the global anti-hunger and anti-poverty initiatives himself.

We also commented on the good relationship that the two had

formed, something often mentioned by the US president since their first meeting in Washington, despite their differences of background. President Lula expressed his concern about the presidential elections in the United States, which were to take place that year, and said that he had asked his ministers not to make any statements of preference between the Republicans and Democrats.

Reflecting a perception that was common in the Brazilian official milieu, but which sounded strange coming from a PT leader, the president said that his government had found it easier to work with the Republicans than with the Democrats, who, he said, were tougher on foreign policy and more protectionist economically. It was a conviction borne out not least by the ease with which Bush and Lula communicated, but also by the events of 2009, when Obama, during the first year of his government, was pressured by Congress to block trade negotiations and step up protectionism.

Also during this February phone call, Lula asked me if I would be working with Olavo Setúbal in São Paulo. The President knew of the close bond I had had with the banker and former minister since my time as chief of staff at Itamaraty. I said that Olavo had invited me to be a consultant to Itaú Bank and that I had accepted the offer, though I had my own consultancy as well.

Before leaving the post, I formally asked the federal government's Ethics Council for clarification on how I should proceed, as I intended to begin my private sector activities as quickly as possible. I knew that other government officials had served a period of quarantine after making similar inquiries.

After analyzing the formal correspondence I had sent to the Council, João Geraldo Piquet Carneiro, president of the organization at the time, told me that, as ambassador, I did not need to undergo quarantine and could start planning my return to São Paulo while taking whatever measures I judged necessary.

I decided to go through all these motions not just because I felt it was the right thing to do, but also as a matter of coherency. When I was ambassador to Britain, I suggested to president FHC and to Piquet Carneiro that Brazil should create an Ethics Council along the lines of the one Tony Blair set up when he became British Prime Minister in 1997.

The festival of farewells in Washington began in January, two months before we were to leave. Normally, the process of transfer or recall takes two to three months, but as we had six, there was plenty of time for gestures of friendship from the diplomatic corps, colleagues and close friends.

A farewell lunch was arranged at the Department of State by the secretaries for Latin America and Economic Affairs, two people with whom I had maintained close contact during the time I served in Washington.

Of the many expressions of appreciation, I especially recall a tribute I received at Congress. An American flag was raised in my honor on Capitol Hill, as recognition for my work toward a deeper Brazil–US relationship. It was later sent to me along with a letter from the Congressman Edward Markey, a democrat from Massachusetts.

The farewell reception was held at the embassy on February 23, and was attended by some three hundred guests, including government authorities, members of Congress and the Supreme Court, my friends from the media and the university milieu, and personalities from the local society.

Our departure was registered in the diplomatic columns of the *Washington Post* and *Washington Times*, with comments that placed us among the *diplomat nonpareil*, in other words, those who had made their mark and would be missed. The local press reproduced some of my sayings from down through the years, and in brief farewell speeches, such as: "Brazil is not for beginners"; "In Washington there are two types of people: who is who and who is still who"; and "Brazil is like Texas. We are big. We think we are bigger than we really are, and we are always at odds with the United States."

Among the many dinners we were given at embassies and friends' houses, two were particularly special. The ambassadors of Kuwait, among Washington's biggest hosts, made a point of organizing a dinner in our honor for about a hundred guests, including major government figures, such as Donald Rumsfeld, fellow ambassadors, congressmen and journalists. On this particular night, Maria Ignez told the CNN presenter Wolf Blitzer about the visit Lula planned to make to Washington in March. Blitzer immediately said he would love to interview the president live on his show and asked her if Lula spoke English. As the response was 'no,' Blitzer recognized that, unfortunately, there would be no chance of a Lula interview.

Another farewell dinner was held on March 10—Maria Ignez' birthday—by a group of our closest friends. The party, which was held at a sprawling mansion belonging to one of the couples, was a veritable carnival. The hosts belted out famous Brazilian songs with the lyrics specially rewritten with sweet and funny references to us.

The most symbolic part of the whole farewell was at a gathering of the diplomatic staff, attachés, and administrative personnel at the chancery.

On this occasion, they unveiled a portrait of me in the ambassador's gallery, satisfying a pet aim of mine ever since my arrival, that of seeing myself up there on the wall alongside my predecessors, illustrious public figures since Joaquim Nabuco, who had honored the post, and amongst whom ranked my wife's grandfather and father.

On the day of our departure, March 31, 2004, I left my successor a beautiful new book on Washington embassies and a letter wishing him every success in his mission. Like myself, Roberto Abdenur had begun his career abroad in the 1960s. We had worked together in London and had always had a cordial relationship. When Abdenur was secretary-general at Itamaraty, during Celso Amorim's term as minister for foreign affairs to Itamar Franco, and I was under-secretary for Foreign Trade and Integration, we spent a few months in close contact, prior to my appointment to the embassy in London. I was very pleased when, as Ambassador to Berlin, he spared no effort to get us two tickets to see *The Mastersingers of Nuremberg* in Bayreuth, the temple of Wagnerian opera in Germany.

FINAL DISPATCH

My final official dispatch to the Ministry of Foreign Affairs, on March 31, brought to a close a forty-two-year cycle. I thanked the Presidents José Sarney, Itamar Franco, FHC, and Luiz Inácio Lula da Silva for the privilege of having represented them abroad. Of those with whom I had worked directly, I mentioned two former bosses, to whom I was extremely grateful for having given me extremely enriching opportunities: Wladimir Murtinho and Olavo Setúbal. From Murtinho, I had learned that nothing is impossible where there is vision and will; from Setúbal, that in public service, as, indeed, in the private sector, the key to success is to have clearly defined the priorities and separated the essential from the accessory.

I also thanked Maria Ignez, who had stood by my side through good and bad, and to whom I owed much of what I had achieved over the course of the career now drawing to a close.

I finished by saying:

> To all my chiefs, to all those with whom I worked, and to the staff at
> Itamaraty and on our missions abroad, I have only words of grati-
> tude for everything I received from the House of Rio Branco.

I endeavored to serve my country with dedication and loyalty,
in all the functions I performed since joining the Passports Division
in 1962, including those of division head, department head, liaison
officer to the congress, chief of staff to the foreign minister, four
under-secretary posts, permanent representative to LAIA, and as
ambassador in London and Washington.

I never shrank from expressing my opinion and speaking my
mind, though always with the national interest at heart. I never
failed to carry out instructions once decisions were reached by the
secretary of state.

My work was always based on the principle that one should
ask nothing of one's country, not even recognition.

The Brazilian Residence and Chancery

The history of the Brazilian residence and chancery in Washington de-
serves a brief note. It is known that, over the last hundred years, particularly since the Second World War, the Brazilian government has
acquired stunningly beautiful embassies in many of the world's capitals. Besides the visibility and prestige these buildings bring to Brazil
from the outside, on the inside, many of them contain furnishings of
the highest quality and works of art by renowned artists from different
periods and origins.

Soon after Brazilian independence, on September 7, 1822, the United
States became the first country to recognize Dom Pedro's proclamation
on the banks of the Ipiranga River. In January 1824, the US president,
James Monroe, received the first Brazilian chargé d'affaires, José Silvestre
Rebello, in Washington. The meeting can be seen as the first diplomatic
mission ever sent by Brazil to the US capital. In 1905, the Brazilian lega-
tion in Washington was upgraded to the embassy category, with Joaquim Nabuco as the first Brazilian ambassador.

In 1934, after occupying numerous addresses, the Brazilian government decided to purchase its definitive premises in the US capital. The
fact that it was during the Depression meant that we were able to acquire a sumptuous mansion on one of the noblest streets in the Dis-

trict of Columbia, Massachusetts Avenue, on the corner of Whitehaven Street. Brazil and Great Britain were the first countries to install embassies on this stretch, better known as Embassy Row, and today it is filled with chanceries and ambassadorial residences.

Our embassy was constructed by the Chicago magnate Robert S. McCormick, later US ambassador to Paris, Rome, Vienna, and Saint Petersburg. It was designed by the famous architect John Russell Pope, known for having designed various public buildings in Washington, such as the Jefferson Memorial, National Gallery of Art, National Archives and a number of important residences, most of which are listed by the Washington Department of Historical Preservation.

Built back from the street front, the embassy has wooded gardens and flower beds, full of cherry blossoms, magnolias, azaleas, and strawflowers, which bloom throughout spring and summer and can be seen from both the house and the street.

The longer face of the triangular plot overlooks Massachusetts Avenue, and the shorter, Whitehaven Street. It was on this street that Bill and Hillary Clinton bought a residence after leaving the White House. In fact, shortly after the move, our new neighbors invited us and other nearby residents over for a housewarming cocktail.

When the building was first purchased in 1934, my wife's grandfather, former-minister Oswaldo Aranha, was given the task of adapting the residence for use as an embassy, and became the first official resident of what was then known as McCormick House. The idea was to preserve the original layout as far as was possible. The furniture and some of the belongings of the former proprietors, Robert and Katherine McCormick, remained in the house, while others were gradually added, such as the large Brazilian commodes in jacaranda wood and the wallpaper featuring landscapes of colonial Brazil, based on paintings by Debret, in the ground floor reception hall, decorated with Imperial furniture. The embassy also has a collection of Brazilian paintings which, according to the taste of each ambassador, often move between the walls of the residence and those of the chancery. The grounds contiguous to the residence, the site of the present chancery, were only acquired from Senator McCormick's heirs in 1942.

In 1964, the US Senate passed a law prohibiting new construction on site, though the Brazilian government was later given special dispensation to extend its facilities on condition that the new buildings be used exclusively as office space—which, in diplomatic language, means chanceries.

The new chancery, in glass and concrete, was designed by the architect Olavo Redig de Campos, a professional of recognized competence in the service of Brazilian diplomacy, who occupied the post of heritage conservator at the Foreign Ministry's Administration Department.

The new chancery was inaugurated on October 1, 1971, when the ambassador of Brazil was João Augusto de Araújo Castro. Despite its bold and modern space, the construction sits in harmony with the older residence. Later, in 1975, the consular services demanded more space, a problem that was resolved by the acquisition of a house on a neighboring plot on Whitehaven Street.

When we arrived in Washington, the big challenge for Maria Ignez, who had redecorated the residence on Mount Street in London, was to make the manor on Massachusetts Avenue more comfortable.

Our predecessors had put almost all of the residence's furniture into storage so to decorate it to their tastes. When they left the post, the original furnishings were recalled from six years under wraps. As was to be expected, almost everything needed to be renovated and restored before being redistributed throughout the various floors of the house.

Decoration had always been Maria Ignez' métier and she devoted herself full time to the task of restoring the halls and rooms to their former glory at the lowest possible cost and within the existing official budget. The idea was to use the original furnishings to make the house functional and comfortable, regardless of the preferences, belongings, or style of any given occupant.

Soon after our arrival, we unfortunately were not ready to receive visitors, for example, Minister Pedro Malan, who was in town for meetings. Only beginning with his next visit and those following, on some of which he was accompanied by his wife, Catarina, were we able to welcome him in our house.

Maria Ignez managed to redecorate the entire house while avoiding the impersonal feel that tends to characterize official residences. I believe the result was well worth the effort, as we never failed to receive praise on the décor, requests for permission to copy this or that idea, and requests from magazines and cultural institutes wanting to photograph the interior, sometimes even at the behest of art collectors from various US states.

During this period, the Colombian publisher Villegas &Villegas published a beautiful book on embassies in Washington (distributed by Rizzoli). Many of those who have leafed through the book say the Brazilian embassy is the most beautiful of all.

CHAPTER 6

Work at the Helm of the Embassy in the United States

"A MAN WHO WANTS OTHERS TO TELL HIM what they know must tell them what he knows, because the best means for getting information is to give it. Hence a city which wants her ambassador to be honored can do nothing better than to provide him abundantly with reports, because men who see that they can get something are eager to tell him what they know."

These words of advice, written by Niccolo Machiavelli on October 23, 1522, in a letter to Raffaello Girolami, who was leaving for Spain as Florentine ambassador to Charles of Habsburg, are especially pertinent to the Ambassador in Washington. The nature of the problems and issues that underpin the Brazil–US relationship demand unimpeded access to the local authorities, the foreign minister and the US president, and building direct communication with these figures takes credibility and quality information.

Public Diplomacy

The promotional program the embassy developed and pursued included the creation of centers of Brazilian studies at North American universities and research centers, such as those at Columbia University in New York, Georgetown University and the Woodrow Wilson Center in Washington. We also set in motion the programs Discover Brazil, for schools; Brazil on the Hill, designed to bolster knowledge about our country at the US Congress; and Recovery Project, a program set up to recover information about Brazil in US archives. I will talk about each of these initiatives a little further on.

STRENGTHENING TIES WITH ACADEMIA

Dialogue with the academic milieu was one of the priorities on the program of work I devised in Washington. I visited thirty American states to speak at hundreds of university seminars and independent research institutes.

I never failed to attend the main gatherings of the leading think tanks in Washington, such as Inter-American Dialogue, the Brookings Institute, the Council of Foreign Relations, the Center for Strategic and International Studies, and the Institute of International Economics, always with a view to introduce Brazil as a theme in the discussions.

The Embassy started organizing annual seminars, the "Brazil Meetings," at universities and other fora throughout the US in order to discuss the most diverse aspects of the Brazilian reality. In all, there were sixteen "Brazil Meetings" in 2000, with ministers of state in attendance, ten seminars in 2000 and twelve in 2001. In 2003 I delivered fifty-three speeches in Washington and was the main speaker at twenty-eight seminars and events in sixteen other cities.

In June 2003, shortly before President Lula's first working visit to Washington, we organized the seminar "Brazil and the United States in a Changing World: Political, Economic, and Diplomatic Relations in Regional and International Contexts," at the Wilson Center. The meeting led to the publication of a book evaluating various aspects of the Brazil-US relationship, not only from the academic perspective, but also with a focus that reveals direct knowledge of the issues raised at the seminar. The book, *Relações Brasil–Estados Unidos: asimetrias e convergências* was published by Editora Saraiva in 2006.

One of my fondest memories of these trips to other American states was my stay in Utah. I had received numerous invitations from local authorities and the governor to visit Salt Lake City. It was somewhere I'd been curious to see ever since reading *A Study in Scarlet*, by Arthur Conan Doyle, in which Sherlock Holmes cracks a murder case in London and heads to Salt Lake City to pursue the perpetrator among hills surrounding the town.

I could finally book the date for the trip. I was received with special honors by the governor of the state, visited the Legislative Assembly and gave a lecture at Brigham Young University, but it was only when I was introduced to some top-ranking Mormons (The Church of Jesus Christ of Latter-Day Saints) that I realized the real reason for the stream of invitations. I learned that Brazil, after the United States, was the country with the largest Mormon population in the world. In 2003, there were over eight hundred thousand practicing Mormons in Brazil and some five thousand missionaries, half of these American. I was told that the missionaries often end up marrying Brazilians who return with them to Salt Lake City.

In the streets, I met many Brazilians and Americans who had lived in Brazil and spoke Portuguese. I discovered that the city also had seven Brazilian restaurants. Another local curiosity is the existence of a highly sophisticated genealogy center where people the world over can trace their lineages.

On this trip, I took the opportunity to resolve a dispute between two groups in Salt Lake City associated with the Brazilian community, both Mormon and non-Mormon, who were having trouble agreeing on who the Brazilian government should appoint as honorary consul to the city. After various consultations, I suggested the journalist Gary Neeleman, a Mormon who had lived in Brazil for many years and who had good relations with the Brazilian community. Itamaraty accepted the suggestion. Curiously, he is the father of the businessman David Neeleman, who became known in Brazil in recent years as the founder of the airline Azul, modeled on its successful US cousin, JetBlue.

I adopted the policy of participating in the highest possible number of meetings on Latin America and Brazil, not only in Washington and New York, but in other cities too. These were often organized by chambers of commerce and trade associations, or Latin American institutes.

In the early 2000s, there were over three hundred university lecturers devoted, wholly or in part, to research on Brazil or the Portuguese language at Latin American Study Centers. Many universities offered Brazilian studies, while others taught Portuguese, and four were part of the Rio Branco Chair Program, set up by Itamaraty and funded by the post-graduate research bureau Capes.

On various occasions I was able to meet with Brazilian professors, such as Roberto DaMatta, at Notre Dame, and with Brazilianists like Albert Fishlow, Tom Skidmore, Werner Baer, Riordan Roett, and Anthony Pereira, among others.

Some months after my arrival in Washington, I organized a seminar at the chancery with some specialists on Brazil. In the embassy archives, we discovered that the only other event of this kind that had been held there, albeit obviously on a much smaller scale, had been thirty-one years earlier. Around fifty lecturers from thirty-five American universities were invited to what became the biggest ever gathering of Brazilianists and scholars of the region within a diplomatic context and, therefore, outside the habitual academic entities, such as the Latin American and Brazilian Studies Associations, LASA and BRASA.

The then minister-counselor at the Embassy and also a university lecturer, Paulo Roberto de Almeida, was fundamental in introducing me to the academic world. At his suggestion, we gathered commissioned works from recognized specialists in specific areas and made a critical overview of the academic output on the region since the mid-1900s.

The result of this endeavor was published in Brazil under the title *O Brasil dos brasilianistas: um guia dos estudos sobre o Brasil nos Estados Unidos, 1945–2000*, organized by Marshall C. Eakin, Paulo Roberto de Almeida, and myself. The American version, *Envisioning Brazil: A Guide to Brazilian Studies in the United States*, was published by University of Wisconsin Press in 2005.

Another embassy initiative was the creation, in October 2002, of the Distinguished Brazilian Studies Scholar certificate of merit, an honor conferred upon the academics Thomas Skidmore, historian at Brown University; Joseph Love, historian at the University of Illinois; Werner Baer, economist at the same institution; and Jon Tolman, professor of literature and Portuguese at the University of New Mexico, and an important BRASA mentor. I conferred the honor posthumously upon the professor and historian from the University of Miami, Robert Levine.

These Brazilianists produced work that was relevant in the social and economic fields and in civilian and military relations, especially during the period 1964–1985, not only because they had access to primary sources in the Brazilian armed forces, unlike their Brazilian colleagues, but because they were the only people who could write about Brazil at a time when there was no place for free thinking in Brazilian universities. The work of these Brazilianists, though written from the American perspective, was highly significant and helped foster understanding abroad of Brazil's particularities. In the field of historical studies, and along the lines of the Baron of Rio Branco Archive Recovery Project—created by the Ministry of Culture that had been developed by Itamaraty with Portugal, Spain, Holland, Italy, and other European countries—I decided to undertake a similar initiative to identify and present documentary sources on Brazil found in the American archives.

Encouraged by Esther Bertoletti, the Recovery Project was an important means of making Brazil and its relations with the United States better known and understood in both countries.

The project was developed by the embassy and carried out by the voluntary work of interns, with generous financial backing from the Vitae Foundation, created by the late José Mindlin. For three whole years, the initiative mapped the main documental archives and other primary sources for historical research on Brazil in the United States and created an inventory with descriptions of content. The most important institutions are in Washington, such as the National Archives, the Library of Congress, and the Oliveira Lima Library at the Catholic University of America (CUA), home to the largest body of information on US soil about Brazil.

As a result of the project, the embassy prepared a reference guide in 2002, entitled *Guia dos arquios americanos sobre o Brasil* (Guide to American Archives on Brazil). The work was published in 2010 as a result of contact I made with the Alexandre de Gusmão Foundation. Luckily, eight years after leaving the embassy in Washington, I was still able to contribute to a better knowledge of our nation through these documents, and for that I thank the then-President of the Foundation, the ambassador Jerônimo Moscardo de Souza.

A lot of American diplomatic papers about Brazil can be found in Brazilian archives—such as the National Archive and Itamaraty, both in Rio de Janeiro—thanks to the pioneering work of the sociologist Luciano Martins and the ambassador Rubens Ricupero. Basically, the Itamaraty Archive contains documents from the nineteenth century while the National Archive holds those from the twentieth century, with some gaps that still need filling.

In 2003, the embassy also undertook the publication of the series "Brasiliana in the United States," which consists of books published in Brazil and translated into English with the support of the Banco do Nordeste, in collaboration with Duke University and the University of North Carolina.

CENTERS OF BRAZILIAN STUDIES

As part of our drive to establish closer links with academia, and in the hope of increasing Brazil's visibility in Washington and New York, I personally raised the funds to create centers of Brazilian studies, as it struck me as unacceptable that there was not even one in the capital city of the world's most powerful nation. I approached American and Brazilian companies and was able to secure roughly US$1.6 million, which enabled us to set up three centers, two in Washington and one in New York.

The Center of Brazilian Studies at the Woodrow Wilson International Center for Scholars (WWC), a non-partisan, publicly and privately funded institution in Washington, was born of a partnership with Lee Hamilton, the WWC director. A well-known former congressman, responsible for an important report on the Iraq War at the end of the Bush Administration, Hamilton was very supportive of the idea for a Brazil center. Brazil as a theme was a new idea at the WWC, preceded only by Russia on the institution's program. I attended several meetings to explain and detail the project and, in counterpart, offered the funds we had managed to raise ourselves (some US$600 thousand), and the initiative got off the ground.

At a lecture he gave some time later, Hamilton declared that he had learned more about Brazil in the eleven months since he had become involved with the center than he had throughout his whole life as a politician and congressman. The Brazilian studies center consolidated and expanded to become what is the Brazil Institute today.

At Georgetown University, also in Washington, we created a Brazilian Studies Program in November 2000. The first director was Arturo Valenzuela, who was also director of the Latin American Study Center at the time. During the first two years of the Obama administration, Valenzuela held the post of secretary of state for Western Hemisphere Affairs.

Professor Naomi Muniz, who coordinated the center with such efficiency and dedication, took advantage of trips to Washington by Brazilian personalities, politicians, and academics to organize monthly seminars and debates on the country in the areas of human rights, the environment, education, and foreign policy.

When I was preparing for my return to Brazil, I was informed by the university that Pedro Paulo Santos, the Brazilian who directed the program between 2001 and 2005, had been defrauding the center's resources. Santos embezzled over US$300 thousand by making payments to fictitious staff and suppliers. He was charged and convicted by the Court of the District of Columbia.

The third project, the Center for Brazilian Studies at Columbia University, was created in New York in January 2001 with the support of private Brazilian and American institutions. We invited the American economist and university professor Albert Fishlow to coordinate the Center. Periodic meetings and seminars with Brazilian authorities, especially in the area of economics, helped disseminate and analyze the internal situation in Brazil, to the benefit not only of the university's students, but also to the benefit of the New York business community.

With the participation of scholars, politicians, and businesspeople from both countries, not a week went by without some discussion on Brazil at one of these three centers.

On one such occasion, in March 2000, former President Itamar Franco went to Washington to speak about Brazil at the Paul H. Nitze School of Advanced International Studies, part of the Johns Hopkins University. The rector at the time was Paul Wolfowitz, who, during the Bush government, became the all-powerful Number Two at the Department of State and one of the most hawkish defenders of pre-emptive strikes against Iraq. I was invited by the rector to attend the lecture by Itamar Franco, who was, at the time, fiercely critical of President FHC. Despite the delicate nature of the situation, as ambassador of Brazil, and out of friendship and respect for the former president, I could not have simply ignored the invitation. Later, Paulo Paiva, then-vice-president of the IDB, called me to discuss the pros and cons of our attending the lecture. For Paiva, there was the question of our loyalty to FHC, but there was also the matter of his being from Itamar's state, Minas Gerais.

In the end, we decided to go to the university to greet Itamar Franco before his lecture. There, at Paul Wolfowitz's side, the former Brazilian president seemed to accept our apologies rather well, but as he leaned in to give me an affectionate hug, he whispered mischievously: "Don't worry, Ambassador, I'll go easy on him."

THE OLIVEIRA LIMA LIBRARY

At the beginning of the twentieth century, the Oliveira Lima Library was donated to the Catholic University of America (CUA) by the diplomat and historian Manoel de Oliveira Lima, who had served in Washington early in his career. After 1913, Oliveira Lima, already retired, devoted himself to academic activities and to touring American and European universities. In 1918, he accepted an invitation from the CUA to teach international law, and settled in Washington. The university offered to pay for the consolidation and transportation of his vast library, then scattered about various cities on either side of the Atlantic: Recife, Rio de Janeiro, Lisbon, London, and Brussels.

Embittered by the treatment he had received from the Brazilian Senate during an episode that involved his recall from Peru, Oliveira Lima decided to donate his extraordinary library of rare books—on fifteenth and sixteenth century Portugal, and on Brazil from later periods—to the Catholic University, along with his collections of paintings and old maps.

The diplomat's will specified that the CUA would have to build proper facilities to house these collections and that the library should be open to all scholars and researchers who wished to use it. To this day, given a shortage of funds at the university, not only has the building not been built, but the collection of books and personal correspondence has yet to be fully catalogued. To my surprise and indignation, while studying this vast collection in 1999, I found a valuable body of some eleven thousand documents shut away in the university basement under the most precarious conditions.

As it is a secular rather than religious collection, down through the years the directors at the CUA have shown very little interest or willingness to raise funds to improve the installations—in stark contrast to the treatment dispensed to the Semitic Library of religious books for which it raised US$3 million for a new building.

The neglect with which this collection, which is of inestimable historical value to Brazil, was treated by the institution, and the repeated phone calls and letters the embassy received from researchers complaining about how hard it was to gain access to the material, led me to try to have the library transferred to some Brazilian academic entity.

The embassy's archives show that in 1985, my father-in-law, Sérgio Corrêa da Costa, then Brazilian ambassador in Washington, had raised the possibility of having the library transferred to Brazil.

After thorough research on the possible legal implications and on the grounds that the CUA had failed to comply with the conditions in the illustrious donor's will, I contacted the rectory and suggested that we have the collection moved to Brazil. I was under no illusions that the proposal would be welcomed.

My discussions with the President of the CUA, Reverend David M. O'Connell, were tense, because the university, predictably, did not want to lose the material. Like all Pontifical universities in the world, the CUA has ties with the Vatican, so I spoke to Oto Maia, then-Brazilian ambassador to the Holy See in Rome, and also with Senator Marco Maciel, a Pernambucan like Oliveira Lima, in an attempt to obtain the space and financial support to house the library in Brazil.

A proposal was drawn up with the support of private partners and was submitted to the CUA for discussions. According to this proposal, the university would be recognized as the definitive owner of the Oliveira Lima Library, but the collection would be given a suitable abode in Brazil, where it would be housed and preserved. The library headquarters would also function as a focal point for other CUA activities in Latin America.

Aware of the difficulties inherent to the project, and taking into consideration the suggestions of Ambassador Sérgio Corrêa da Costa, I set about making exploratory contact with the rectories of the Catholic University in Brasília, the University of Brasília, and with the Pontifical Catholic Universities of São Paulo and Rio de Janeiro to sound out their interest in receiving the Oliveira Lima collection.

As was only to be expected, the sullen response of the rector, received days before I left Washington, was in the negative. In the end, I did not have time to take matters further, not even with the Brazilian universities. I hope that someday one of my successors manages to repatriate this precious collection, which has a lot to contribute to our fuller knowledge of the history of Portugal and Brazil.

BRAZIL IN SCHOOLS

Having realized that the knowledge shortfall about Brazil in the United States will only be redressed through ongoing information programs in the media and academia, I decided to set up promotional projects about our country in public schools across twenty-four American states.

When I was ambassador to Britain, I structured the Brazil in the Schools program, which, with the support of local educational authorities, distributed a wealth of material on Brazil to thousands of secondary schools. The program generated excellent results and was adapted for use in the United States, under the title Discover Brazil. Launched in February 2002, the program sent material to fifty thousand teachers and reached roughly one and a half million students.

In order to stimulate student interest in the material, which focused on Brazilian geography, history, and culture, we established an annual Brazil-themed essay competition. The winner won a week's vacation in Bahia, while the teacher of the winning student received a computer manufactured in Brazil.

To enhance our contact with American students, the embassy opened channels for direct consultations—a thousand per year, on average—via telephone or e-mail, all of which were addressed and answered.

After the launch of the Discover Brazil program, we also started

receiving weekly school visits, with lectures delivered by our diplomats. Between 2002 and 2003, roughly 2,500 students attended these
gatherings.

Every student who contacted us for information on the country was
given a copy of two of the embassy's publications (*Brazil in Brief* and
Brazil and the USA—What Do We Have in Common?) which deal with
Brazilian history and broach some of the main development issues facing Brazil through parallels with the US reality.

To maximize this student contact, we created a Kid's Corner on the
Embassy website, with links to "Meet Brazilian Kids," a pen-pal system
for children and teens.

The success the Discover Brazil program achieved, thanks to its
originality, was a source of enormous satisfaction to me. I personally
participated in the program by visiting schools to talk about Brazil, often
accompanied by Virginia Williams, the mother of Anthony Williams,
the mayor of Washington, who was an enthusiastic fan of our work.

Building Credibility

At the Rio Branco Institute, we were taught that the ambassador's role is
to inform and represent. Today, the information is generated and transmitted by news agencies like CNN or Reuters, and it's the ambassador's
job to interpret and analyze it. In terms of representation, it behooves
the ambassador to handle issues under the embassy's jurisdiction and
act upon the instructions issued to it by the Foreign Ministry. However,
if the embassy is not to be accused of being omissive in fulfilling its mission, it is important that it have a plan of action of its own. To illustrate
my point I will mention a couple of situations that show how valuable
the official stance of the ambassador can be.

DEALING WITH ISSUES OF TRADE AND ECONOMICS

When the FTAA and the Doha Round of multilateral talks were at the
top of the agenda, I took part in TV and radio programs, and academic
debates at think tanks and with foreign trade institutions. Our aim was
to carve out a space for Brazil in these specific debates. From 2003 on,
there was someone from the USTR and EU at every meeting on trade—
and the ambassador of Brazil as well.

I endeavored to keep the US authorities always informed about the
viability of Brazil's program for economic stability and fiscal reform,

either through direct contact or the countless conferences and seminars I attended.

During the currency devaluation crisis of 1999, it was important that we got the message across to the economic agencies, authorities, and investors that our economy would rebound quickly. During this period, the finance and planning ministers made frequent visits to the US. The embassy's support proved extremely useful in explaining what was going on and the measures being taken.

In comparison with other Brazilian diplomatic missions, the embassy in Washington enjoys a privileged position: not only does the ambassador tend to the bilateral relationship between the host and home countries, but he also mediates among visiting governors and ministers and the World Bank, IDB, and International Monetary Fund (IMF).

In fact, on one occasion I signed agreements with the IBD and World Bank on behalf of these state and federal authorities. Each year, practically every governor in the federation passed through Washington.

We maintained the procedure of establishing contact with the American government and, specifically, encouraged working meetings between ministers from the economic area, such as Finance Minister Pedro Malan, and their US counterparts. Malan's visits to the FED and to the chairman of the Federal Reserve, Alan Greenspan, were excellent opportunities to make and broaden contacts. This practice proved extremely valuable during the 1999 currency crisis, only months before my arrival at the embassy. On that occasion, the support we received from the US government spared Brazil from the trauma Argentina would go through not long afterwards.

US solidarity with Brazil was felt once again in 2002, when the IMF granted a US$30 billion loan that enabled us to avoid a financial crisis threatening to erupt on the eve of the presidential elections. In October that same year, this economic instability was heightened by fears in the US and EU that the election of the PT candidate might signal a shift in the economic policy that had proved so successful under FHC.

However, the reckless declarations made by Treasury Secretary Paul O'Neill, who spoke negatively about the new deal the Brazilian government was negotiating with the IMF, triggered a depreciation of the Brazilian real against the dollar, fanning the flames of market instability and fueling rumors of a deepening crisis. According to O'Neill, the IMF should not issue rescue packages to certain countries without guaranties. As he saw it, Brazil, Argentina, and Uruguay, "US friends and allies," and especially the first two, had to adopt policies to ensure that the funds they received were used "on concrete benefits and did not end up in Swiss bank accounts."

The Treasury secretary's ill-considered comment was made on *Meet the Press*, one of the Sunday shows with the highest ratings on American TV, only days before he was scheduled to visit Brazil, on the eve of the country's new agreement with the IMF and at the height of the election campaign. The Brazilian government was naturally indignant and the furor almost caused a diplomatic incident.

The Brazilian reaction was stern and expressed in strong declarations from President FHC and the ministers Pedro Malan and Celso Lafer and in contact I made with the Treasury and State Departments. At the suggestion of Robert Zoellick, from the USTR, Lafer tried to speak with Condoleezza Rice, but as she could not be found, he ended up talking to Ambassador John Maisto, from the National Security Council, who got in touch with her and conveyed our protests and concerns over the effects those declarations might have. Maisto got back to me and said that he had taken part in a meeting with Bush and his cabinet, also attended by Bob Zoellick, at which the President had expressed his appreciation and total support for Brazil.

In Brazil, US Ambassador Dona Hrinak contacted Minister Celso Lafer to try to soothe the effects of O'Neill's unacceptable remarks. Hrinak said that the American government was very sorry about the whole affair and agreed with Lafer's observations about the importance of Brazil and the US working in synch in the face of international economic adversity. Celso Lafer said that if no adequate explanation was forthcoming, the President would probably refuse to meet with O'Neill.

After numerous excuses, including one from the White House spokesman Ari Fleischer, and Bush's reiterated declarations of support for Brazil, Minister Celso Lafer put the subject to rest. As a result, Paul O'Neill's visit to Brazil a week later went without incident. At the meetings with FHC, the minister of finance, the president of the central bank, and the chief of staff, the gaps were filled and the way paved toward the conclusion of negotiations. After lengthy talks, Brazil had secured a loan package with the IMF that would see the country through the turbulence.

The announcement of the agreement with the Monetary Fund had huge repercussions abroad. It was the largest financial package the IMF had ever approved for a single nation, and it represented a major change in Bush's policy toward US support for countries hard hit by economic crisis. Brazil featured heavily in the international press, which recognized the soundness of its macroeconomic policy and the measures taken by the FHC government. With this boost to Brazil's image, I was invited to appear on Jim Lehrer's *News Hour* alongside Peter Hakim, director of Inter-American Dialogue, to talk about the political and economic situation in Brazil and the IMF loan. The American attitude not only showed a shift in opinion toward IMF loans in general, but recognition of Brazil's growing importance to US interests in the region.

From the Brazilian perspective, the loan package was part of a political transition strategy drawn up by President FHC to ensure economic stability in the wake of the presidential elections. At his request, each of the presidential candidates expressed agreement with the terms of the IMF loan, which Lula was able to pay back, in full, to great fanfare, during his first mandate.

This US engagement in Brazil's favor at that moment in time contrasted starkly with their indifference toward the crisis in Argentina.

Our neighbors had complained about a perceived lack of Brazilian support during an earlier crisis (2000–2001), a subject discussed at the time by Presidents Carlos Menem and FHC. The Argentinean ambassador to the United States, Diego Guelar, complained to me on numerous occasions about the Brazilian representative to the Fund, Murilo Portugal, who he said was not backing Argentina's applications. I was able to verify with both our IMF representative himself and with Minister Pedro Malan that the opposite was the case, and that Brazil had been actively supporting Buenos Aires. Portugal, however, with the full backing of the Brazilian government, had merely expressed his concerns when Argentina threatened to default on its repayments to the IMF, as Brazil would have had to cover the unpaid installment. I had personally seen Pedro Malan vouch for Argentina at the IMF and World Bank, and FHC intercede on the country's behalf in talks with Bill Clinton and George W. Bush, repeatedly urging them not to leave Argentina adrift. In our opinion, Argentina's recovery was essential to the region's stability. However, despite Brazil's best efforts, and for a number of political and economic reasons—particularly the Argentinean government's adoption of unorthodox policies and rolling of its foreign debt—the American government could not be moved to assist our stricken neighbors.

During the "mad cow" crisis in February 2002, the channels of communication that I had opened with the US agriculture secretary enabled the imbroglio to be swiftly resolved. The problem began when Brazil failed to provide information on sanitary conditions that Canada had requested some six months earlier. Alleging non-compliance with deadlines, the Canadian government decided to withdraw all Brazilian meat products from its supermarket shelves and asked the US and Mexico to do the same under the NAFTA agreement. The US market, though closed to Brazilian meats *in natura*, is a major buyer of our processed meats, so a potential suspension on these imports was cause for serious concern to the federal government and our meat exporter sector.

I phoned the then-Minister for Agriculture Marcus Vinícius Pratini de Moraes, who was in Boston, and asked him to come to Washington early the following week. He promptly agreed, so I was able to arrange a meeting with Agriculture Secretary Ann Venneman. At this meeting, which I attended, the ministers decided on the immediate suspension of the embargo by the US quarantine authorities.

THE CAYMAN DOSSIER

Another example of just how far you can go on the strength of a good conversation conducted in the spirit of mutual trust was my contact with the Justice Department on the so-called Cayman dossier.

During FHC's re-election campaign in 1998, rumors began to circulate about the existence of a dossier that supposedly proved some US$300 million in shipments abroad, more precisely to the Cayman Islands, to accounts belonging to FHC, Mário Covas, José Serra, and Sérgio Motta, all front-line members of PSDB. Urged by opponents to FHC's re-election, the press hyped the story of this dossier, which had been fabricated in Miami and offered to opposition parties in Brazil at astronomical prices.

For some time, the fake dossier hung in the wings, fulfilling its purpose of slowly tarnishing the reputations of these political leaders, all from the state of São Paulo. News even began to circulate that the US government had launched an investigation into the accusations.

When the subject resurfaced in 2002, toward the end of FHC's second term, I rang the President Cardoso to tell him that I planned to contact the Justice Department to discuss the matter. Not only did FHC give me authorization to talk to the US authorities to see if there really was an investigation in progress, but asked me to lodge an official request for whatever documentation the department had gathered. The

Brazilian government wanted to make the findings public, whatever their content.

At a meeting with authorities from the Justice Department, I raised the issue of the dossier and presented the President's request to have the department's intelligence on the matter sent to Brasília so that the government could disclose the information and dispel any lingering doubts about the inveracity of the accusations. Naturally, the Justice Department had found nothing at all, so we were able to corroborate what FHC, Covas, and Serra had declared all along, that the dossier was a fabrication fed to the press for electoral purposes and bore absolutely no relation to the facts.

Later investigations proved that the dossier was a fake and that its contents had been forged by people with ties to political adversaries of the politicians involved, and the matter ended there.

Brazilian Information Center

The creation of a Brazilian information center abroad was an old idea I had been trying to develop since my time in Brasília, in conjunction with the advertising entrepreneur Jorge da Cunha Lima. Back then, we had drawn up the charter for such a company to be discussed with President FHC, but the project went no further.

In 2000, however, the idea was resuscitated and I created the Brazilian Information Center (BIC), a nonprofit private American company set up to support the Brazilian private sector in the United States and to liaise with Congress.

I chose as BIC director journalist Flavia Sekles, who had just left her position as Washington correspondent for the *Jornal do Brasil*. After three days—proof of her efficiency and of how easy it is to open a company in the US—she had registered the BIC with the authorities and the center was up and running.

Completely independent of the embassy and official organs in general, the company ran on donations received from Brazilian companies with business interests in the United States.

In partnership with the BIC, we established Brazil on the Hill, a program tailored to the US Congress, with the aim of promoting lectures and debates for Congressional audiences.

In addition to these initiatives, others included the Brasiliana project, sponsored by Banco do Nordeste, which published and republished Brazilian titles in the United States; "Brazil Meetings," a series of twenty seminars held in different US cites; an e-zine hosted on the embassy website, featuring articles about Brazil; and the Brazil Economic Briefing, a collection of studies on the main economic trends and events of interest to the American investor.

Working with Congress

The Congress plays an extremely relevant role in the US political system. Although the regime is presidential, as opposed to parliamentary, the US Congress wields considerable political power, perhaps even greater than Parliament does in Britain. It would be no exaggeration to say it is *primo inter pares*, that is, the congress of all congresses, and its power derives from the very origins of the American state.

Given the specificities of American society, the office of the president is actually controlled by the congressional powers, as established under Article One of the Constitution of 1787. Interestingly, the power to regulate trade with foreign nations lies with Congress, not with the Executive.

In itself, the power to regulate trade is more than sufficient reason for diplomats and foreign businesspeople to pay special attention to the work of legislators in the two Houses of Congress.

With this in mind, from the very beginning of my ambassadorship, I strove to make contact with congressmen and their staffers, as these have a great deal of power and autonomy in their own right. As the authors of the speeches and bills of law presented at Congress, these professionals are extremely influential.

In 1999, I encouraged the creation of the Brazil Caucus at Congress, which included forty-nine representatives with whom I maintained regular contact throughout my time in Washington.

In 2005, the Brazil Caucus was stunned when its president, the Republican Congressman William Jefferson of Louisiana lost his seat after police found US$90 thousand in bribes in his freezer. In August 2009 he was convicted and sentenced to thirteen years in prison. As far as we know, this unusual idea of a hiding place for money has yet to be adopted in Brazil. However, the Jefferson incident aside, the Caucus has been a constant and effective presence in the relationship between the two countries. One particularly telling episode, recounted in more detail in Chapter 7, was when the president of the Caucus threatened to stand down over Brazil's involvement with Iran.

As a result of my initiatives to establish closer bonds with US congressmen, I was the first Brazilian ambassador to be invited to participate in a session about Brazil at Congress, an invitation extended to me by the Latin American subcommittee of the Committee on International Relations. The debate, held in February 2002, was valuable in terms of our bilateral relations, but also, on a personal note, for the special opportunity it gave me to present Brazil's view of the relationship directly.

The bridge built with Congress meant it began to feature on the agenda of Brazilian authorities visiting Washington. Minister Luiz Felipe Lampreia was the first to have meetings with the chair of the Foreign Affairs Committee and with the Brazil Caucus.

In order to make more personal informal contact, we arranged regular visits to the embassy by congressmen and their advisors, complete with a genuine Brazilian barbeque in the gardens once a year. The number of congressmen attending these get-togethers never ceased to grow and was of great benefit to the embassy's work.

In order to foster knowledge about Brazil, the embassy also organized a series of meetings in Congress on themes relevant to our international agenda. It was essential to continue working to improve the information that House representatives, senators, and their aides were receiving about the country, so as to correct certain distorted perceptions of Brazil that abounded in Washington.

We also supported Brazilian congressmen on missions to the US, producing reports, detailing internal and external aspects of US politics, drawing up programs, and participating in meetings. In return, many members of the US Congress made visits to Brazil, where they were received by the highest authorities of the Executive, Legislature, and Judiciary.

However, despite our good contact with the US Congress, we also had our fair share of difficulties. One of these concerned the issue of environmental conservation and Amazonian deforestation, a theme of great concern to American and European NGOs.

Early in 2002, the US authorities, under pressure from NGOs, impounded shipments of Brazilian mahogany that had been cleared for export under a preliminary court ruling. The certification that extractors were required to obtain was not always respected and accusations of corruption were common in relation to these shipments. There was a tug of war: on one side, the US government was taking measures to ob-

struct Brazilian lumber imports, while, on the other, American import-
ers were lobbying sectors of Congress to have the shipments cleared.

The contradictions between laudable intentions and pragmatic actions by American companies in the service of concrete interests were
perfectly demonstrated by the behavior of Trent Lott, the powerful senate minority leader from Mississippi. The invitation I received to meet
the well-known Republican senator was a good example of how ambassadors sometimes have to stand firm in the national interest in the face
of political hardball.

With enormous arrogance, the senator mentioned that a mahogany
importer based in his home state was losing lots of money and might
even go bankrupt unless some shipments of Brazilian lumber were released for export. Lott spoke at length about free trade and how the US
wanted to increase its imports from Brazil, but insinuated that unless
the issue was resolved to his satisfaction, he would take the subject to
President Bush, Secretary of State Colin Powell and President FHC. He
also said that if the dispute continued, he would block the Trade Promotion Authority (TPA), one of the priorities of the Bush government's
foreign trade policy, from being voted on in Congress.

After listening to Lott's aggressive and inflamed speech, I flagged his
rudeness and proceeded to address his arguments point for point. At the
end of the meeting, his chief of staff, surprised by my reaction to the Republican leader's truculence, declared that the meeting had been great,
"for you and for him."

Throughout 2002, the US authorities permitted the importation of
most certified-lumber shipments up to the limit stipulated by the Brazilian Institute for the Environment and Natural Resources. Seven im-
porters sued the US government to secure the release of sixteen other
shipments retained at ports nationwide, and some of these won. However, in mid-2003, the US authorities definitively ruled against allowing
the rest of the retained lumber into the country.

Press Relations

Periodically, I had contact with the major media vehicles in the United
States and with journalists from the Brazilian press, including some
Washington correspondents. I paid equal attention to the Portuguese-
language newspapers and channels that were popping up in the US in
response to the growing Brazilian population there.

Since my arrival, I did my best to promote Brazil widely in the press. I systematically arranged breakfast meetings at the embassy to foster relationships with editors, specialized journalists and reporters from the *New York Times, Wall Street Journal, Washington Post, Miami Herald, Los Angeles Times*, and *Financial Times*.

Frank and ongoing contact with the media was a key element in the promotion of Brazil in the United States during the intensification of our bilateral relationship.

My interaction with members of the Brazilian press covering the various financial and political institutions in Washington was always easy. Our contact was constant through press conferences, exclusive interviews, and off-the-record chats in which I was able to remain abreast of the political and economic situation back home. Before releasing our annual report on trade barriers against Brazilian products and services on the US market, I used to call a press conference with local reporters and foreign correspondents to go over the findings.

The internet became a fundamental tool, not only in transmitting news that appeared on Brazil in the US media, but in enabling us to conduct periodical qualitative and quantitative assessments of the country's media presence and the dynamism of our image in the United States. The internet showed that American interest in Brazil spiked at the start of the 2002 presidential election campaign.

On official visits to various American states, I also sought to meet with the editors of the main local newspapers and to speak about Brazil's specific interests in that particular state or region. This initiative led to news reports which I believe helped dismantle certain stereotypes associated with Brazil and generate more interest in the country.

Promoting Trade

Considering individual nations rather than blocs, at the beginning of the 2000s, the US market was the single largest recipient of Brazilian goods, absorbing over 25 percent of our total exports, almost 80 percent of which was high value-added manufactured goods.

Boosting our exports was, from the commercial point of view, the number one priority of the work I did in Washington. There were basically two fronts on this: the elimination of chronic trade barriers against certain competitive Brazilian sectors, and the promotion of new products within new markets.

In terms of the elimination of trade barriers, we began a project to garner efficiency in our always difficult negotiations with the United States executive. We began to work more closely with Congress and sectors of the US economy that shared commercial or political interests with Brazil. The aim was to forge alliances that would help us to overcome specific points of resistance to the opening of target markets. I was personally involved in negotiating changes to the subsidies the US granted to cotton growers, which were clearly illegal under WTO rules, and extremely prejudicial to this sector in Brazil. Alongside Pedro de Camargo Neto, then secretary for production at the Agriculture Ministry, we supported a WTO suit against these US subsidies. One of the decisive meetings on this issue took place at the embassy in Washington. Itamaraty did not always look favorably on my involvement, because a positive outcome was far from assured. As they saw it, making a case against the subsidies meant securing support from other countries and establishing a highly complex causal connection between the subsidies granted to cotton growers in the US and the harm caused to those in Brazil. The Ministry of Agriculture, on the other hand, held the opposite view. For the Ministry, cotton was not only the most serious problem, but also the most actionable and winnable. I was convinced that the Brazilian cotton growers had a genuine grievance and that the case would be decided in our favor, as finally occurred in 2009, when the WTO recognized the illegality of the subsidies and authorized Brazil to take countermeasures until they were discontinued.

One of the embassy's roles was to accompany the annual renewal of the Generalized System of Preferences (GSP), a program that sets reduced tariffs for certain countries and which, at the time, encompassed 15 percent of Brazil's exports to the US.

Another constant concern of ours was Brazil's inclusion on the priority watch list of countries that, from Washington's perspective, refused or failed to protect intellectual property rights, especially in the area of pharmaceutics. PhRMA, the US association of pharmaceutical companies, frequently questioned measures taken in Brazil and the policies the country adopted to force down prices. The most caustic of these confrontations occurred in the United States in October 1999, soon after José Serra, then minister for Health, signed a decree authorizing Brazilian drugs manufacturers to break pharmaceutical patents, in conformity with the WTO's Intellectual Property Agreement (TRIPS). The PhRMA directors contacted me almost immediately to lodge their protests and complaints, to which I had to respond vehemently in defense of the legitimacy of Brazil's position.

In general, up until 2004, our trade disputes with the United States grew constantly. In Washington, I accompanied numerous Brazilian delegations to meetings with US authorities to defend the interests of our producers and exporters of steel, orange juice, soya, cotton, ethanol and shrimp, all sectors which had suffered from US barriers in breach of WTO regulations.

In relation to trade promotion, the embassy created a program of business meetings and rounds of talks with the private sector in ten states which we had identified as priorities to Brazil's commercial interests: Florida, California, Texas, Illinois, New York, New Jersey, Pennsylvania, Indiana, Michigan, and Ohio. The idea behind these meetings was to identify niche markets and expand our trade channels for seven product types (auto parts, furniture, footwear, textiles, ceramics, marble, and granite), in accordance with a special export program established by the Brazilian Agency for the Promotion of Exports and Investments (APEX).

The embassy also actively maneuvered to expand Brazil's participation in other sectors, such as software, tropical fruits, and meats. Each year, we organized dozens of business meetings and informative seminars in the main US state capitals.

In the particular case of *in natura* meats, our innumerable attempts to remove sanitary restrictions against Brazil were frustrated by protectionist resistance from the Department of Agriculture, which continues to bar Brazilian fresh meats from the US market.

In 2001, the embassy created the Brazil Group, designed to support Brazilian companies in the US in their trade demands. The Brazilian Information Center (BIC) functioned as a sort of executive secretary for this group. Embraer was one of the first companies to engage the initiative by offering its Florida headquarters as the venue for the Group's inaugural meeting. In a show of support for the embassy's initiative, the meeting was attended by Apex President Juan Quiróz, representing Minister Luiz Fernando Furlan.

The embassy also worked to collate and distribute relevant information. Each year we published studies on trade opportunities in the United States and a report on US trade barriers, which were widely reported on in the Brazilian media and distributed to interested associations.

Ethnic Markets

African American minority organizations frequently contacted me at the embassy to ask for our help in developing ties with similar groups in Brazil.

In October 1999, the Center for Business Integration, a business association recently created in São Paulo to support the Brazilian Program for Supply Chain Diversity and Inclusion (Integrare), made some initial contact with its counterpart in the United States.

To stimulate joint action, leaders from various segments of the African American community sought the embassy's support in contacting the Brazilian institution. During one of my trips to Brazil, I visited the Integrare headquarters to meet its director, Carlos Nascimento, and encouraged him as best I could to look for ways to make the organization grow and strengthen its ties with the United States.

In our search for points of common interest, the embassy decided to support Nascimento's initiative to talk to Brazilian and US authorities about creating a direct flight between Miami and Salvador. The Black community, especially in New York, had discovered Bahia and its multiple ethnic, cultural and religious aspects of African origin. The inflow of Afro-American tourists might grow if there were a direct flight to Salvador.

Integrare made some solid contacts with representatives from the National Minority Supplier Development Council (NMSDC) and the Congressional Black Caucus Foundation (CBCF), which helped in the effort to identify business opportunities in the areas of trade and tourism.

In an attempt to pursue the possibility of opening new flights between the US and Bahia, I contacted the tourist department in Salvador and the air traffic bureau in Brasília. Negotiations were started with some small airlines interested in establishing and operating a direct Miami–Salvador line, but nothing further could be done at that time.

Later, in 2009, as the result of action by former Minister for Tourism Marta Suplicy, a regular Miami–Salvador flight was opened, with potential for larger and more constant tourist flows between the two cities.

I also worked to stimulate commercial exchange between Brazilian companies and the ethnic market in the United States and to awaken interest within our government and private sector to redress the lack of strategies to expand economic relations with this market and our exports to it.

The private sector's lack of aggressiveness and the inexistence of fixed priorities for certain promising markets for Brazilian products in the US had always struck me as a terrible waste.

The US market is the largest, most dynamic, and one of the most open in the world. With a GDP of US$11.5 trillion and imports above 1.5 trillion in 2002-2003, the United States was a mine of opportunities for the attentive exporter, interested in discovering and exploring niches in so diverse a market.

Two segments that fit well into the medium- to long-term strategic vision and which stood out for their sheer potential for the Brazilian exporter were the Latino and African American segments.

At the beginning of the decade, the Latino market, which numbered some thirty-eight million people across the United States (with nearly two million Brazilians), was beginning to attract attention from Brazilian companies. At the same time, the Black population was in the region of thirty-six million, and it was a mature consumer market for Brazilian products and a sure tourism target.

In terms of geographical distribution, the ten states whose Black populations had the highest acquisitive power in 2003 were New York (US$65 billion), California (US$53 billion), Texas (US$50 billion), Georgia (US$46 billion), Florida (US$41 billion), Maryland (US$38 billion), Illinois (US$37 billion), North Carolina (US$31 billion), Virginia (US$29 billion) and Michigan (US$28 billion).

If considered as a nation, the Afro-American market would have been the eleventh largest economy in the world in 2002, and therefore larger than Brazil that year. According to the study *Buying Power of Black America*, the overall consumer clout of this sector was US$631 billion in 2002, an increase of 4.8 percent over 2001.

According to the publication *Black Meetings & Tourism* (BM&T), during the period 2002-2003, the African American population spent US$35 billion on travel for business and leisure.

The growing buying power of this segment was becoming increasingly clear. For BM&T, the Afro-American tourism market was the most dynamic in the sector, registering 16 percent growth in 2001 and 2002, while tourism overall grew a mere 1 percent over the same period. At the beginning of the decade, the Black population in the US accounted for roughly 17 percent of leisure travel, while its relative share in terms of total travel was 13 percent. The growing number of chartered flights between New York and Salvador during this period was a reflection of this tendency.

The strong Black influence on our culture and the similar origins shared with the Black population in the US constituted a unique market differential, and opened abundant prospects for commercial exploration.

Tourism

Throughout my time in Washington, tourism to Brazil was always a subject of major interest.

At a private dinner at the residence during President Lula's visit in June 2003, I raised the controversial issue of absolute reciprocity on visas, which, as I saw it, was prejudicial to Brazil. The demands and high processing fees charged on tourist visas were the same in Brazil and the US. This meant that Brazil was losing competitiveness to destinations closer and cheaper to the US traveler, such as the Caribbean and Central America.

The idea was to revise the visa policy in order to facilitate entry for US citizens, considering not so much the reciprocity issue as the country's interest in receiving tourist revenues. President Lula turned to Minister Celso Amorim and asked what he thought of my suggestion. In a formal tone, Amorim said he was totally against any loosening of visa requirements because it was, as he saw it, a question of sovereignty on which Brazil could not give ground. To this day, the policy of reciprocity continues to hold, to the detriment of Brazilian tourism.

One of the embassy's main actions in the area of tourism was to create the "Visit Brazil" program. The aim was to promote Brazil as a destination for US tourism and investments through events in the main American cities (Los Angeles, Houston, New York, Miami, Chicago, Atlanta, and San Francisco).

The president of Embratur at the time, Caio Luiz de Carvalho, who later became Minister for Tourism, always attended these events, which attracted upwards of two hundred participants—tourist agents, operators, and the specialist press. The exhibitors generally included Brazilian state and municipal tourist boards, airlines, large hotel chains and Brazilian tour operators catering to the foreign traveler.

The trade show brought heightened interest in Brazilian tourist destinations and in establishing offices and agencies in Washington, with Embratur support. In 2003, as a result of this work, the embassy's Tourism Promotion sector was named the best South American travel office in the United States at the World Travel Awards.

Also in 2003, the embassy published Portuguese and English versions of the brochure *Brazil at the Smithsonian—Brazilian Presence in the Collections of the Smithsonian Institution*, showcasing the Brazilian items in the institution's museums in Washington. One aspect that drew a lot of tourist attention was Brazil's mineral wealth, the true measure of which was little known in the United States.

Military Attachés

Given the importance to the United States of the Armed Forces, Washington is the only foreign post that has military attachés with the rank of officer generals.

In order to integrate the Brazilian military attachés into the wider work of the embassy, I invited them, as a matter of policy, to participate in the regular coordination meetings I held with the diplomats.

After September 11 and at the beginning of the war in Iraq, I encouraged the attachés to sound out sources at the Defense Department and attachés from other countries. It was important that we knew how things were going in Iraq and what was being done to tackle terrorism. Information on sensitive issues, however, was not easily given to countries like Brazil, which had positioned itself clearly against the invasion of the Arab nation.

The annual visits of the Almirante Saldanha navy training ship served to show Brazil's prestige in the military sphere. Every year, Senator Edward Kennedy contacted me to get the Brazilian navy to repeat the now traditional and much-awaited call at the Port of Boston, in his home state of Massachusetts.

Brazil's three services have their own offices in Washington from which they procure spare parts for equipment used on land, sea and in the air, an endeavor not made any easier by the bureaucracy and the Defense Department's delays in filling our orders.

The embassy and its diplomats ended up having to intervene in negotiations between the Air Force Command and the US Defense Department for the purchase of replacement parts and supplies needed to maintain and run Brazil's aircraft. Besides the US Foreign Military Sales (FMS), there was really nowhere else Brazil could procure these parts, as much of the equipment was obsolete after decades of budgetary restrictions.

Obtaining the spare parts was even more crucial at that time because Brazil was in the middle of setting up its Amazonian Protection and Surveillance System across the nine states in the Legal Amazon. When I took over at the embassy, the construction of the system, by Raytheon of Boston, was already underway. In addition to the military aspects of defense, the system was also designed to collate environmental data and control Brazilian airspace with a view to attaining higher levels of security for our civilian and military aircraft overflying the rainforest. During the installation of the equipment and the engineering work, Air Force planes were essential carriers of materials. It was therefore essential that we obtained those replacement parts from the FMS.

The bid to speed up the supply process took countless meetings and discussions with the Defense and State Departments.

In an attempt to reduce this external dependence, I repeated something I had done in London and rallied the commanders of the three armed forces to approach the Ministry of Defense to propose a program designed to strengthen Brazil's defense industry. The strategy was to produce those spare parts in Brazil through national companies, in association with foreign manufacturers, and therefore eliminate any dependence on the FMS. The idea gained momentum later on and was included in the Strategic Plan for National Defense issued in December 2008.

CHAPTER 7

Developments in Brazilian Foreign Policy toward the United States

(APRIL 2004 TO MAY 2011)

HAVING COMPLETED MY ACCOUNT of the developments in Brazil–US bilateral relations during my time in Washington, it struck me as useful to give an update on some of the dealings between the two countries between April 2004, when I left the embassy, and May 2011, when the Portuguese version of the book went to print.

As I showed at the beginning, the signs President Lula was giving early in his first term indicated that the government would recognize Brazil–US relations as central to our foreign policy and proceed with the core tenets and attitudes of the FHC administration. However, after the first months of Lula's government, it became clear that foreign policy in general and toward the US in particular would be conducted in a rather different manner.

The Lula government introduced a new and very personal vision of the world into our foreign policy. From the beginning, the official rhetoric was, in effect, that the government was not willing to accept the world order as it was and that it would strive to change it in pursuit of a more democratic and equitable international order.

The government's spokespeople spared no criticism of the deep social divides between countries rich and poor and looked to the Third World in search of alliances and new foreign policy priorities for the southern hemisphere, always underscoring the growing asymmetries between the developed and developing worlds.

The rhetoric in favor of strengthening multilateralism, itself a traditional Brazilian position, was spun to incorporate a shift in Brazil's trade coordinates and to create the conditions from which to undermine the uni-polar world so fully and vigorously prevalent under George W. Bush.

Describing his foreign policy as assertive, Lula branded the previous approach as "subservient," a mere "acceptance of directives issued by the major power hubs: the United States and Europe."

The party-politicization of Brazilian foreign policy was unmistakably clear from the beginning of Lula's first term, as the influence of the Partido dos Trabalhadores (PT) was increasingly felt on the decision-making process at the Foreign Ministry. The first sign of this was the appointment of Marco Aurélio Garcia, a PT stalwart, to the position of international advisor to the presidency, a post customarily occupied by a diplomat. In March 2003, Minister for Foreign Affairs Celso Amorim indicated this partisan bent when he observed, in a speech, that two aspects need to be taken into consideration in every change of government and of policy orientation: first, a natural affinity with the position adopted by the government, the president, and the minister of state; and, second, professional competence. We are a professional corps par excellence, but, he added, we have to be enthusiastically engaged with certain lines of policy, with certain leanings.

The party's growing influence saw Amorim officially join PT in the closing months of 2009, something hitherto unheard of among diplomats who held the post of foreign minister, who must act in the interests of the state, not of a party.

As for International Advisor to the Presidency Marco Aurélio Garcia, I have to recognize that throughout my time in Washington, I never noted any direct or indirect attempt to interfere in issues of Brazilian interest in the United States, contrary to what seemed to be happening in relation to the formulation and implementation of policy toward South American nations.

The international advisor's only visit to Washington during my ambassadorship was toward the end of 2003, as related earlier. On that occasion, anti-Americanism was welling among certain sectors of the Lula government, although it had not yet assumed clear contours.

Although new in principle, I don't see anything particularly wrong with a party representative international advisor playing a part in foreign policymaking, especially given his proximity to the president and to the president's office.

From the beginning of the Lula government, foreign policy was cast in the mold of a PT vision of the world and was guided by the party's programs. This approach to foreign policy was a sort of compensation to PT for its quiet support and neutrality in relation to Lula's decision to continue with the economic policy inherited from FHC.

Itamaraty made no attempt to conceal the fact that it was following party lines, and foreign policy ceased to represent purely and simply the permanent interests of the Brazilian state, but was now put into the service of party-political platforms.

The South–South priority in foreign relations, with its focus on developing countries and new partnerships with other emerging nations, shoved the developed world into the background—not that it was altogether ignored, but Brazil now met its proposals in an increasingly reactive way.

A document approved by the PT Congress in February 2010 left no doubt as to the real aims of Brazil's foreign policy toward the United States.

> Objectively, the foreign policy of the Lula government sees Brazil as competing with the United States. Compared with other powers, our competition is low in intensity, seen as our official doctrine is one of peaceful and respectful cohabitation (frank cooperation and serene divergence with the United States). However, in the light of our proximity to the United States, Brazil's competition is of immense geopolitical importance and has the potential to become a threat to the US over the medium term. This is confirmed . . . by the Obama administration's insistence on maintaining a policy of bilateral agreements and displays of brute force (IV fleet, bases in Colombia, coup in Honduras and the ongoing embargo against Cuba). It is against this backdrop that the debate on the overhaul of the Brazilian Armed Forces has been set, including the nuclear submarine and the purchase of jet fighters from the French.

Over the course of Lula's two terms, relations with Washington did not progress, but they did remain within the bounds of normality, without any serious problems in the political or diplomatic fields, with the exception of Brazil's policy toward Iran, in 2010. In terms of trade flows, the natural disputes were all handled at the WTO and resolved as per the normal means and without contaminating other areas of common interest.

At the end of Lula's visit to Washington in June 2003, we had every reason to envisage the institutionalization of Brazil's bilateral relations with the United States and the creation of conditions for expanded co-operation in the areas of energy, trade and agriculture. However, little or no concrete action was taken to realize that potential.

Lula's disinterest in deepening relations with the United States was made evident on his second visit to Washington. Not only did the president display a certain irritation at having to prolong his stay by one day—and it was very much in Brazil's interests for him to do so—but he gave the impression that to rub shoulders with the Americans was a sort of betrayal of the working class.

Despite his rhetoric to the contrary, from the second semester of 2003 onwards, our relations with the United States slumped into stagnation punctuated with isolated incidents that demonstrated our dissatisfaction with US policies. The programmatic PT approach was also largely employed internally, especially in relation to FTAA negotiations, as a means of reinforcing grassroots support.

While Itamaraty was becoming more radical on ideological positions in its foreign policy, the US government was beginning to give Brazil special treatment, visible not only in the format of the meetings on the Presidential visit of 2003, but also in the nature and diversification of the bilateral themes under discussion.

In Brazil's official rhetoric, the relationship was always at the best possible level, and this description of Brazil's relations with the US was no exception to the way the Lula government presented its foreign policy actions and their results.

I recall one attempted rapprochement with the United States that ended up being thwarted by Brazil's own behavior. Toward the end of July 2004, Treasury Secretary John W. Snow visited Brazil to participate in a working group on growth and stressed the importance of trade liberalization, both globally and hemisphere-wide. Minister Palocci, his counterpart, signaled his agreement and mentioned Brazil's interest in reinvigorating the FTAA, which had been stalled since the Miami summit in November 2003. Palocci offered to lead a drive in this direction and bring the trade understanding between the two countries to a new level, especially in the area of services, taking an opposite line to Itamaraty, which he hoped to re-engage in the talks. There was even a possibility of resuscitating the 4+1 trade agreement between Mercosur and the US. In a meeting Snow and Palocci had with Lula, the Minister tried to get the President to support his position, but Lula gave no response and stuck with Itamaraty.

From 2005 onwards, President Bush visited Brazil twice and Lula made one more official trip to Washington. During the G8 and G20 meetings and at the UN General Assembly and other multilateral fora, Lula maintained regular contact with Bush and, later, with Barack Obama.

The joint communiqué issued in November 2005, after a meeting at the Granja do Torto, the Brazilian Presidential residence, made the first reference to a strategic dialogue between the two countries. The intention was to broaden the political discussion in order to make the relationship more mature and enhance agreement on sensitive matters. The United States maintained similar relationships with only a handful of countries, such as Russia, China, India, and Japan. The ground was prepared for this dialogue months ahead of the meeting at Granja do Torta, on the sidelines of the United Nations General Assembly, in talks between Secretary of State for Political Affairs Nicolas Burns, and then-political undersecretary at Itamaraty, Antonio Patriota.

Throughout 2006, Burns–Patriota interlocution and meetings between the ministers of state prepared for a series of presidential meetings in 2007. During the campaign period in 2006, the Brazilian government had once again sought to allay any fears the American authorities might have had about the future directions the bilateral relationship would take. According to the report of the United States embassy in Brasília, Gilberto Carvalho, Lula's chief of staff, in talks with US diplomats, asked for "understanding if the electoral rhetoric had occasionally seemed too critical of the United States," adding, once again, that the relationship with the US would remain "central" during Lula's second term.

Meetings between ministers and high-ranking government officials remained constant and fluid, although the results of discussions with Colin Powell (late 2004), Donald Rumsfeld and Condoleezza Rice (2005), national security advisors from the Bush administrations, with Obama and Hillary Clinton (2010), trade secretaries, trade representatives, and secretaries for agriculture and justice yielded results that were more rhetorical than concrete.

Though these visits tended to accentuate the positive, they could not eliminate the divergences between the two countries. The multilateral agenda generated tension, mostly on the spur of clashing interests and dissonant positions on such global themes as the environment, human rights, terrorism, UN reform, and Brazil's campaign for a permanent seat on the UN Security Council. On this particular point, Brazil sought US support to no avail, largely because, as Ambassador Clifford Sobel put it in his communications with the Department of State, Brazil had failed to demonstrate the kind of leadership that might have made it a strong candidate.

One thing that was clear during this period was that Brazil and the United States were assuming positions on multilateral, regional, and bilateral trade negotiations that were not always convergent. That said, trade disputes and conflicting stances on negotiations were, quite rightly, seen as just part of the game, without offending sensibilities or causing any undue commotion.

Washington continued to view Brazil and President Lula as a moderating factor in a region that was increasingly divided by rising anti-Americanism in places like Venezuela and Bolivia. Brazil was still seen as "a regional power . . . ready to become a world power," to use the words of Condoleezza Rice during a charm offensive that certainly pleased Brasília.

The visits exchanged by Presidents Bush and Lula reinforced this optimistic impression, and with the PT government's full endorsement, but when seen in historical perspective they reveal themselves to have been purely symbolic. On one hand, with his weakened support at home, Bush was in no position to make any concessions on trade, as was clear from his refusal to examine the elimination of barriers affecting Brazilian products, particularly ethanol; on the other, with Lula just beginning his second term, there was no reason for the Americans to expect any significant change of course in Brazilian foreign policy.

In the absence of a proactive attitude on the part of the PT government, the United States proposed a positive agenda focused on energy. This subject dominated discussions on Bush's second visit to Brasília, in 2007. Though immensely important, the memorandum of understanding on expanded and standardized ethanol production was not fully executed by the end of Lula's presidency. It was an issue of just as much importance to the US, given its priority of diversifying energy sources and on reducing oil dependency, as it was to Brazil, one of the countries with the highest capacity to increase its output of renewable energy.

The agreements looked good on paper, but their results would only be felt when and if the two administrations acted to implement the decisions the presidents had made on these Brazil–US visits.

The Latin American–Middle Eastern summit held in May 2005 introduced a new point of tension with the United States. The US and Israel were spared no criticism during this summit meeting, which also revealed a growing presence of China and Iran in the region, with potentially serious national security implications for the United States, given the possibility of collaboration on nuclear energy and also agreements re-routing Venezuelan oil away from the US and toward China.

Adding further fuel to the fire were the American government's restrictions on the sale of components for a satellite Brazil that was building in conjunction with China, and US objections to the sale of Embraer's Super Tucano aircraft to Venezuela. On the Brazilian side, there was the decision to exclude US-built F-16 fighter planes from the bidding of items up for renewal as part of the Air Force overhaul.

When Lula visited Bush at Camp David in 2007, the pair emulated FHC and Clinton by declaring a commitment to deepen the strategic dialogue between Brazil and the United States. In their joint statement, they endorsed expanded bilateral relations based on shared democratic values, respect for human rights, cultural diversity, liberalization of trade, multilateralism, environmental protection, defense of international peace and security, and the promotion of socially just development. In their direct talks, energy, the Doha Round, South America, Africa, and UNSC reform topped the bill. The meeting also gave rise to the Innovation Forum and CEO Forum, as well as to a trilateral cooperation program with Haiti, the Dominican Republic, El Salvador and Saint Christopher, and Nevis. The two governments committed to the conclusion of an agreement on double taxation and renewed a memorandum of understanding on education and a partnership on science and technology.

Without changing the axis of its foreign policy toward the United States, some positive signs were to be noted in the official Brazilian rhetoric on the developed economies, which had, up to now, been shunted into the background, and the US economy in particular. There was, therefore, reason to expect a more pragmatic approach to policymaking and trade negotiations, but no such measures were taken, and fresh areas of conflict emerged.

On the other hand, the new store the United States placed on Brazil was demonstrated by an initiative taken by the House of Representatives

Committee on Foreign Relations to approve a resolution on the bilateral relationship. In a resolution passed on October 9, 2007, the US Legislature recognized that "the United States and Brazil have reached a strategic confluence in their interests," citing Condoleezza Rice's remark that "the United States sees Brazil as a regional leader and a global partner."

In response to the critics of the 'new' foreign policy indicated by these more positive nuances in official Brazilian declarations about the United States, Minister Celso Amorim classified as myth any assertion that Brazil would start placing more emphasis on its relations with the US and Europe. Later, toward the end of 2007, in the face of a backlash in the media and at the Brazilian Congress against certain directions in Brazilian foreign policy, Amorim seemed to have changed his tune, declaring that Itamaraty was looking to create a reinvigorated relationship with the United States. In yet another exercise in rhetoric, he said that Brazil–US relations were at a positive juncture, with growing reciprocal trust and mutual respect. The reality, however, was very different indeed.

The election of President Barack Obama in 2008 was met with expectations and demands from the Brazilian government. In his message of congratulations to Obama, Lula repeated a slogan that had been part of his own campaign and that of the president elect: "Your Excellency knew how to transmit a vision of the future, showed a capacity for leadership and certainty that hope is stronger than fear."

As it had done upon the election of George W. Bush, the Council on Foreign Relations in New York drew up a new report with recommendations on US relations with Latin America, and this was sent to Barack Obama in 2009. The document recognized that if the US had once exercised hegemony over Latin America, those days were gone and that Brazil should now be viewed in a different light by Washington's policymakers. According to the Council's report, Brazil today warranted different treatment than eight years before, as it had become an increasingly important player not only in Latin America, but in the world. The text recommended that the US government negotiate a Biofuels Pact with Brazil. To this end, it suggested lifting disincentives on the production and sale of these products and recommended the creation of incentives for gasoline distributors in Brazil and the United States to increase ethanol availability. For the Council on Foreign Relations, energy is a matter of national security, and Brazil had an important role to play in that sphere.

During the first meeting between Lula and Obama, in March 2009, in parallel with the G20 meeting, Itamaraty strove to stress what it called the "intellectual affinity" between the two presidents—which may well have been an overly optimistic turn of phrase. "Obama is like us," said Lula, who Obama had referred to at an earlier meeting as "the guy" on the international scene.

This meeting in Washington was important for its symbolism, but little changed in practice. The one-to-one signified recognition of Brazil's importance as a protagonist—and Brazil presented itself as a nation with global interests—and took us one step closer to individual standing vis-à-vis the South American context as a whole.

According to the coverage of the meeting, Obama and Lula dealt with the same global themes as ever, such as the international economic crisis, the G20 summit in early April, protectionism and energy, but only touched on bilateral issues. It was interesting to note the overlap of these themes. The bureaucracies of the two nations appear to have been unable to interpret adequately what was said by the presidents, as their many declarations of intent were followed by restrictive observations on the Brazilian side.

The agenda for the private discussions contained, as always, bilateral, regional, hemispheric, and global themes. Among the bilateral subjects were the decrease in trade flows, restrictions on Brazilian ethanol, and cooperation on energy and medicines in third nations, especially Haiti and African countries. On the hemispheric level, the presidents discussed the Summit of the Americas, to be held in mid-April 2009, and, regionally, the US relationships with Venezuela, Bolivia, and Ecuador. The reintegration of Cuba into the Inter-American system with the suspension of the US embargo was "an inevitable issue," to use the words of Minister Celso Amorim, though Obama was not very receptive on this, as he had already loosened the Bush-era restrictions on travel to the island and on cash transfers to family still living there.

Differences of position on trade negotiations and protectionism became very clear. While Lula wanted to continue the conversations on the Doha Round and criticized US protectionism, symbolized by the Buy American campaign and continued restrictions on ethanol, Obama recognized that, amidst such a serious crisis, it would be difficult to progress on multilateral trade negotiations and suspend the barriers on Brazilian produce. Continent-wide energy security, the environment, and climate change were also discussed, but without conflict, given Obama's course-correction on these issues earlier in his term.

From the outside, I saw that two aspects of the visit went largely unnoticed. First was the didactic tone of the press conference, at which Lula, assuming the role of regional spokesman, saw fit to lecture Obama to the effect that the United States ought to look at Latin America through the "correct lens," i.e., recognize the political and social changes of recent years and stop acting as an overseer imposing solutions, but instead as a genuine partner. The second noteworthy aspect was that Lula, addressing the Brazilian public, laid the blame for the global economic crisis, Brazil's own economic slowdown, and the rise in unemployment squarely at the US door. Trying to exonerate his government of all responsibility for negative results, he shunted the blame onto the United States and pressed Obama for measures that could redress the 'wretched legacy' left by Bush.

In October 2008, with the financial crisis caused by the real-estate bubble in the US, the higher echelons of the Brazilian administration resumed their attacks on the US government. "It is not fair that the poorer parts of the world should end up paying for the errors of the wealthier few. Nor is it fair that countries that worked hard to rebuild their economies should have to carry the burden for the recklessness of those who caused this crisis," said President Lula.

At the G20 meeting in São Paulo in November 2009 there was public disagreement over how the financial system should be run. Brazil argued for a global coordination model, while the US wanted to stick with the current model of national regulations.

On other issues, the Brazilian government ascribed the failure of the Doha trade negotiations and the unsatisfactory results of the Climate Change Summit in Copenhagen to US action and inaction.

Nevertheless, Washington's view continued to be that the former union leader had made a democratic, moderate center-left president and that the interests and values Brazil defended coincided with US foreign policy priorities for the region: democracy, political and economic stability, a crackdown on narco-trafficking and support for free trade.

As Brazil's participation on the world stage grows and our interests become more global, our relationship with the United States will become crucial to those interests. This convergence would be facilitated if certain political-ideological concerns that pervade our foreign policy were set aside, as occurred at many meetings between Lula and

American presidents. However, everyday reality has done its best to ignore and undo the good results these brought. If Brazil had pursued a pragmatic approach like that adopted by China, which kept its ideology to itself, the benefits for the defense of our national interests would have been far greater.

Despite the government's lack of strategic vision and these unnecessary tensions, some advances were made, such as the Brazil–US CEO forum and the private sector's efforts to set a positive agenda. Two significant agreements were signed: one on military cooperation—the first in the Defense area since 1975—and another of a consular kind, which extended the validity of tourist visas between the two countries from five to ten years. A memorandum of understanding was also signed concerning cooperation on biofuels, including the introduction of international standards that would help transform ethanol into a commodity, and on an exchange of tax information. The Washington government proposed negotiations on a Trade and Investment Framework Agreement (TIFA) and another on double taxation, which was of major interest to Brazilian companies in the middle of an internationalization process. Neither proposal advanced during the Lula government.

Beginning in 2008, trade and investment started to grow at slower rates and Brazilian exports lost dynamism. This was not exclusively due to exchange rate appreciation and economic slowdown in the US in the wake of the global crisis, but also to Itamaraty's failure to support the promotion of trade, which was now geared more toward developing countries in the southern hemisphere.

In practice, the Lula government missed a great opportunity not only to put pre-2008 economic growth and trade with the US to better use, but also to deepen cooperation in areas of interest to Brazil.

Itamaraty did not exactly inhibit expanded bilateral cooperation, but it did nothing to encourage it either. The low priority given to relations with the United States and the undisguised anti-Americanism of certain sectors of the government could be surmised from the fact that during the first years of the Lula government, Minister Celso Amorim only visited the US to attend a meeting of the UN General Assembly in New York and for gatherings of the OAS secretary-general's support group for Venezuela in Washington. It was only on these occasions that he met with his peers at the Department of State.

As Itamaraty and the international advisor to the Presidency stepped up their rhetoric on the United States, the US pretended to ignore the public declarations coming from certain quarters of the Brazilian government. It was obvious that the USA was continuing with its policy of no-conflict with the country it touted as the moderating influence in the region, and that Brazil stood to gain nothing from highlighting these divergences.

At multilateral and hemispheric assemblies, the foreign policy positions Brasília adopted underscored its combative tendencies. Celso Amorim is known to have compared US trade representatives to Nazi propagandists while President Lula declared that the global economic crisis had been caused by the "irrational behavior of blue-eyed whites."

During Lula's second term, Brazil's action throughout South America was decisive to the creation of institutions that excluded the United States and strove to enfeeble the OAS. The government applied an inverted version of the Monroe Doctrine, the nineteenth-century plan by the US President to weaken European influence on Latin America; in other words, Brazil tried to exclude the US. The establishment of the Union of Southern Nations (UNASUL), the South American Defense Council and the Community of Latin American and Caribbean States (CELAC) are examples of this policy. Divergent positions between the United States and Brazil on Venezuela, Cuba, and, more recently, Honduras, reinforced this opposition to US policy.

The attempt to discuss regional conflicts and differences among South American nations only, within UNASUL or the South American Defense Council, obtained only limited success. The more sensitive issues—concerning Colombia and Venezuela and the agreement the former signed with the US in 2009, granting US military consultants usage rights to several air force bases in Colombian territory—were not handled in these forums due to opposition from Bogota.

The release of a US Air Force report to Congress recognizing the strategic value of these bases in terms of strike capacity against potential South American enemies was cause for further strain on the relationship between Brasília and Washington. The crisis in Honduras was another example of a situation aggravated by the rejection of Brazil's proposed solutions to the critical political problem created by the ouster of President Manuel Zelaya.

The Lula government's aspirations toward a more effective leadership role and a higher profile outside the western hemisphere go some way toward explaining Itamaraty's actions. Electoral motivations must also be factored in, considering that Brazil's growing presence in the world scene and opposition to the United States were exploited throughout the 2010 presidential campaign as major achievements of the Lula government.

Brazil's relations with the US during Lula's second mandate can be described as "correct," which, in diplomatic terms, means neither nation showed any enthusiasm for the bilateral relationship.

Never free of tension, the relationship that we saw was peppered with disagreements on hemispheric affairs and divergences on specific trade issues, such as the WTO's decision to impose trade sanctions on the United States for having broken international rules on cotton subsidies.

The policies the Brazilian government adopted on Honduras, Cuba and its dissidents, and on Iran and its nuclear program exacerbated the political friction with the United States and contributed to the overall deterioration of our relationship with the superpower. The Brazilian government's affirmative stance on what it saw to be the nation's interests at the time was presented by Itamaraty in an increasingly arrogant and self-congratulatory manner, and this radicalization ended up causing more harm than good for Brazil.

Foreign policy activism abroad indicated that Brazil was looking to exert influence beyond the South American context, and this made it harder for Brazilian diplomacy to identify where Brazil's real national interests lay.

The pursuit of Brazil's position as a global political agent, as President Lula described it, attempting to solve conflicts through negotiation, presupposes a capacity for evaluation and information-gathering that the Brazilian Foreign Service is perfectly equipped to perform.

It is worth remembering other points of friction, too, such as Brazil's stance on the Honduras crisis and its clashes with the United States at the OAS on Tegucigalpa's return to the organization, and the way the Chancellery handled the issues of human rights in Cuba, democracy in Venezuela, and the concession of Colombian military bases to the United States. Competition with the US on Haiti shortly after the earthquake was another example of unnecessary attrition with Washington. These episodes are sufficient to demonstrate how foreign policy treaded paths that led away from our best diplomatic traditions and permanent national interests.

As the US government saw it, according to the cables released by WikiLeaks, Brazil adopted a "confused" policy on Honduras and "took a backseat" while waiting for the US to sort things out.

Our northern neighbor's reservations about Brazilian foreign policy in the region were made clear in 2004, when, again according to the WikiLeaks cables, President of Colombia Álvaro Uribe said that Lula was doing his best to create an anti-American alliance in Latin America and asked the US to do something to curb Brazil's ambitions. The Paraguayan foreign minister, Leila Rachid, twice affirmed—first in 2004 and again in 2005—that Brazil's agenda was to minimize US influence in South America in order to ensure its own dominion and that she was concerned that Brazil was trying to become a voice of leadership in the region. According to these communications, Rachid reiterated Uribe's request that the United States take steps to contain Brazil.

Apparently, at no time did the US government make any attempt to 'contain' Brazil, as our Colombian neighbors wished it would.

The visit to Brazil by the new western hemisphere secretary, Arturo Valenzuela, in December 2009, and the initial contacts made by US Ambassador Tom Shannon with Celso Amorim and Lula, early in 2010, revealed the ambiguities of Brazilian foreign policy toward the United States. The leaked diplomatic cables between the Embassy in the US and Brasília prove as much.

Valenzuela attended meetings with Itamaraty, the Ministry of Defense and the international advisor to the Presidency, meetings at which it was patent that Brazil's representatives did not wish to exacerbate the already growing differences between the two nations and that they wanted to work with Washington on a number of issues, such as the crisis in Honduras, the need to defuse tensions in South America (particularly between Venezuela and Colombia), Haiti, and cooperation on eliminating narco-trafficking in Bolivia. At the presidential level, the emphasis was on the issue of Iran and the conflict in the Middle East.

As tensions rose, President Lula kept on telling the new ambassador of his continued interest in forging a strong personal bond with President Obama and his desire to pursue an active rapprochement through an exchange of visits in order to realize the enormous potential of our bilateral relations. The areas Lula identified as ripe for cooperation between the two countries were Haiti, negotiations on climate change, Iran, and the Middle East peace process.

On the other hand, Minister Celso Amorim, in a breach of protocol, met with Shannon on his first day in Brasília and spoke of how anxious he was to begin a new phase in Brazil–US relations. Underscoring the importance of intense dialogue between the two capitals, Amorim referred to cooperation in the economic sphere, on climate change, on the issue of Iran and the conflict in the Middle East and, regionally, on Honduras and the defense agreement between Colombia and the United States.

Despite the attempts on both sides to minimize the tensions and accentuate the few advances that were actually being made, the uranium enrichment agreement with Iran, negotiated in Turkey in 2010, provoked the most serious divergence with the US during the eight years Lula was in power.

As this was the first time Brazil was getting involved in a serious international crisis, taking concrete actions that ran counter to what the US considered to be in its national security interest, it is important to examine in greater depth the broader implications of this first encounter between the two nations outside the South American continent.

Brazil's intervention in the crisis between the United States and Iran, concerning the suspicion that the theocratic regime in Tehran was developing a nuclear program for military rather than purely civilian purposes, was presented as something positive by the Lula government, which proposed diplomatic negotiations as a means toward overcoming the difficulties and distrust between the two nations.

However, given the manner in which the country went about this, it proved that we still have a long way to go before we have the maturity or credibility to go around waving the flag of world peace.

We could have offered our good offices on conflicts closer to home, trying to help Argentina and Uruguay to work out their differences on the installation of a cellulose plant on the border, for example, or on disputes between Colombia and Venezuela, which almost led to war. In both cases, Brazil did very little, preferring to carry the white flag to the Palestinians and Israelis and to try to intercede between the US and Iran.

These decisions called into question the sound judgment of our foreign policymakers and their ability to determine Brazil's true interests and to make objective analyses of the information collated by Itamaraty's efficient intelligence network.

Here is not the place to go into the rights and wrongs of the crisis itself, but merely to show how clearly it evinced a series of misevaluations by the Brazilian government when it undertook to negotiate an agreement with Iran, which Tehran then threatened to break if sanctions were brought by the United Nations. In November 2009, Celso Amorim declared that "Iran is the new strategic partner in the country's foreign policy."

The Brazilian government miscalculated the weight of the strategic and commercial interests China and Russia have with Iran and their willingness to support Brazil's efforts. Brazil's measure of the United States's determination to push for sanctions against Iran at the UN Security Council was also misjudged.

Itamaraty ignored the internal and external pressure on the Obama government that ultimately forced it to break off its negotiations with Iran, and warnings as to Washington's predictable response to the interference of new players in matters it monopolistically considered its sole preserve.

There was no adequate assessment of the damage supporting Iran could cause Brazil. By wading into such a sensitive situation involving US national security in search of prestige, Brazil would seem to have made little of the potential backlash. The very real possibility of souring our relations with the United States was basically ignored in favor of the PT line that the US was a waning power and that others had to step up and make the world more multipolar. While this may be true on the economic and political fronts, where the US can no longer impose its will on emerging nations, it was a grave error to assume the same applied to issues of strategy and defense, on which the United States remains the world's one and only superpower, without any sign of decline.

Analysts abroad tried to show that, given his lack of familiarity with regional problems outside South America and his blatant anti-Americanism, Lula was poking a hornet's nest with a short stick.

Worse still in relation to Brazil's interests was President Lula's express recognition that the agreement with Iran was a risk from which the country had nothing to gain. According to the news, a high-ranking government official was noted as saying that Brazil's discussions with Iran may well have cost it a permanent seat on the UN Security Council and that it could be exploited by the opposition during the election campaign as a reckless adventure and failure. Even so, he said, it "was worth sticking to the policy."

In November 2009, soon after the visit to Brazil by the Iranian president Mahmoud Ahmadinejad, the view in the US was that Brazil had not yet understood the dynamic surrounding Iran and the Middle East, as was clearly stated in cables issued by the US embassy in Brasília. In conversations with the American embassy in Buenos Aires, Argentinean diplomatic staff said that their warning lights were flashing on the directions Brazil's nuclear program was taking. However, they admitted that they were not unduly concerned, as they did not believe that Brazil would break international and bilateral agreements on nuclear armaments.

The Lula government's criteria for determining the national interests were by no means clear at the time. If obtaining a permanent seat on the UN Security Council was one of the main foreign policy priorities, why risk blowing whatever prospects we had of being accepted onto the board that presides over international peace and security?

Another theme that pitted Brazil against the US was the quinquennial revision of the Non-Proliferation Treaty (NPT). The main problem was the introduction of an Additional TNP Protocol, with demands from the IAEA concerning inspections at uranium enrichment facilities and other installations under the nuclear program. The new regulation clashed with Brazil's policy of not allowing unscheduled inspections at Brazilian nuclear facilities.

The ambiguous wording of the final document meant that both Brazil and the United States were able to claim that their concerns had been fully addressed. As publicly recognized in the National Defense Strategy, Brazil had no need to sign the document at all, because, according to Brazil's interpretation—not accepted by the nuclear powers—the protocol "is a non-compulsory document that does not oblige Brazil to receive the IAEA inspectors." Thus, Brazil cannot be questioned on its nuclear program, especially on its enrichment of uranium.

The relationship between the two countries was seriously affected by this combination of facts. The President of the Brazil Caucus at Congress, Eliot Engel, democrat representative for New York, contested Brazil's policy on Iran at a terse meeting with the then-ambassador in Washington, Antonio Patriota. Engel later publicly criticized Brazil's support for Iran and threatened to stand down as Caucus President.

According to the WikiLeaks cables, the view at the US embassy was that Brazil was not yet mature enough to be a global player. In another communication, Ambassador Clifford Sobel recounts that he asked our government to discuss its initiatives with the US only to hear, from a high-ranking staffer at Itamaraty, that "Brazil does not need US permission to follow its own foreign policy."

The visit by Secretary of State Hillary Clinton, in early March 2010, can be seen as a further slump in Brazil–US relations. The main theme of the meetings with President Lula and Minister Celso Amorim was Iran.

Their public disagreement raised the temperature of the press conference at Itamaraty, when Amorim responded to Clinton's criticisms of Iran by likening the pressure the Obama administration was applying on Tehran to that preceding the invasion of Iraq in 2003. The Brazilian Chancellor added that Iraq's reputed arsenal of chemical and biological weapons never materialized and the cost to the world was enormous. "Brazil thinks with its own mind and will not bend to a consensus it disagrees with," said Amorim, practically giving advance notice of how Brazil would vote on the Iran sanctions at the United Nations Security Council.

The situation became even more delicate in the face of Brazil's machinations during the UN Security Council deliberations on the sanctions called for by the US, Britain, France, Russia, and China. Since the very beginning, Brazil had refused to take part in the discussions because it disagreed with the sanctions. At the last minute, it managed to sway Turkey away from abstention to a vote against the resolution, which meant that, given Lebanon's abstention for reasons of internal politics, it did not end up being an isolated naysayer. Brazil's vote against sanctions was the first at the UNSC on a resolution backed by all five permanent members.

The damage to Brazil's standing and to the personal reputations of Lula and Celso Amorim among the influential circles of Washington's decision-makers was unprecedented. In the closing months of Lula's government, all communication between the two countries' presidents and ministers of state was interrupted, such was the mutual loss of trust.

The unilateral sanctions brought against Iran by the US Congress included, for the first time, restrictions on the sale of ethanol to Iran and the monitoring of all ethanol exports to the country.

The renewal of talks between Brazil, Iran, and Turkey in an attempt to participate in discussions of the Vienna Group, created within the IAEA and including the US, Russia, China, France, Britain, and Germany, further ratcheted the tensions between the two Departments of State. With the US refusal to admit Brazil and Turkey as informal members, Minister Celso Amorim resumed his criticisms of the United States after a meeting with President Ahmadinejad, saying that it must be very difficult for someone to share control after wielding it so absolutely for so long. Always eager to deny any impact Brazil's positions had on the bilateral relations, Amorim repeated that not one single aspect had been affected.

When the president of Syria, Bashar Al Assad, visited Brasília in June 2010, he stressed Brazil's role in the Iran crisis and defended the country's participation as a new interlocutor in the Middle East, particularly as a broker between Palestinians and Israelis, in which we would certainly not have received support from either the US or Israel.

In early August, Washington sent a mission to Brasília to pressure the government to comply with the sanctions approved by the UN Security Council.

In the middle of this imbroglio, with the clear intention of avoiding yet another problem with Washington, the Lula government decided to delay the imposition of WTO sanctions against the US because of its failure to remove cotton subsidies, even though the US proposal presented in Brasília was not satisfactory. The Brazilian government had passed legislation through Congress that would have allowed for countermeasures against US produce and cross retaliation against American brands and patents, measures that would have seriously aggravated the dispute had they been implemented. To avoid this, Lula left it to Dilma Rousseff to decide what to do about the authorized sanctions, pending the Congressional vote on the US Farm Bill in 2012, which planned to maintain the subsidies to upland cotton growers.

In practice, Brazil ended up compensating for its defense and support of Iran, in defiance of the US, by relinquishing its right to impose countermeasures against the US for their cotton subsidies, to avoid further straining already deteriorated relations with Washington. In other words, once again, the national interest was sacrificed at the altar of ideological posturing.

During the eight years of the Lula administration, Brazilian foreign policy found itself mired in paradox. In its bid to be seen as a regional power, Brazil had to distance itself from the US, but in order to have its international ascension recognized, it still needed Washington on its side.

The fact that Brazil broke ranks on certain consensus positions among the international community, as was the case on Iran, did not end up crippling Brazil's aspirations toward a permanent seat on the Security Council. What the government's actions demonstrated was a desire to defy Washington. The emphasis the official rhetoric placed on multilateralism and multipolarity indicated Brazil's interest in exploiting the United States's flagging influence in the world in order to assert its own.

In September 2010, despite the dark clouds gathering in the diplomatic sphere, talks continued between the two countries on the Brazil–United States Trade Dialogue, conducted by the Ministry for Development. The main themes of these discussions were US trade restrictions, investment, trade promotion, and the terms of the Trade and Economic Cooperation Agreement (TECA). This accord would create a permanent forum for dialogue on disputes in these areas. The commitment was that the document would be signed at the end of Lula's government, but this, too, was left to the administration of Dilma Rousseff.

On that particular occasion, Minister Miguel Jorge resumed talks on the 2009 framework agreement (TIFA) to establish rules for investors and more agile mechanisms for settling trade and investment disputes. In conjunction with the double taxation agreement, TIFA would benefit Brazilian companies investing in the United States. Political resistance within the government prevented these negotiations from progressing, and ensured that another accord, on the exchange of financial information, negotiated as the preliminary phase of a double taxation agreement, foundered at Congress.

In defense of its interests and mindful of the need to bring down its trade deficit, the Obama government launched an ambitious program that September to double the country's exports in five years. Brazil became one of the few countries with a trade deficit with the United States, a fact compounded by a reduction in Brazilian exports.

In 2002, over 25 percent of Brazilian exports went to the US market. By the last year of the Lula government, this percentage had dropped to 10 percent.

In this context, the CEO Forum and the Brazil–US Business Council could do little to expand the economic and commercial relationship. The lack of official support and of an active policy to promote trade and attract investment was clearly reflected in the cold numbers of the statistics.

In a lecture to US and European military and strategists at a seminar on international security in Geneva, Celso Amorim said that Brazil only profited from not joining the FTAA and that its rejection gave rise to a new regional arrangement. In one more example of the distance between rhetoric and reality, Amorim declared that the FTAA had been replaced by an effective trade area in South America and that the region had ceased to be the United States's backyard.

Also in September there was an important announcement on a trade liberation agreement in the air transport area. This accord, known as Open Skies, meant that, as of 2011, Brazil and the United States would eliminate all caps on the number of flights and domestic flight destinations between the two countries. The US Congress delayed the decision on whether or not to maintain Brazilian products on its Generalized System of Preferences (GSP) until 2011, which raised doubts as to the continuation of advantageous tariffs for Brazilian companies.

In often paternalistic tone, the US embassy reports leaked by WikiLeaks signaled to foreign policymakers in Washington that Brazil would have to be encouraged to assume responsibilities and would need to learn to confront other countries if and when necessary.

On various occasions during the election campaign in 2010, President Lula referred to Brazil's new way of dealing with the United States. Paying no heed to US sensibilities, he resorted to provocative analogies in describing Brazil and the United States's disputes at the WTO: "An elephant is a huge animal, its trunk alone is worth maybe ten rats, but all it takes is one little rat to make it crap itself with fear."

In November, at the G20 Summit in Seoul, South Korea, there were further signs of disgruntlement between the presidents and their economic ministers, Guido Mantega and Timothy Geithner, of the Treasury Department. Visibly ill-at-ease, Lula and Obama spoke for five minutes, certainly about the divergent positions they had just presented at the Summit. Mantega, who had coined the term "currency war," proposed the idea—summarily rejected—of putting an end to the hegemony of the dollar and legitimizing capital controls for countries facing currency appreciations caused by an influx of foreign funds. It was an oblique reference to the US$600 billion flushed into the market to irrigate the US economy, but which, given the cautiousness of American investors, ended up being transferred to emerging countries. "We cannot suffer losses in order to help the United States," said Central Bank President Henrique Meirelles. The exchange of barbs continued with Geithner's public reaction against Brazil's positions. Along the same lines, President Lula said that the G20 needed to recover its solidarity and that the group had become "every man for himself and God for all." Amorim added one more critical argument by stressing that the FED's decision distorted trade by forcing the currencies of emerging countries to appreciate, and that this was a tactic that rendered multilateral trade negotiations irrelevant.

In the context of these fast-deteriorating relations, in the build-up to the Seoul Summit, President Barack Obama, on a visit to New Delhi, endorsed India's application for a permanent seat on the UN Security Council. While the main goal had been to gall China, which was against India's entry, the gesture hit Brazil hard.

After years of trying in vain to secure the same support from Washington, the Brazilian government sought to downplay Obama's decision to back India by taking the gesture as a sign of renewed US interest in the United Nations. In reality, Obama had moved a pawn by endorsing India, but without accepting any change to the number of Security Council seats. Recognizing the realities of global power and the role of the United States, President Lula said that Obama ought to make his commitment to India a profession of faith and effectively open the Council up to other countries. "The United States is just one voice within a Council of five," he continued, contradicting himself in a bid to diminish the importance of Obama's declaration.

"If the price of admission into the Security Council is to say yes to everything, then maybe it's not worth it," said Amorim, aware that that was not India's style, much less Brazil's. Minister Amorim was perhaps responding to Obama's declarations that any candidate for a permanent seat on the Council had to work to ensure that its authority was respected by the international community. The United States certainly did not believe that Brazil had done anything to strengthen the institution by voting against the sanctions the major powers had brought against Iran and its nuclear program that June.

The issue of human rights was another example of misalignment between the two countries. At the UN Human Rights Council, Brazil abstained on a resolution condemning Iran for violations of human rights and for its use of stoning as a punishment. Once again, Celso Amorim defended the government's position of going against the international community on censuring Iran.

These divergences had been building up for years, as the WikiLeaks documents revealed. Since 2006, the United States had noted a certain hypocrisy in Brazil's positions. For the US, Brazil withheld its criticism of certain nations when it was in its interest to do so, but was quick to criticize the United States on such issues as Guantanamo Bay, and to rail against Israel's offensive against Hezbollah in Lebanon in 2006.

These public disagreements with the United States continued down to the final days of Lula's government, due to strategic perceptions at different forums and settings. Two examples of this—one involving NATO and the other Palestine—warrant special attention.

Within the context of NATO's revised strategic concept, the organization's role outside the North Atlantic came under consideration, with talk of its expansion as an Atlantic Treaty Organization. Brazil's problem with this was that it would enable the US, through NATO, to interfere in the South Atlantic without consulting the United Nations Security Council. Brazil's concerns chiefly lay with the protection of its pre-salt oil reserves and the fact that the United States had not ratified the 1962 UN Convention on the High Seas.

Brazil's recognition of the Palestinian state within the 1967 borders, published in an official statement in December 2010, was nothing new, as it merely repeated the country's traditional position. It was, however, a political gesture in response to a direct request made that June by Mahmoud Abbas, the President of the National Palestinian Authority (NPA). The decision to issue the statement, done in December so as not to interfere with the October elections, revealed Brazil's continued desire to influence the course of the peace process in the Middle East. Israel reacted negatively to the announcement, which it said had been made in an underhanded manner: on the eve of publication, Israeli Deputy Prime Minister Silvan Shalom had met with Celso Amorim at Itamaraty and not a word was said on the subject. Informally, the US government made known its surprise at not having been informed in advance of Brazil's position.

Perhaps spurred by an interview given by former president Jimmy Carter in which he praised Brazil's initiative of recognizing the Palestinian state and encouraged the nation to become more deeply involved in the Middle East peace process ("Brazil can help because it has a lot of influence among developing countries. Brazil can be one of the leaders of this process") President Lula went back to making public statements about the United States. With only ten days left in his Presidency, Lula said that he was "convinced there will be no peace in the Middle East so long as the United States is the peacemaker. In order to negotiate the issue of peace in the Middle East it is important that other agents get involved, other countries. It is not just a US issue."

On December 27, during a breakfast with accredited journalists at the Planalto presidential palace, Lula made one of his most severe criticisms yet of Barack Obama and US policy on Latin America and the Middle East. He called the US an "empire" and said that Obama had "to recognize the importance of our region, a place experiencing democracy more intensely than anywhere else on earth." He went on to repeat his view that "so long as the United States is brokering the peace process in the Middle East the Palestinian–Israeli conflict will never end. Countries like Iran and Syria cannot be left out of the negotiations." The agreement Brazil and Turkey made with Iran on exchanging uranium in natura for enriched uranium was defended in the strongest possible terms. Considered by Lula as one of the foreign policy high points of his administration, despite being rejected by both the international community and the UN, the president added, in typical style: "I think it hurt their pride. All of a sudden along comes a Third World country, which is how they've always seen Brazil, and it gets more out of Iran than they've ever managed to get; it must have caused a certain envy, a little jealously, or whatever."

Of course, by this stage, the international community was taking the outgoing president's declarations with a pinch of salt, aware that it was all just demagogy for domestic consumption.

The leaked internal correspondence between the state department and its embassies, particularly the embassy in Brasília, revealed by WikiLeaks, corroborated a lot of the observations I made in my account of my experience in Washington.

In the cables released up to the end of 2010, it was clearly the perception of the US diplomats that there was a deliberate intention to upset relations between Brazil and the United States and that the main obstacles to expanding the bilateral relationship were the head of Itamaraty and the president's international advisor.

As in many examples cited in US official communications, this attitude did not prevent cooperation and a frank exchange of opinions between the two countries on sensitive areas, such as the fight against terrorism, the reception of prisoners from Guantanamo, and the issues of Iran and Venezuela, in which Brazil offered, in vain, to assist in establishing direct contact with Hugo Chávez.

Over the eight years in question, what we saw was an ideologically-driven foreign policy that hardly disguised the intention to oppose the United States and Washington's policies in defense of what were understood to be Brazil's interests. In practice, however, the Lula government always looked to exploit minor policies as an opportunity for posturing and displays of independence from Washington, and to score points on the home-front among the PT militancy, especially close to elections. It is interesting to note that President Lula, his close advisors, and cabinet members always did their best to keep an open channel of communication with Washington and the embassy in Brasília. In many cases, the public rhetoric against the US was tempered by a more conciliatory tone behind the scenes.

For reasons rooted in the more distant past, long before the PT government, and which had a lot to do with the perceptions of autonomy and manifest destiny that historically pervaded the work of Itamaraty, on many occasions mutual distrust took hold and influenced the course of the internal decisions made in relation to the United States.

Given the degree of animosity in Washington toward the Lula government, it is hardly surprising that all the work that went into building credibility and trust that had been so successful up to the mid-2000s should have been lost and now need to be reconstructed by governments to come.

In his memoir, published in 2010, George W. Bush said that Brazil became a regional leader with support from the United States. However, he does not mention the Brazilian president once in his book, which is certainly a reflection of the general state of relations between the US and Brazil and his disappointment at the meager results that came of all those countless meetings and statements of intent. For very different reasons, Hugo Chávez and Álvaro Uribe were given much more space in Bush's memoir than Lula.

As was to be expected, the US government continued to downplay the repeated criticism of closing months of the Lula government. On a visit to Brazil in mid-December, the political under-secretary with the Department of State, Nicolas Burns, opted to look forward rather than back. In November 2010, President-Elect Dilma Rousseff had openly criticized the human rights situation in Iran. "The United States is optimistic about the future government, which made some excellent criticisms of Iran, and we look forward to renewing our relationship with the Brazilian government." After her election, Rousseff was invited to meet with Barack Obama in Washington in December 2010. Ambassador Tom Shannon informed the government that it was in both countries' interests to have a meeting at the earliest possible convenience. He added that there was a positive expectation that the two nations could deepen their relationship and that they were sure this would be possible with Rousseff. The official Brazilian News Agency confirmed that she would meet with Obama before her inauguration and that he would be welcome in Brazil once she had taken office. However, on the very same day, sources inside PT announced that the US visit could not be made because of a scheduling problem. Reflecting the PT line, Minister Celso Amorim said that the visit was not indispensable at that juncture and that the president-elect would have plenty of time to go to Washington after the inauguration. It was apparently more important that Rousseff visit Argentina first, as it symbolized the government's achievements in South America.

The fact that Secretary of State Hillary Clinton was sent as Obama's representative at Rousseff's inauguration on January 1, 2011, was a signal of initial interest in mending the bridges.

"The key words for Brazil–US relations are mutual respect and cooperation. The focus on convergences means a strategic partnership, like we have always had, but not the abdication of our independence, sovereignty, and freedom of action." This position announced by Dilma Rousseff—who maintained the broad strokes of the Lula government's policy toward the United States—might change over the course of her administration, if the traditional partnerships are preserved and expanded, as the candidate's government program seemed to indicate. The president-elect's first public declarations, including an interview with the *Washington Post* late in 2010, were positive and indicated certain changes of direction in foreign policy.

Barack Obama's visit in March 2011, though set against a backdrop of global uncertainty and instability, can be considered a milestone in Brazil–US relations, given the prospects Obama promised to usher in over the medium and long term.

After a period of tension that had practically lasted throughout Lula's two terms of office, the newly-inaugurated Rousseff administration decided to open a new chapter in Brazil–US relations, setting aside the turbulence of recent years.

The joint statement the two presidents released at the end of the Obama visit presented a new roadmap for global and bilateral partnership, and not, as it was pragmatically touted, the reaffirmation of a strategic alliance, which could not exist, as it would presuppose a slow building process between equals.

It is important to note that, on this visit, Obama and Rousseff made the decision to raise the dialogue on certain key issues—such as the global, economic, financial, and energy partnership—to presidential level. Ten agreements were signed with a view to exploring new possibilities for cooperation in the areas of trade, education, innovation, infrastructure, air transport and aerospace, major sports events, biofuels for aviation, and cooperation on work with third-party countries, especially in Africa.

The Rousseff-Obama meetings set the tone and the bedrock for how the bilateral relationship should develop over the coming years, opening up the possibility of concrete progress being made that could benefit the governments and private sectors of both countries. On the crest of the major changes underway in the world and the two nations' interests, mention was made of partnerships in areas that, should they actually materialize, could lead to a qualitative improvement in the bilateral relationship, with concrete gains on both sides.

The US government is interested in becoming a key buyer of the oil produced by Brazil's pre-salt reserves and the Brazilian government, for its part, wants to move ahead with its space program by rebuilding the Alcântara base with the help of US companies. Major infrastructure projects could attract investment and North American companies could help Brazil to meet the stringent deadlines for the delivery of facilities and equipment for the World Cup and Olympic Games. The Pentagon, the world's largest buyer of aviation-grade kerosene, is keen to attain energy security through the production of biofuels to power its fleet, and this could open up countless opportunities for the private sector in both countries.

Dilma Rousseff will have to oversee a Brazil–United States relationship rife with tensions, but free of ideological contamination.

Given the dynamic of international relations, it is likely that the two countries will find themselves on a collision course again in the years to come, as their agendas include differing interests, priorities, and visions.

Brazil will continue to enjoy growing international reputation and, should it be willing and able, will find a role deserving of its voice and serve as a mature and honest broker on global issues. Of course, the road to that level of standing and genuine influence on the world stage will be both tough and long. It presupposes a learning curve of trial and error, but also depends on objective assessments, based on a clear vision of the country's permanent interests and not on the party-political priorities of whoever happens to be in power.

One last comment is in order here, and it concerns the Lula government's reaction to those who argue for fuller advantage to be taken of the opportunities that arise out of Brazil's relationship with the United States, seen through a pragmatic and objective understanding of what the world's largest and most important market has to offer.

In recent years, perhaps because of their constant concerns about their image at home, the Lula administration and Itamaraty seemed to fear that a good relationship with the United States would give the population the impression that we were being pliant. However, far from submissiveness, the real result of improved relations with the US would be enhanced independence and concrete political and economic benefit. After Lula's two terms, Brazil's relationship with the United States is in bad shape, and our political weight and moderate image have begun to be questioned, as can be seen from the friction between the two countries on the agreement with Iran.

In the outmoded language of the Cold War, those in favor of a good understanding with the United States and of the opportunities it could yield in areas of our interest were customarily branded "sell-outs." Times have changed and this perception has become less radical, but no less removed from the reality. The attitude of those who defend an improved relationship with the United States are still seen as "joiners" or as suffering from a "nostalgia for subservience."

As then-Assistant Secretary for Western Hemisphere Affairs and current US Ambassador to Brazil Tom Shannon rightly predicted back in 2008, Brazil–US relations will determine how events unfold not only in Latin America, but in many parts of the world.

Over the last sixteen years, and especially over the last five or six, Brazil has achieved wider international visibility than ever before. The United States represents only a part of the Brazilian agenda, and perhaps that is why the country has yet to decide what it really wants from its relationship with its northern neighbor.

A certain disharmony in Brazil–US relations was only to be expected, given the transformations the two countries have undergone in a changing world with Asia as its driving force. Both nations need to adapt if they are to tackle the challenge this poses and take measures to protect against the future disagreements that will come as a matter of course outside the American continent.

With regard to Brazil's growing influence, the United States does not yet see Brazil as a potential strategic partner or crucial economic player on critical issues of security, and it tends to view Brazil's policy on human rights, democracy, and nuclear non-proliferation as erratic and confused, as the American analyst Peter Hakim, a close associate of Washington's policymakers, pointed out.

This is the context in which Brazil's foreign policymakers have to work today, with the national interest as a point of reference.

CHAPTER 8

Historical Perspective

By way of conclusion, I thought it useful to give a brief historical overview of relations between Brazil and the United States. This is by no means an exhaustive or even detailed diplomatic history, much less an academic analysis penned for specialists, but merely a description in broad strokes with no other intention than to give the reader some background to the events my book relates. As such, this chapter will be divided more or less arbitrarily into five phases.

The first deals with the period up to the late nineteenth century and is primarily concerned with the Empire. The second concerns the Republic, culminating in the early decades of the twentieth century. The third begins during the inter-war period and spans the Second World War and post-war years up to the late 1950s. The next phase, which defines many of the contours of our bilateral relationship with the United States even today, covers the buildup to the coup of 1964—which put an end to the democracy in place since 1946—and runs through the authoritarian regime, ending with the Sarney government. The current phase, the last in our account, deals with the re-democratization movement and beyond, down to the present day.

Let me reiterate that this division is somewhat arbitrary because the changes in relationships between nations do not follow any calendar and many of the processes of convergence or conflict are invisible to the naked eye; most of the time, we only realize that a cause has occurred by the effect it yields. Yet, however arbitrary it may be, it will serve to underline some of the most relevant aspects of these complex and constantly changing relations between our two countries.

Historically speaking, we cannot really talk of Brazil–US relations prior to the nineteenth century, when Brazil declared its independence and the United States consolidated its territory and politics. The American Revolution, at the end of the eighteenth century, with its ideals of democracy, constitutional government, and Republicanism, had a strong intellectual influence on the Brazilian elite, inspiring insurgencies and laying the bases for an affinity that made the United States of America the first nation to recognize Brazil's independence from Portugal. For the Americans, taking the side of a former colony in the New World against an Old World metropolis was the natural thing to do, especially when the colonizer in question was an old and loyal ally of the British Empire.

From the outset, the main foreign aim of these new nations was to ensure the legitimacy of their independence and the integrity of their territory—or its expansion, in the American case. They also shared the condition of *avis rara* on the continent, two giants looked upon with no great enthusiasm by their Spanish-speaking neighbors: the United States up north, with its diversity of language and customs and propensity toward territorial expansion; and Brazil to the south-east, which, in addition to its difference in language and its own expansionist aspirations, was also a monarchy. All of this meant that both, for better or for worse, were kept at arm's length and out of Bolivarian initiatives toward integration.

The historical roots of the distrust and suspicion between the two countries lie in this period.

The relations between the United States and the Brazilian Empire were established amid misgivings and suspicion, explained by the difference in regime and structure of their societies. The United States considered Brazil's monarchical regime an "anomaly," while Brazil saw the United States as a hive of subversion.

As such, the relationship between the US and Brazil did not run as smoothly as it is often supposed.

The independence of the Kingdom of Brazil on September 7, 1822, was not immediately recognized. In 1823, José Silvestre Rebello was appointed chargé d'affaires and plenipotentiary minister in Washington. Though he was reluctantly received by Secretary of State John Quincy Adams, the recognition of Brazil as an independent state only came, in practice, when Rebello met with President James Monroe. Officially speaking, recognition of Brazil was only given on October 29, 1825, after Portugal accepted Brazil's independence.

America's influence was not just ideological, in terms of promoting the republican mode of government. Political and commercial interests saw the United States become involved in nearly every domestic upheaval throughout the nineteenth century, such as the various separatist revolts—Sabinada (Bahia, 1837), Cabanagem (Grand-Pará, 1835), Balaiada (Maranhão, 1838), and the Farroupilha Revolution (Rio Grande do Sul, 1835).

During that period, the Brazilian government suspended diplomatic relations with the US on three occasions (1827, 1847, and 1869), despite the fact that it had been the biggest importer of Brazilian goods, especially coffee, since 1848. The relationship between the two countries only began to improve after 1870, when Brazil became dependent on the American coffee-buying market.

Relations became tense again when the US attempted to colonize the Amazon. They proposed the transfer of part of their Black population to an area north of the Amazon River and the creation of an Amazonian Republic. Aware of the northern neighbors expansionist tendencies, the Brazilian government did not receive the proposal in good spirit. At the same time, US pressure to open the Amazon River to free transit convinced the Brazilian government that they risked losing the Amazon to the Americans.

Brazil was now alert to the fact that the United States had designs on the region, a suspicion reinforced by US insistence that the Amazon River would be opened to its vessels by fair means if possible, or by force if necessary. Brazil held its ground, and the river remained closed to US ships and any colonial intentions they may have brought.

During the government of Abraham Lincoln (1861–1865), however, the United States returned to its old proposal for Brazil to receive Black American immigrants and establish a Negro colony in the Amazon River basin, an idea Brazil continued to reject.

These overtures may linger in the national subconscious, which would explain Brazil's concerns about Amazonian occupation to the present day.

On the other hand, during the American Civil War, Emperor D. Pedro II financed the immigration of white confederates, perhaps pining for their ranches full of African slaves. Settled mostly in São Paulo (those who went to Alcântara in Grão-Pará failed to survive the inhospitable conditions there), these confederate ranchers left their mark in the foundation of the towns Americana and Santa Bárbara and certain educational institutions.

In 1865, the relationship between the two countries was plunged into crisis once again when the US started to support Paraguay, with which Brazil, as part of the Triple Alliance formed with Argentina and Uruguay, was at war (1864–1870).

From 1870 on, diplomatic relations improved, but the distrust lingered. In 1887, President Grover Cleveland proposed the formation of a Zollverein, or customs union, with a duty-free exchange of goods. Emperor D. Pedro II was for the idea, but the Brazilian government ended up not following through on the proposal.

The twentieth century dawned with huge changes for both countries. Brazil became a republic and reorganized its economy in the wake of abolition. The US, on the other hand, started military and commercial expansion that led, first of all, to war with Spain for control over US coastal waters, the Antilles, and Central America, and, later, the Philippine archipelago. It also wrangled with the British for commercial and financial control over Latin America's economies, hitherto dependent on the European superpower.

Brazil was the first in Latin America to note the decline of the British Empire and the rise of the new northern power, with which it was pursuing a promising trade partnership. The Baron of Rio Branco, then foreign minister, played a relevant role in this process. Sharing America's suspicions of the European powers and its views on the risks inherent to military and political instability in Spanish America, Rio Branco coordinated Brazil's actions across the continent in order to avoid conflict and reinforce the convergences between the two countries' interests.

However, in order to implement this policy, Rio Branco first had to overcome the reciprocal suspicions concerning the territorial issue with Bolivia. The situation had become increasingly delicate since 1899, given the presence of US investors acting through a company called the Bolivian Syndicate, the creation of which had been negotiated with La Paz, with support from Washington. After various incidents, such as the unauthorized entry onto Brazilian waterways of a warship carrying a US consul, negotiations with the Bolivian government that granted the territory of Acre to the Syndicate, and threatened US intervention, Rio Branco decided to close the Amazon River to international navigation in order to protect the Brazilian interest. This decision blocked the access of Syndicate staff to the disputed territory and forced the investors to capitulate. In 1903, the issue was resolved with the payment of compensation to the Syndicate and border negotiations with Bolivia.

With this episode overcome, the bilateral relationship flourished to such an extent that it came to be seen in the history books as an unwritten alliance between the two countries: Brazil supported, and rallied support for, US initiatives, or at the very least displayed no open opposition, while the United States tacitly supported Brazil in its endeavors to obtain favorable border demarcations from its South American neighbors. Brazil and the United States seemed to agree on both the Monroe Doctrine—though Brazil had its own understanding of what that meant—and the issue of pan-Americanism.

The First World War (1914–1918) did not change the relationship between the countries, and both declared neutrality as hostilities began. The war drastically affected normal trade with Europe, and from 1927 on, the US surpassed England to become Brazil's biggest trading partner. In October 1917, Brazil broke its neutrality and joined the war effort alongside the United States, which had declared war in April of that year. Brazil supported initiatives by President Wilson, from the Peace Conference in Paris to the creation of the Society of Nations, and Wilson endeavored to secure Brazil a non-permanent seat on its Council.

Between the wars, the New York Stock Exchange crisis of 1929 and the Revolution in Brazil in 1930 rocked the growing convergence between the two nations. The United States withdrew into itself, and years went by without any attempt at effective economic recovery. Brazil turned its external focus onto negotiating its foreign debt, obtaining new lines of credit, and ensuring minimum prices for its commodities. In search of alternatives to our dependence on US trade and investment, Brazil adopted a policy of friendship and cooperation that oscillated among Paris, London, Berlin and Rome, powers increasingly at odds in Europe.

As the Second World War loomed, two perceptions nurtured by the Brazilian elite were brought to bear decisively on our relations with the United States. On one side, the opportunity arose to exploit the rivalries born of the two European blocs' need for secure political allies and loyal suppliers of foodstuffs and strategic materials, something Getúlio Vargas achieved masterfully. On the other, the arms race in Europe and Asia was underlining the fragility of the Brazilian society and economy and the country's military vulnerability.

The Armed Forces, whose generals had all been trained in Europe—France and Germany—realized that unless the country rapidly industrialized its productive sector and modernized the state, the country would find itself at the mercy of military action in the advent of war. When the US joined the fray in 1941, pressure on Brazil to side with the allies against the Rome–Berlin–Tokyo axis became unbearable, with Brazil breaking off diplomatic relations in 1942, declaring war in August that same year, creating the Brazilian Expeditionary Force in November 1943, and engaging the enemy in Italy in July 1944.

Before this, starting in 1941, the two countries had established a number of agreements that enabled Brazil to acquire weaponry and supply strategic raw materials. There was also an agreement that financed the creation of Brazil's first industrial estate, in Volta Redonda, and a secret accord granting the US access to military bases in the Brazilian northeast. With great symbolic fanfare, Brazil signed the United Nations Declaration, which gave rise to the UN.

The alliance with Brazil during World War II also brought the US certain political advantages, given Brazil's mobilization of Latin American nations in favor of the war effort, which resulted, for example, in a strengthened Inter-American Security System.

Immediately after the war, expectations were running high in Brazil. The United States was expected to honor its commitment to support the modernization of Brazil's economy, its Armed Forces and state apparatus, transferring the scientific knowledge and technologies needed for sustained development. From the political perspective, in the postwar period Brazil found itself punching above its weight in negotiations on the creation of a new institutional framework that included the UN; the Bretton Woods Conference, which created the international financial system—the World Bank and IMF—; and the creation of the GATT (present-day WTO), as well as being the US candidate for a permanent seat on the UNSC, though this was lost to France due to a British and Russian veto.

However, as the Cold War crept in and the need arose in the mid-1940s to stem the flow of Soviet expansion, the United States's regional goals took a backseat and Brazil was relegated to a position of little relevance in the face of growing international commitments. In this new panorama, Europe, especially a now divided Germany, was the prime focus of American foreign policy. Unlike other peripheral areas, such as the Middle and Far East, Latin America (and thus Brazil) lost most of its strategic importance.

The national elite—particularly the state bureaucrats, diplomats, and military—resented the fact that the country's problems persisted even though it had made the right choice during the Second World War and had honored all of its commitments. Despite having broken off all commercial and diplomatic relations with the Soviet bloc, opened its market to trade and floated its currency, and politically supported the US in all forums, Brazil was still left short on resources with which to tackle its trade deficit, foreign debt, and mediocre growth rates.

The honeymoon period in Brazil–US relations did not last long into the post-war years and soon cooled into ambivalence on both sides, especially so from 1949 on. What followed was a lengthy impasse on such themes as the renegotiation of Brazil's foreign debt, new investments, support for the development and modernization of the Armed Forces, scientific and technological transfers, particularly of a strategic nature, and commitments on nuclear non-proliferation. Nevertheless, the governments of Dutra and Jânio Quadros—when Brazil introduced its so-called independent foreign policy—formed what was known as the period of "automatic alignment" with the US.

The phase that included the governments of Jânio and Jango and the military regime, marked by with its disputes and failed attempts at cooperation, was to a degree foreshadowed by the intense external activism of the Juscelino Kubitschek government. This had a direct impact on relations with the United States, a combination of political and military alignment with constant friction in the areas of trade, non-proliferation, disarmament, and direct official investment. After 1958, facing mounting debts, stagnating exports, and rising inflation, Juscelino skillfully played with a mix of nationalist rhetoric and liberal economic diplomacy. At the same time, he was very active in attracting alternative foreign investments and opening new markets, including to socialist nations.

The United States looked suspiciously on these initiatives, and Brazil showed its dissatisfaction with the results of Operation Pan-America—a Juscelino initiative—that fell short of expectations. The OPA, as it became known, envisaged an economic development plan for Latin America involving foreign-debt relief, special trade regimes with protection against fluctuations in commodity prices, official investment in a wide-ranging industrial development program, and transfers of science and technology.

The OPA initiative began with a letter from Juscelino to President Eisenhower during a visit by then-Vice-President Nixon to Latin

America, during which he was met by widespread and hostile demonstrations. The backbone of the Brazilian argument was that the lack of industrial development condemned Latin America to poverty and backwardness, which, in turn, would serve as an insurmountable barrier to convergence on America's Cold War goals. It was an argument later applied to underdeveloped nations in general.

Some Operation Pan-America objectives were actually reached, such as the creation of an investment bank for the region, the Inter-American Development Bank, designed to serve a similar function to the World Bank in Europe. Later, President Kennedy launched his Alliance for Progress, modeled on the Brazilian program, but without its backbone, the much-awaited "Marshall Plan" for the subcontinent.

This fresh disappointment with US indifference toward what Brazil saw as a standing debt after such intense convergence during World War II continued to affect the bilateral relationship. With the independent foreign policy implemented by Jânio Quadros and consolidated by João Gulart, Brazil gave up any hopes it had of receiving political or economic rewards for "good behavior," that is, for its alliance and allegiance to US interests and goals. The central argument was that the Cold War and its nuclear arms race would lead only to misery and insecurity, if not destruction. Peace would only be achieved through disarmament and prosperity, through financial and technical aid to underdeveloped nations.

The so-called "ideological borders" only really prevailed for one brief moment, during the first military government of Castelo Branco, on the presupposition that the interests and objectives of the American bloc were subordinate to those of the Cold War. However, the idea that Brazil's commercial, financial, and scientific interests would be pursued universally, wherever necessary or possible, prevailed as the core of the bilateral relationship, establishing limits for collaboration and the bases for conflict between the two partners.

This backdrop of conflict continued throughout most of the military period, despite a certain margin of political alignment, especially on themes affecting the "ideological borders." One example of this was Brazil's participation in the Inter-American Peacekeeping Force (1965), created under Brazilian command to support US intervention in the Dominican Republic. Another was the support on the effort to destabilize the socialist government of Salvador Allende in Chile (1973).

During the authoritarian military regime, there were growing suspicions concerning foreign interest in occupying the Amazon. Studies by the Hudson Institute in Washington on the creation of a massive lake in the region and a perceived external threat to Brazilian control over the mineral resources there served to deepen the distrust in relation to US ambitions.

When Ernesto Geisel came to power in 1974, the domestic conditions in both countries were undergoing relevant changes that would have a major effect on the bilateral relationship. In the United States, there was growing opposition to political and military interventions abroad, especially in support of corrupt and authoritarian governments, as in Southeast Asia, and this led to a general reining in of US activism, including in Latin America. The Jimmy Carter government took this policy to the other extreme, as the dirty war waged by military regimes across the continent, with the support of US security agencies, hitherto seen as a virtuous endeavor, was now viewed as a punishable sin in need of correction.

In Brazil, the "economic miracle" was stalled by the first oil crisis, which triggered an international recession and a major retraction in industrial growth. In his inaugural address, Geisel defined his foreign policy priorities in terms of the national interests, namely international trade, vital raw materials, and supplies for industry and consumption, and access to state-of-the-art technologies. In different statements, Brazilian diplomacy made it clear that the country's bilateral relations with the US and its multilateral relations in general would now be focused on practical targets, with no more thought for convergences or divergences. Independent foreign policy continued now under the label of "responsible pragmatism."

As was bound to happen, the divergences were not long in coming. On energy policy, there was an urgent need to diversify lines of oil supply and develop alternative energy sources, with one of the options being the construction of nuclear power plants. The Carter government was, at the time, engaged in combating nuclear proliferation and adopted restrictive measures on the supply of nuclear materials and equipment, frustrating Brazil's completion of its Angra dos Reis plant, under contract to an American company, Westinghouse.

As in the case of President Juscelino, who when faced with US reluctance to invest in an automotive manufacturing plant considered a strategic step toward Brazilian industrial autonomy, Geisel looked toward Europe for potential partners and secured a deal with pro-US West Germany on the co-development of an alternative uranium enrichment process. The Carter government applied all the pressure it could muster to have the contract rescinded, frustrating Brazilian and German aspirations.

Carter-era activism on such issues as indigenous rights, non-proliferation, defense of democracy, and human rights almost led to a severing of diplomatic relations after Congress published a report on human rights that was extremely critical of Brazil. Brazil retaliated by withdrawing from the military assistance agreement, inoperative in practice but a symbolic jewel of the post-war special relationship between Brazil and the US.

This was the most turbulent period in the bilateral relationship, and it was exacerbated by measures Brazil took on issues sensitive to both countries, such as Brazil's diplomatic recognition of the Angolan Liberation Movement, which precipitated its international recognition as a free state in 1975; Brazil's vote at the UN General Assembly in favor of the resolution that declared Zionism to be a form of racism (1975); the Amazonian Cooperation Treaty (1978) between Brazil and other nations from the region, which served (with no practical results) as a sort of Monroe Doctrine to keep foreign nations—the US and other industrialized countries—from attempting to meddle in the region's affairs; and a nuclear cooperation agreement with Iraq (Figueiredo government, 1980).

With the restoration of democracy, Brazil maintained its policy of autonomy from the United States, but with less friction. On one side, it was important to exorcise the demon of foreign debt, which was negotiated largely with US creditors with IMF mediation. There were also the matters of hyperinflation, which was scaring away investors and inhibiting a return to growth, and a closed economy—with price and currency controls and discrimination against foreign companies—which meant Brazil was unattractive to the international community as a trading partner.

The efforts democratic Brazilian governments made to dispel suspicions in the areas of human rights, the rights of Indian tribes and other minorities, the resolution of social conflicts, especially in the hinterlands and in the Amazon, and Brazil's positive contributions in certain important international forums, such as GATT and the IMF, went a long way toward feeding a positive agenda with the US. With regard to opening and modernizing the economy, regional economic integration was a strategic element of policy. The creation of Mercosur was the first step toward a South American free trade zone and the subcontinent's infrastructural integration. In contrast, American attempts at economic integration across the continent, including Bush Sr.'s Enterprise for the Americas Initiative and the negotiations on the Free Trade Area of the Americas during Clinton's government, were warily received in Brazil.

The main areas of convergence between the two countries therefore shifted from policy and investment to the regional sphere, especially with regard to trade. In the case of the Enterprise for the Americas Initiative, a project geared toward Latin America that envisaged foreign debt relief accompanied by modest investments and a none-too-clear free trade proposal, though warmly received across the region, was met with reservations on the Brazilian side, which announced the creation of a common market agreement with Argentina, Uruguay, and Paraguay— Mercosur. Without Brazil's support, the Enterprise for the Americas Initiative did not prosper.

The proposal for the creation of a continent-wide free trade area (FTAA) during the Clinton administration was received with even more suspicion. Sectors of the government and society in general believed that the FTAA would interrupt the development of the promising Mercosur agreement, which was not only increasing our volume of trade in the region, but also our trade balance, powered by industrial exports, which garnered quality to our portfolio. It was also feared that the agenda would target markets that were relevant and sensitive only to Brazil, such as industrial products and services, but which in no way threatened the vast majority of countries across the continent, which would have left Brazil isolated when it came to defending its interests.

Brazil was the United States's main interlocutor throughout the whole negotiation process on the FTAA, which it co-chaired with the US during the final phase, when able diplomacy on our part yielded something far more palatable to Brazil. However, with the changing domestic contexts in both countries and in the negotiations on the Doha Round, the talks on the FTAA were aborted, during the Lula government, by tacit agreement among the main players.

We find ourselves now in the contemporary phase, which spans the latter part of the Fernando Henrique Cardoso government and the two terms of office of President Lula. This period has been more thoroughly discussed in earlier chapters, especially that on the more recent developments in our foreign policy toward the United States, between April 2004 and May 2011.

Index